RAW GUIDE

to

GREATER MANCHESTER

DEBBIE RIDEHALGH & MIKE PARKER

HARRAP
LONDON

First published in Great Britain 1991
by HARRAP BOOKS Ltd
Chelsea House, 26 Market Square,
Bromley, Kent BR1 1NA

ISBN 0 245-60274-7

Designed by Roger King Graphic Studios.
Printed in Great Britain by
Guernsey Press

PREFACE & ACKNOWLEDGEMENTS

Preface

RAW is about looking at places with a keen, sometimes cynical, often irreverent eye. Guide books over-rely on pictures of misty churchyards at sunrise and sun-dappled glades superimposed with the ramblings of some local poet. ***RAW*** celebrates the diversity of the cities and the regions of the British Isles and believes that London and the south-east of England do not have a monopoly on culture, excitement and vitality.

This guide should help you sort out the rhetoric from the reality, and to learn to look at Greater Manchester's world with a fresh eye. Some things mentioned may take a dash of perseverance to find and appreciate; you may vehemently disagree with some of the opinions expressed. If so, then tell us. But we hope that, if you do bother to do more than merely scratch the most obvious of surfaces, you will agree that this is a very exciting time to live and breathe Manchester. Enjoy!

Acknowledgements

MAPS

Network NorthWest map (page 8) reproduced by kind permission of Greater Manchester Passenger Transport Executive.

Maps on pages 7, 9 by Roger King Graphic Studios based on maps from DE ROUCK Cartography.

CONTRIBUTORS

Chris and Florence Ridehalgh
Jon Clarke

CONTENTS

	MAPS	
	Manchester area	7
	Network NorthWest	8
	Manchester and Salford City Centres	9
	INTRODUCTION	11
1.	ORIENTATION	16
	Travel and Transport	16
	Accommodation	23
2.	ROOTS	27
	Towns, Villages and Districts	27
	History and Politics	31
	Local Media	34
3.	MILK AND HONEY	39
	Restaurants and Cafés	39
	Pubs and Bars	47
4.	JOY RIDES: DAYS OUT AND ABOUT	57
	Museums and Galleries	57
	Tours and Walks	65
	Parks and Houses	69
	Kids' Stuff	72
	Special Events	72
5.	THE TWILIGHT ZONE	74
	Nightlife and Music	74
	Cinema, Theatre and Classical Music	80
6.	DALES, HILLS AND DARK SATANIC MILLS	87
	Lancashire, West Yorkshire and up to the Lakes	87
	The Peak District	98
	Cheshire	100

7. SPORT AND LEISURE 105
Shopping 105
Sport 112

8. THE MORAL MAJORITY 120
Women 120
Black and Ethnic 124
People with Disabilities 126
Lesbian and Gay 128
Youth 131
Environmental Groups and Concerns 132
Working in the Voluntary Sector 133
Continuing and Further Education 134

9. GREATER MANCHESTER POTTED DIRECTORY 135
Tourist Information Centres 135
Useful Contacts 135

INDEX 137
Pubs Index 141

MANCHESTER AREA

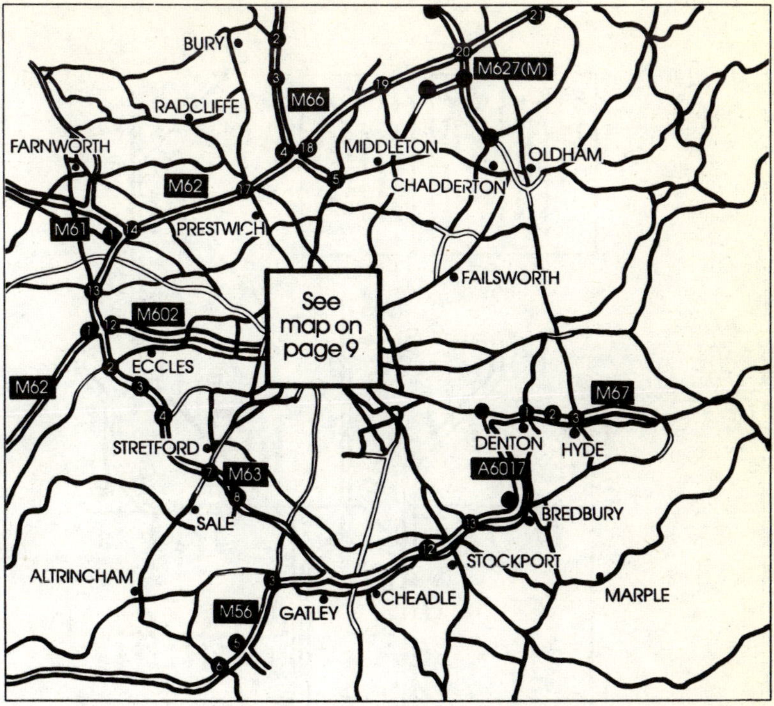

NETWORK NORTHWEST

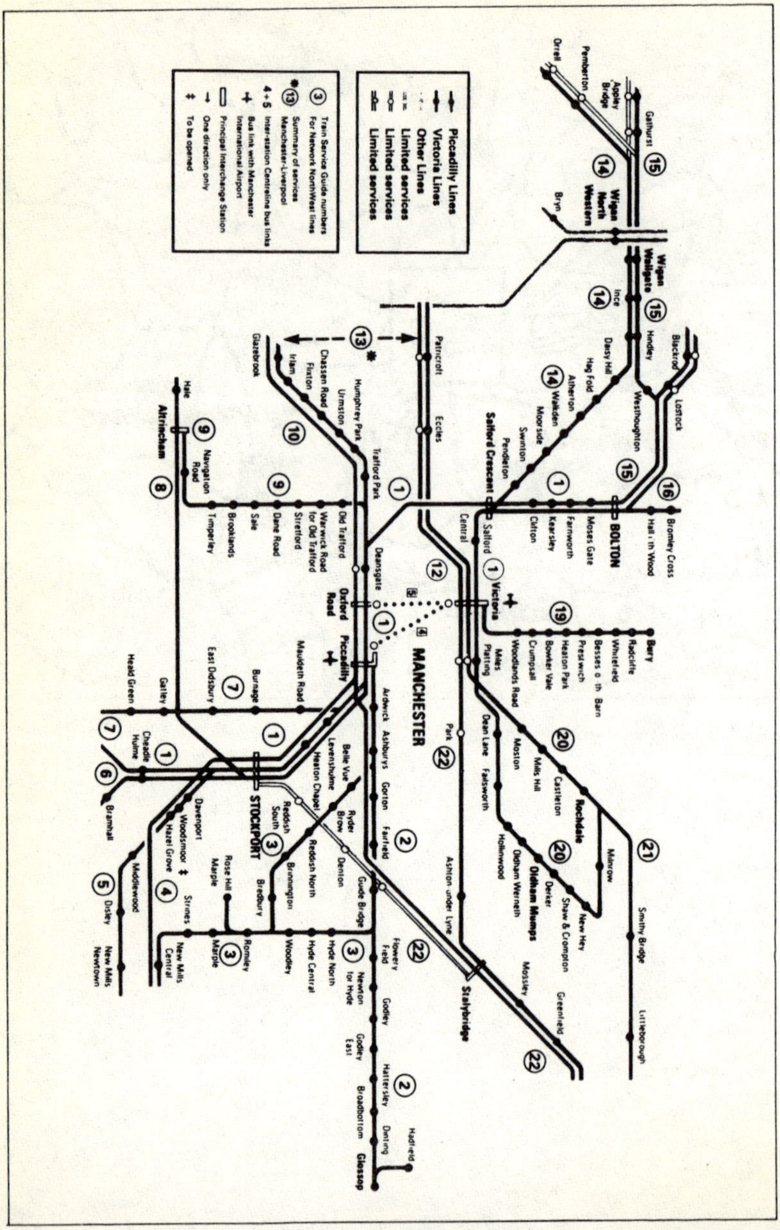

MANCHESTER AND SALFORD CITY CENTRES

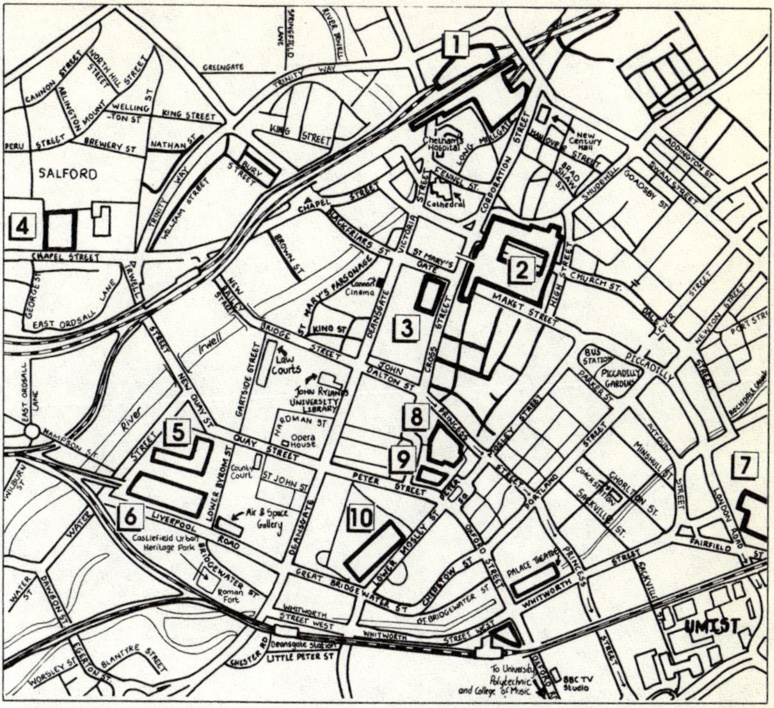

1 Victoria Station	6 Science Museum
2 Arndale Centre	7 Piccadilly Station
3 Royal Exchange	8 Town Hall
4 St John's Cathedral	9 Central Library
5 Granada TV Studios	10 G-Mex Exhibition Centre

INTRODUCTION

It's the city that has suddenly sprung to international recognition. Go on holiday and tell foreigners that you're from Manchester and they will shake your hand. A survey of American students placed the city above London as the European city they would most like to visit. Manchester made the cover of *Newsweek* magazine; its bands are topping the charts; its fashion is being paraded down South Molton Street; its clubs are drawing hordes of eager ravers from opposite ends of the country. At last, the *Evening Standard's* teeshirts claiming 'There Is No Life North Of Watford' are gathering dust while shirts emblazoned with the message that 'On The Eighth Day God Created MANchester' are selling like Eccles Cakes. In the space of two years, an image of dour industrialism has changed to one of hedonism and innovation; London is looking to Manchester for the latest trends as Dick Whittington re-knots his spotted hanky and travels North – applications to Manchester University alone rose by thirty per cent in 1990.

In the young worlds of fashion and pop, a connection with Manchester has become a marketable asset: a phenomenon similar to that of the 1960s when Liverpool led the way. Then, however, the northerners who gained recognition took their trendy roots and planted them in the more affluent soils of the South. London snapped her fingers and the young and talented offspring of the North migrated. It is hardly surprising that the barren North was hardest hit by the recessions of the 1970s – but out of the hardship grew a determination to succeed, and the results are becoming evident. London's soil has become sterile, crowded and unpleasant while Manchester stands poised to capitalize on the capital's demise, smacking its lips with relish.

Nonetheless, should the hype die down, and the music and fashion press suddenly turn their benevolent gaze from the North and decide that they have condescended to pay attention to Manchester for long enough, few Mancunians could care less. They have been proud of their city for a good deal longer than the fickle pundits, even though many of them still don't realize how much potential the city has. Bands from Manchester have not suddenly emerged from nowhere – they have been building up a thriving music scene for years with nothing short of solid graft. Likewise, the young fashion designers have worked long and hard to be noticed, and – whether the rest of the country falls obediently into line or not – Mancunians will continue to dress as they like, with a spirit of sartorial independence evident since the early days of the Industrial Revolution. Mancunians don't need crowds of folk from the Home Counties on a day-trip up North to tell them that they've got it right. They are merely surprised that it took them all so long to catch on!

Success isn't merely limited to the industries of youth culture: the business and leisure communities are also booming. Having been consistently ignored by the capital during the difficult years of the 1970s, Manchester has developed a sense of independence and has worked hard to promote itself as a major world city. Unlike Liverpool, where independence was pushed almost to the point of isolation, Manchester saw the need for a loud voice in the North-West, and began painstakingly building up international links, bringing investment to the area and developing a new period of growth. The results are already clear to see. Thus, though unemployment in England has risen sharply at the beginning of the 1990s, the worst increases have not been in the North, but in the South-West and East Anglia. The North-West learned harsh lessons in the 1970s and used the more affluent 1980s to rebuild shattered foundations so as to ensure, as far as possible, that a 1990s recession would neither cripple nor maim. Manchester has benefited most noticeably from this philosophy largely because it hasn't promoted itself as merely the major city of the North but as a major world venue.

A large international airport has boosted this image, as have the concerted efforts of a dedicated city council, the Central Manchester Development Corporation and such individuals as Bob Scott (MD of the Palace Theatre and Opera House, director of the Royal Exchange, Hallé Orchestra, Buxton Festival and Manchester Arts Festival, chairman of the Cornerhouse and the brains and inspiration behind Manchester's Olympic Bid). He believes that:

> The first requirement for Manchester to regain real importance internationally is for its citizens to think well of themselves and their own city. We cannot expect others to take us seriously unless we take ourselves seriously first. I am convinced that Manchester thinks better of itself than it did a few years ago, and we now have things we are really proud of like the airport, Salford Quays, the Royal Exchange Theatre and our universities. By the end of this century, we must have a new concert hall, a new national stadium, new hotels and much, much more besides.
>
> The image that we have of ourselves is the image that others will have of us. When we complain about our image, we are actually complaining about ourselves!

Stirring words, and sadly very true. The people of Manchester are still suffering from the inferiority complex inflicted upon them by the North/South divide that has dominated the nation's political geography for a large part of this century. It was partly due to this that even Mancunians found it difficult to believe that they could compete against the likes of Athens for the Olympics. This was a misconception founded upon the unfortunate fact that, while Manchester is an altogether prettier place than Athens, the former suffers from the lack of an attractive image while the latter benefits from an over-romanticized one. It is this whole question of image that lies at the crux of the problem highlighted by Mr Scott.

Images *are* developing and changing in the city, and while they may seem to be at odds with each other at first glance, they are in fact closely related. Manchester's new images of hedonistic zest and energy are symptoms of a growing stature and confidence taking place at most levels throughout the city. The topic of image is further complicated by the hangover of an industrial history. Visions of Lowry's Salford and scenes from *Coronation Street* are about as representative of Manchester as Samuel Pepys and *EastEnders* are of London, and yet the North still cannot shake off southern preconceptions of flat caps and whippets. In reality, smog-filled skies are long gone in the city that first introduced a smokeless zone; cobbled streets, where they exist, are considered quaint; clogs form part of the exhibits in our heritage museums and flat caps are a more common sight upon the 'hooray Henries' of the county set than the working classes of the city. Manchester has moved on.

But has this warped image developed with any degree of justification? It can't be denied that after the 1970s, Manchester was left with a whole pile of disused factories, warehouses and over thirteen miles of oil-slicked and putrid canal. In addition, the doped-out town planners of the 1960s had further enhanced the already formidable beauty of the city with a massive orange and yellow monstrosity and countless tower blocks of council flats that were presumably some hippy way of reaching heaven, as they could never seriously have been intended for habitation. Admittedly, the end result was a bit of a mess. Like many other cities, Manchester decided to clean up its act. Unlike many other cities, Manchester decided to use its existing fabric and buildings rather than simply razing it all to the ground to be covered with endless shopping precincts. Too many other cities – such as Leeds and parts of Birmingham – fell into this bottomless pit. Instead, Manchester attempted to update the old city in as sympathetic a way as possible, taking care not to lose the original inspiration. The results undoubtedly speak for themselves -- two of the most remarkable examples being the innovative Royal Exchange, resembling a giant glass creature squatting in the Victorian splendour of the city's old trading exchange, and G-Mex, a huge concert hall/ exhibition centre housed within the dramatic shell of the old Central Station.

Not that this kind of imaginative approach and entrepreneurial spirit is new to the city. It was Manchester, after all, that became the third busiest port in the British Empire, despite the fact that it lies forty miles inland! The Bridgewater and Manchester Ship Canals were symptomatic of Mancunian innovation. And it was in Manchester that Roget compiled his Thesaurus, the first commercial computer was developed, the atom was first split, the first test-tube baby was born and the first public library was established. Not bad for an industrial backwater! All this epitomizes the city's reach for new horizons and ideas -- as relevant in the 1990s as the 1890s.

And what of the image of the city's people? The clog-bedecked folk on the streets of Lowry's Salford and the thrifty characters of early *Coronation Street* episodes were born into a life of hard toil and extreme poverty. Resulting from this came a pride and camaraderie not easily broken, something still evident on the streets today. Visitors from all over the world are amazed at the Mancunian humour and friendliness. 'No donkey could guarantee the safety of its hind legs in this garrulous city' wrote the *Daily Telegraph*. Juan Antonio Samaranch, President of the International Olympic Committee, commented: 'The thing I came to see was the people, and you have obviously got the right people'. Shame that there wasn't the Coca-Cola HQ to go with it....

The Mancunian 'front' *is* garrulous, open and friendly, often with a very sarcastic sense of humour. This has evolved as a form of defence and has become a source of pride. Mancunians laugh a great deal; they talk at bus stops and in shops and are genuinely interested in hearing what you may have to say. It is a quality that cannot fail to make you feel at home in the city, and one which is sadly non-existent in so many others.

Much of the cosmopolitan atmosphere of the city lies in the diversity of its population. There are large and vibrant ethnic communities, coming especially from Chinese, Indian, Greek, Italian, Irish, Afro-Caribbean and Jewish backgrounds. These contribute enormously to the cultural, social and political life of the city, as does Britain's second largest (and arguably most visible) lesbian and gay population. In addition, one of the biggest student populations in Western Europe lends an increased vitality to the city, which has greatly helped its development as a centre for youth culture. The contributions made by all the above groups play as valuable a part in the city's cultural heritage as do those traditional Lancastrians who were part of the Industrial Revolution. Together they make the city wealthy.

The population of this cultural hotchpotch realize that there is a great deal more to Manchester than its international gloss. Most importantly, not all aspects of life here are glossy and cool – many are simply grotty and cold. Thousands of people live well below the recognized poverty line in appalling conditions. Many are homeless, and many of those who have homes live in areas where burglary, vandalism and drug pushing as have come to be accepted as everyday occurrences.

Gradually, the scummier parts of the city are being bulldozed and replanned. A good start was made in Salford in 1990, when eight tower blocks were demolished. To the east of the city, major housing projects are taking place and slowly but surely, problems of homelessness are being tackled. On a more commercial side, redevelopments such as Castlefield (the first urban redevelopment scheme in the UK) and the construction of the Metrolink system (a light transport system unmatched in the country) enhance the city for visitors and, hopefully, residents alike. Other problems, noticeably the disturbing rise in racism (forcefully shown in the repulsive desecration of Jewish graves in the city), need a desperate solution – as do the battles for control between the growing numbers of drug barons and the increase in organized crime. The Greater Manchester Police, eager to calm public jitters, have focused on easy targets like the Konspiracy, while the real culprits melt into the shadows and escape untouched. All very worrying, but take heart from the results of a survey published in the United States in 1990: Manchester is the eleventh safest city in the world, standing head and shoulders above any other major city in Britain. Let's hope that the city has the faith and the spirit to tackle its dark side, even if it isn't so bad as the dens of iniquity elsewhere in the world.

1. ORIENTATION

Travel and Transport

NATIONAL AND INTERNATIONAL

Blessed with an extensive transport network, Manchester has those all-important high-accessibility credentials. Yes, siree. Fed intravenously by a network of motorways and one of British Rail's more successful Inter-City Links, it is one of the easiest British cities both to approach and to flee. Those who wish to do either may find the following numbers useful.

Airport Information Service	(24 hours)
Manchester Airport	061-489 3000
British Rail Information	061-832 8353
National Express Enquiries	061-228 3881
Credit Card Bookings	061-236 2120

LOCAL TRAVEL

Unfortunately, once approached, the city is not so easy to travel through. The nucleus of the city centre itself suffers from severe congestion, and a bird's eye view of rush-hour traffic resembles more closely a stagnant, multi-coloured worm convention than an effective road transport system. This, we are reliably assured, is about to be miraculously cured by the introduction of the Metrolink system (see *Metrolink*), and a long-overdue Ring Road.

The reality remains to be seen as neither project is yet complete, but at least action is being taken, and don't forget that transport miracles are not new to Manchester. This, after all, is the city that first built a passenger railway, that first provided a public bus service, that linked up to the first motorway and that introduced Mr Rolls to Mr Royce.

Car Owners

Lucky, lucky people! But did you know that your car is contributing to over 100,000 tons of toxic gases in the atmosphere? An alarming figure, and more so in view of the fact that most cars carry only one passenger. Environmentally friendly help is at hand in the form of the

Car Share Project (061-224 3171), a non-profit group based in Longsight but covering the whole city. Drivers are allowed to claim money from passengers as long as it doesn't exceed the running costs of the car. (That doesn't include the installation of a new CD stereo system!)

Driving through and parking in Manchester can be pretty frustrating, especially if you only want to park for a short period of time. Although there are loads of car parks (details on 061-234 4111), street parking is a nightmare. The rules are one of the unsolved mysteries of the Universe, and be warned, Mancunian traffic wardens move in mysterious ways. Some angry car owners have gone so far as to accuse the city council of 'carist' and 'parkophobic' policies, but few will champion their cause for fear of appearing ecologically unsound.

In spite of hassles in the city centre, a car is a useful commodity when moving around the suburbs or even right out of the city. There are no fewer than six motorways converging on the conurbation (although the M62 is more of a car park) and all the towns surrounding Manchester are easily accessible by road. The new ring road, aptly named the Inner Relief Route ('inner relief' referring, perhaps, to the driver's karma) is due for completion in early 1992. It will clear the city centre of 'through' traffic, and provide direct access to developments at Salford Quays and in the east of the city.

For day trips and weekends away, car hire is a perfect solution. There are hundreds of companies in Manchester, and it's worth checking the *Yellow Pages* for local firms who give the best value. Many offer special weekend rates, and although the bigger chains are handy for dropping off cars at different places, it's often better to use a smaller company if you are coming back. As a rule, car hire firms require a driver to be over the age of twenty-two with a clean licence, or over the age of twenty-five with penalty points. This is all connected with some weird and not very wonderful insurance policy, but seems to be a pretty universal rule.

Cyclists

Being fairly flat, Manchester is surprisingly easy to cycle around. Being fairly congested, it is also surprisingly easy to end up as flat as the city: be careful! Having said this, there are a number of cycle lanes around, and many people are taking Norman Tebbit's advice and getting on their bikes. Unfortunately, many people are also returning to their bikes to find that someone else has been getting on them. The police do actually recover a surprising number of lost bikes and, if unclaimed, sell them off at the end of the year at bargain prices. Check your local cop shop for details. If you are the proud owner of a bicycle, do ensure you take several notes of its serial number and invest in a secure lock.

The **Greater Manchester Cycling Project** (061-794 1926) is the answer to most of a cyclist's problems. They can tell you where to buy or hire a bike, give you details of the easiest, safest and most direct routes in the city (as well as routes for rustic rambles out of the smoke), and provide other general safety, security and legal advice. Unfortunately, in spite of a great need for the organization, it is under threat from suggested reductions in funds. It seems somewhat paradoxical that such facilities are being cut back in an area supposedly so committed to the environment. In any case, the Cycling Project intend to continue services, providing advice not only for cyclists in the city but also in Bolton, Tameside, Oldham, Stockport, Salford, Rochdale, Trafford, Wigan and Bury. If you telephone them at the number listed, they will be happy to provide you with maps and information as required.

Local Trains

There are three important mainline stations in the city centre: Piccadilly, Victoria and Oxford Road -- Manchester's attempt at a miniature wooden version of Sydney Opera House. Confusingly, but actually quite helpfully, some destinations are served from both Piccadilly and Victoria (though trains from one do not call at the other), while many (but not all) Piccadilly trains call at Oxford Road. Emphasizing rather blatantly the stereotypical split between the north and south of Manchester is the local rail system. All local trains to the North leave via grotty, cold and depressing Victoria Station and those to the South leave from modern and bright Piccadilly Station. A trek between the two consists of a ten-minute dash up Market Street, or a longer trip on a bus moving slowly through city traffic. This problem is apparently a hangover from the nineteenth century, and will in part be solved by the Metrolink. Otherwise, the rail network is relatively extensive and reliable, if slow. Another rather curious trait of Network NorthWest is its ticket system. You can buy a return to some destinations, but only if you come back on the same day, otherwise a return doesn't exist. A day return is cheaper than a single. The two facts put together would suggest that there is some conspiracy to keep Manchester's population in Manchester. Is this related to high levels of non-payment of the poll-tax?

Back on the right tracks (ouch!).... There are several stations in, or just out of, the city centre. **Deansgate** is handy for **Castlefield**. **Piccadilly** for **Chinatown** and **Market Street**; **Victoria** for **Cross Street** and **Manchester Cathedral**; and **Oxford Road** for the **Polytechnic**, **University**, and the **Cornerhouse**.

Moving out of the city, from Victoria, the towns of Bolton, Wigan, Blackburn, Bury, Rochdale, Oldham, Salford and Stalybridge are easily reached, as are the attractions at Hall i' th' Wood, Bromley Cross, Heaton Park, Shaw, Hollinwood and Ashton-under-Lyne. From Piccadilly, towns like Warrington, Altrincham, Chester, Wilmslow, Macclesfield and Buxton can be reached directly, as can attractions at Old Trafford, Sale, Styal, Hyde and Glossop. (See *JOY RIDES* and *DALES, HILLS AND DARK, SATANIC MILLS*).

Travel is made cheaper with a variety of concessionary cards. **Network NorthWest Day Ranger** tickets and **Wayfarer** tickets offer extensive use of any trains in Lancashire, Cheshire and the northern Peak District. Wayfarers also include buses within the area, although if you are not planning to hop around, it isn't the cheapest alternative. If you make several repetitious journeys, perhaps in and out of work, between two stations, season tickets are available from most rail stations. Information on local rail services can be obtained from the **Greater Manchester Passenger Transport Executive** (061-228 7811 / 061-273 5341).

Local Buses

Since the buses were deregulated a few years ago, no fewer than forty operators have begun or continued to provide services in the city. As a result, getting a bus is a more complicated experience than you first anticipate. Relief arrives in the form of a central, co-ordinated body that can help with any local transport queries, the **Greater Manchester Passenger Transport Executive** (061-228 7811 / 061-273 5341). They also produce a map showing all bus services. If you can make sense of it, you can probably understand *Satanic Verses* and find your way out of the Arndale Centre unaided.

The GMPTE also produce a vast number of timetables that are invaluable sources of comfort when you have been waiting in the pouring rain for two hours for a bus that never materializes. This can sometimes be avoided by consulting the *Manchester Evening News's* Information Page on Mondays, which lists changes in bus routes and timetables.

By far and away the largest operator is **Greater Manchester Buses**

(061-273 5341), characterized by big orange-and-white double-deckers seen lurching noisily through all parts of the city and beyond, an annoying 'people on the move' logo and an abundance of (admittedly very useful) leaflets telling you how to get around.

Together, the buses serving Manchester provide a pretty good and reliable service given that they have to contend with high levels of congestion, but their journeys are not particularly cheap. Passes make things a little bit easier on the pocket: **clipper cards** can be bought for a snip, covering ten bus journeys of a limited value, saving time as well as some of your precious pennies. They are available at any of the outlets listed below. If you need something more comprehensive, **Everybus Saver** tickets give unlimited travel for seven or 28 days, or 52 weeks. For these cards, take a picture of your own fair mush down to one of the following bus stations and get a membership card:

Arndale	Mon-Sat		0700-1825
Ashton-under-Lyne	Mon-Fri		0700-1755
	Sat		0830-1655
Bolton	Mon-Sat	(closed Weds)	0700-1755
Bury Interchange	Mon-Fri	(closed Tues)	0715-1755
Eccles Market	Sat		0830-1655
Hyde	Mon-Fri		0930-1630
	Sat		0930-1655
Leigh	Mon-Fri		1000-1230
			1300-1630
	Sat		0900-1700
Middleton	Mon-Fri	(closed Tues)	0930-1245
			1330-1640
	Sat		0930-1730
Oldham Town Centre	Mon-Fri		0700-1755
	Sat		0830-1655
Pendleton Precinct	Mon-Sat	(closed Tues)	0930-1630
Piccadilly	Mon-Sat		0700-1830
Rochdale	Mon-Fri	(closed Tues)	0700-1800
	Sat		0700-1700
Stockport	Mon-Sat		0700-1755
Walkden, St Ouen	Sat		0930-1630
Wigan Bus Station	Mon-Fri	(closed Weds)	0930-1315
			1345-1630
	Sat		0930-1315
Wythenshawe	Mon-Sat	(closed Weds)	0930-1630

Night Buses

In recent years, Manchester's nightlife has been given a real boost. Young ravers hit the town every night of the week until the wee tiny hours of the morning from all over the city. Living on fairly small budgets, night buses are a welcome and much-needed source of transport home. But what's this? Services only run on Fridays and Saturdays? Surely not! Oh yes indeedy, someone at the head of bus services is behind the times. Only the W42, running between Piccadilly and Didsbury, works on a nightly basis – and even that excludes Sundays. Still, the following limited services do run on Fridays and Saturdays – but be prepared to freeze your buns off: only two or three journeys on each route take place, and hardly any leave after 0230. For more comprehensive details, pick up a leaflet from the GMPTE or from one of the bus stations listed above.

Existing services include:

10	Manchester-Eccles-Cadishead
28/36	Manchester-Bolton
42	Manchester-Withington-East Didsbury
46/7	Manchester-Chorlton-Southern Cemetery
50	Manchester-Kingsway-East Didsbury
57	Manchester-Bank House
82	Manchester-Oldham
106	Manchester-Northenden-Wythenshawe
161	Manchester-Royton
162	Manchester-Middleton-Rochdale
164	Manchester-Middleton-Langley
192	Manchester-Stockport-Hazel Grove/Marple
211	Manchester-Hattersley
216	Manchester-Ashton-under-Lyne
222	Manchester-Hyde
256	Manchester-Urmston-Partington
263	Manchester-Sale-Altrincham
705	Manchester-Prestwich-Bury
W42	Manchester-Fallowfield-West Didsbury-East Didsbury

Metrolink

Manchester's new demigod, Metrolink has been pushed forward as the answer to all the city's transport problems. It is not necessarily a new idea as it has been modelled quite closely on that yuppie train set the Docklands Light Railway in London, but Manchester's designers claim that this is going to be the best in Britain. Unlike other systems, Metrolink can run on existing railway tracks, which has meant that the lines can be more extensive and easily maintained – thus ensuring its success as a major form of public transport and not just a touristy city centre convenience.

An unusual amount of consideration has gone into the needs of the passenger – usually the last priority but in this case seemingly the first. Each Metrolink carriage was designed to be fully accessible to people in wheelchairs or with walking disabilities, and to those with prams or impaired by heavy shopping. Platforms at existing stations have been altered to include lifts, ramps and level access, while at street level a profile platform is being introduced to ensure that all sections of the carriages will be 'get onable and offable', with space for two wheelchairs at either side of the door. Plans are all very well in theory, but the good news is that the platforms have been tried, tested and approved by disabled groups, turning a theory into a welcome reality.

Phase One of the project is a line from Bury to Altrincham, due for completion in 1991 with many others to follow. More information can be gleaned from Metrolink (061-228 1228), from the GMPTE (061-228 7811 / 061 273 5341) or from the little tinpot Metrolink office in Piccadilly Gardens, which, judging from the state of the place, is a temporary offering during construction.

Taxis

There are hundreds of black cabs and mini-cabs throughout the city, but three 'top tips' apply, as they do all over the country. First of all, if possible, use a mini-cab: fares are infinitely cheaper as they are based on mileage and not time spent in traffic. They can also be booked in advance, and most companies only charge from the pick-up point, so check when you ring – numbers are listed in the *Yellow Pages* directory. Secondly, if using a mini-cab, arrange a fare before you go. Many now have meters anyway, but a price indication will avoid having to do a runner when you realize you haven't got enough. Finally, make sure you take a registered cab, with a little plate on the back of the car: crank drivers frequently stop to give lifts, and while they may just be trying to con a bit of money, all too often people are attacked and robbed. Be careful!

Taxi ranks can be found outside all British Rail stations and black cabs can often be hailed as they shoot up and down the main roads of the city.

Accommodation

LONG-TERM ACCOMMODATION

Despite the city's claims that there is housing a-plenty for all in Manchester, the many bodies littered in shop doorways would seem to suggest otherwise. The crisis in accommodation has hit even the hitherto privileged student community, many of whom arrived to start courses at Manchester University in 1990 to discover that their first few weeks of fresherhood were to be spent on other students' floors. In South Manchester the price of rented accommodation is constantly inflated by the huge demand, especially in the more upmarket studenty areas of Withington and Didsbury. Further south and to the west, where suburbs desperately try to cling to their Cheshire credentials, rents are even higher than in the city centre. The northern suburbs, being less popular, are inevitably cheaper to rent in.

Council Housing

Salford has recently knocked down some rotten eyesores, and has embarked upon a comprehensive housing scheme based on the unfashionable assumption that everyone has a right to a decent home. Manchester and Tameside councils have joined forces to complete a massive housing scheme in the east of the city. Major problem areas such as Hulme are under the scrutiny and observation of the powers that be, and eventual redevelopment is beginning to get under way. The situation is far from ideal, but at least there seem to be moves in a positive direction.

Council housing is allocated on a points system, and the more desperate your personal conditions, the more points you accumulate – rather like some sick game show. To be fair, Manchester's housing shortages are less acute than those in many other major cities, and a roof is usually found for desperate cases. Sadly, you really would need to be desperate for some of them. For housing advice and information, contact the housing departments of the local councils on the following numbers:

Bury	061-705 5000
Manchester	061-234 5000
Oldham	061-678 4610
Salford	061-737 0051
Stockport	061-474 4235
Tameside	061-330 8355
Trafford	061-872 2101

Housing Associations and Co-operatives

There are many. But they are also very much in demand, and frequently operate on similar points systems to council accommodation. The central co-ordinating body is the **Housing Corporation**, based at Elisabeth House, 16 St Peter's Square (061-228 2951). They will be able to give you extensive lists of housing associations and co-operatives as well as offering advice on finding somewhere to rest your weary head. Local authority housing departments can give specific advice for your area.

Private Rented Accommodation

Rent ain't what it used to be. Prices have rocketed with the growth and popularization of the city. A room in a shared house will set you back around £30 per week, and if you're searching for a one-bedroom flat with all the trimmings, you'll be forking out at least £60.

The *Manchester Evening News* publishes comprehensive lists of flats and shared houses, and *Loot* has some accommodation advertised. Surprisingly, listings in both are pretty thin on the ground. The trusty and unsophisticated card in the newsagent's window can often be the best way of finding yourself somewhere to live.

If things are getting desperate, you can always go through an accommodation agency. Legally, they are not allowed to charge you for anything before they have found you somewhere to live, but you should nonetheless be very vigilant in trying to ensure that there are no hidden extras before you register with them. Many estate agents have a section for rented accommodation, although they might not advertise it and are frequently particularly snotty about this part of their service. Grit your teeth, go in and ask.

If you're already well ensconced in your little dream pad but are having those oh-so-unusual problems with your landlord, or if you need advice on escaping the rent trap and entering the mortgage prison, contact **Housing Aid** on 061-234 4750. They will advise on mortgages, fair rents, deposits and agencies. They also operate a 24-hour eviction hotline on 061-234 4815.

SHORT-TERM ACCOMMODATION

Hotels and Bed & Breakfasts

This section should give some brief pointers for those who have come to the Costa del Salford for their annual holiday or for those who want to house a few guests.

The upmarket hotels are out of the price range of just about anyone who would read a book like this. All the same, these could give you a good laugh. The swankier hotels range from £95.00 per person per night at the **Midland Hotel** on Peter Street (061-236 3333), to the positively reasonable **Castlefield Hotel** on Liverpool Road (061-832 7073), which chimes in at a mere £40.00. These biggies are mainly frequented by fat cats with suitably corpulent expense accounts, but many offer discounts for weekend breaks to fill the rooms that they've left behind.

Of the smaller hotels, one of the cheapest in the centre is the **City Road Inn** (061-236 3820) on Albion Street, at £15.00 per night. For further lists and extensive information, contact the Tourist Information Centre on 061-234 3157/8. Out of the city, many places are cheaper still (often charging under £15.00 for bed and breakfast). Some of these are detailed below.

South

Lincoln Service Flats and Hotels, 16-18 Wilabraham Road, Fallowfield, Manchester M14 6JY (061-224 5658)
Verdene Hotel, 454 Moss Lane East, Rusholme, Manchester M14 (061-224 1576)
Hotel Martinez, 126 Palatine Road, West Didsbury M20 (061-434 3337)
Blezards Guest House, 191 Slade Lane, Levenshulme, Manchester M19 (061-224 7753)

Salford

Prince of Wales, 165 Oldfield Road, Salford M5 (061-832 5716)
White Lodge Private Hotel, 87-9 Great Cheetham Street West, Broughton, Salford (061-792 3047)

Tameside

Lancaster House Hotel, 17 Richmond Street, Ashton-under-Lyne (061-330 1350/1639)

Norman's Guest House, 33 Hyde Road, Ardwick M12 (061-273 1059).

Other short-term accommodation

Out of term-time the **Universities** and **Polytechnic** offer short-term accommodation in their halls of residence. Manchester University (061-275 2888) and Manchester Polytechnic (061-247 3490) are seriously overpriced for the privilege of sleeping in a narrow bed and suffering an institutional breakfast. Salford University is generally more reasonable. Details on 061-745 5457.

Those old champions of penny-pinching youth, the **YMCA**s and the **YWCA**s offer budget places to sleep, perchance to dream. The main YMCA is on Peter Street (061-834 6035), next to the Midland Hotel, which means that you can always hang around there and pretend to look wealthy before nipping into your hostel. There is also one in Castlefield on Liverpool Road (061-839 2567). The gals' equivalents can be found at 73 Carlton Road, in the south of the city (061-226 2768), or way out in Altrincham (St John's Road, 061-928 2107) – not that the women have been marginalized in the outer suburbs or anything!

For the classic budget resting place, the **Youth Hostel** is at 166 Deansgate (061-834 7119) and caters for members of both sexes.

This list can only be sketchy; by far and away the best way to find a humble short-term abode is to telephone or visit the local Tourist Information Centre.

2. ROOTS

This chapter is designed to afford you the opportunity to step back from mind-boggling lists of telephone numbers and information and take a broader look at the region and the things that make it special.

ROOTS covers the sprawling and diverse conurbation, its suburbs and surrounding towns, as well as giving a brief insight into their history and politics.

Towns, Villages and Districts

The area of Greater Manchester is split into the major districts of Trafford, Tameside, Salford, North Manchester and South-east Manchester (all coming under the jurisdiction of Manchester City Council), with small bordering areas like Stockport, Oldham and Bury existing happily and independently on the edges. The differences contained under the 'Greater Manchester' umbrella are enormous, making the city a lively place in which to live and an exciting one to explore.

TRAFFORD

Trafford incorporates the districts of Urmston and Stretford to the north, and the very affluent areas of Sale and Altrincham to the south. The area boasts the lowest poll-tax rate in Manchester and one of the largest industrial parks in Western Europe, as well as the internationally renowned sports grounds of Old Trafford. **Stretford** is one of the few working-class areas, where housing costs are still comparatively low. There is more of a community atmosphere here than in the commuter belts of the south or in **Flixton**, a very middle-class area lying slightly to the west. Much of the population is employed at nearby Trafford Park, along with many of the citizens of **Urmston** – the ones that haven't retired, that is. Judging from the differences in their shopping centres and pubs, it would appear that once you have spent your working life in Stretford, you make a dignified retreat to Urmston.

Until the railways came in the nineteenth century, **Sale** didn't exist. Now it is an exuberant area, proudly possessing a water park and trying desperately to associate itself with Cheshire in spite of its 061 telephone code! Both Sale and its role model **Altrincham** go a good way to explaining the Conservative bias in Trafford's politics, not to mention the generally high price of housing and rented accommodation in the area.

SALFORD

Poor old Salford has suffered terribly from recessions and depressions, and more recently from image problems left over from the Industrial Revolution. Salford University has not benefited half so much from the hype surrounding Manchester as has its near-neighbour on Oxford Road, and the city has always been more sensitive to fluctuations in the economic climate. Now, at long last, Lowry's images are being plonked firmly on the walls of galleries, and the realities on the streets are being spruced up. The massive developments down at Salford Quays have enhanced the image of the city no end, so that more and more visitors are impressed by its attractions. The good, solid community has much to boast of in the city: a reputable university, a multi-screen cinema, a large section of Castlefield, some excellent pubs, a beautiful cathedral, and out to the west towards **Worsley**, some pretty countryside.

Eccles, to the west of the City of Salford but within the council boundaries, is a fairly independent and old-fashioned area. It boasts many Real-Ale pubs, nearly all full of locals, all of whom seem to know each other. The area gives the impression that it is far away from the city, whereas in fact it is very close. East Eccles is much more traditionally industrialized than the west, where it gives way to Chat Moss. Just below lies Trafford and just above sits **Swinton**, about which there isn't a great deal to say.

NORTH MANCHESTER, BURY AND OLDHAM

With the exceptions of **Prestwich** and **Whitefield**, North Manchester is distinguished by cheap housing and a healthy community spirit. The two areas mentioned above suffer from delusions of Cheshirism and are relatively countryfied, boasting Heaton Park among their attractions. **Cheetham Hill** and **Crumpsall** have pride in the diverse claims to fame that they can brag of – among them the Abraham Moss Community Centre and local hero, comedian Henry Normal. They are seedy areas, the sort of places that Southerners imagine the whole of Manchester to be like, but they have a cosy and vibrant spirit, contributed to by a large ethnic community.

Bury and **Oldham**, although technically parts of Greater Manchester, operate very independently of the city, and are more in tune with neighbouring old Lancashire towns. They run their own affairs and offer all the benefits of life in a localized, independent centre – such as cheap housing and excellent facilities – while still being close enough to the city for work and play. Bury boasts some large redevelopment projects including the Warner B twelve-screen cinema complex and a Megabowl centre. Oldham, on the other hand, has not been so adventurous but remains traditional and content on the edges of the moors. They are both very handy for escapes into Yorkshire and Lancashire.

Former exceptions excluded, **North Manchester** is actually the only area which doesn't get trendier the further you progress out of the city. Unlike the situation to the south, house prices actually fall with distance: the towns to the north are cheaper places to live all round, and are infinitely more interesting than the commuter belts of the Cheshire border.

TAMESIDE

With the exception of villagey areas like **Stalybridge** (the far east still remains the most desirable place in the district to live, although areas around Debdale Park in **Denton** are also popular and pretty upmarket), East Manchester has suffered in the last twenty years from declining fortunes and unsightly landmarks. The once-affluent and ironically named **Belle Vue** sank heavily in the 1970s but has recently re-emerged to become the major leisure area of the city. Along her stretch of the Hyde Road, sit a multiplex cinema, a greyhound racing track, a ten-pin bowling emporium, and one of the city's best athletics grounds. Further down in Hyde itself, a massive water complex has been completed, and the entire area is now attracting much attention.

Like many other parts of Manchester and Lancashire, **Ashton-under-Lyne** has used its heritage to advantage and is developing as a major town out of the city. Whereas Belle Vue and Hyde have been marketed as leisure suburbs for the general use of everybody (Tameside's own residents footing the bill in the form of the poll-tax), Ashton has more carefully distanced itself and focused on its community.

The developments in Tameside have been undertaken with the close co-operation of Manchester City Council, and other schemes such as new housing are proposed. With Salford, Tameside is one of the major indications of Manchester's changing fortunes.

SOUTH-EAST MANCHESTER

Being the area where the vast majority of students reside, this is one of the most highly populated and vibrant parts of the whole city. Nearer to the centre lie the areas of **Moss Side** and **Hulme**, where violence and crime are commonplace in the ghettoized council districts. This was not always so: during the Industrial Revolution both were relatively affluent. The *Morning Chronicle* in 1849 reported that 'Hulme presents the most cheering spectacle, on account of its comparatively broad and airy streets'. Difficult to believe it's the same area! The police working in Moss Side have recently done much to enhance their image with a 'softly, softly', supposedly community-based approach, but it remains to be seen whether that will intimidate the big bad wolves of the drug scene.

It sometimes seems that the whole Wilmslow and Oxford Roads stretch is one great hall of residence. **Rusholme** is renowned for its Asian community and high student population, the latter being also very much in evidence in **Fallowfield** and **Withington** – home to Christie's, the internationally renowned cancer hospital and research centre. To the south, the more affluent (and hence more expensive) areas of **Didsbury** and **Chorlton** boast the more discerning students, curiously interspersed with the older, well-heeled local community. The benefits of such a large student population are evident in the nightlife of these areas, but there are drawbacks, especially in the high costs of rented property raised by sheer demand. **Whalley Range**, between Moss Side and Chorlton in every way, is another cheap and lively area. Moving south-eastwards from the city centre, **Longsight**, **Levenshulme** and **Ladybarn** are unglamorous but inexpensive.

Further south, **Wythenshawe** (the proposed site of a new multi-million pound hospital causing much controversy in all parts of the city) is caught in the curious situation of being a Labour constituency within a very blue area. One of the southernmost suburbs, it is more closely akin to Altrincham than Manchester, and the area is more prosperous than it used to be. Some good things have come out of Wythenshawe – namely, the first bus service for disabled people and an excellent theatre, the Forum. The areas of **Cheadle**, **Burnage** and **Gatley** are also pretty independent and relatively student-free: ideal if you want the benefits of the south-west without clamouring for accommodation.

History and Politics

In the beginning, Manchester was a 'mere village' in a county dominated by Liverpool, the centre of the slave, tobacco and sugar trades. Livelihoods inland from the Mersey were made in agriculture or cottage industries such as textile weaving until suddenly, in 1774, the government lifted the ban on British production of cotton and those tiny cottage industries woke up to a revolution. Manchester stepped forward and grabbed growing potential by the cotton balls.

Almost overnight the tiny hamlets surrounding Manchester (such as Hulme, Pendleton and Salford) became amalgamated into the smoky mass of Cottonopolis, and the mere village became the 'dear, old, dull, ugly, smoky, grey, grim Manchester' of Elizabeth Gaskell's industrial novels. Further out to the north, east and west, independent towns cloned into 'Little Manchesters', and around them textile villages sprang up. Whereas once upon a time cottages clustered around the castle, cottonages now clustered around the mill.

The growth was fast and extensive: the population boomed, inventors crawled out of the woodwork to make fortunes and opportunists flocked to the North to become rich. Yet while all this was going on, the working classes worked longer hours in more cramped conditions for little money, and a new form of slavery was born. Children had to be handed over to incompetent nurses while mums went out to work; many were drugged on laudanum, which ensured listless lives and early deaths. The situation did not really improve until the twentieth century, in spite of the introduction of Health Authorities in 1858. In Wigan, those who survived went into the mines at the ages of four and five, and elsewhere seven or eight was the average working age. Pregnant women all over Lancashire were expected to work until they dropped: work days lasted as long as the work that had to be done, and twenty-four-hour shifts were not uncommon. As a result of the poverty and working conditions, death rates were high, and quality of life was low, but the spirit of the people remained unbowed.

Instead of bowing, the working classes fought back. They campaigned for the Ten Hour Act; they campaigned for the vote; they campaigned for the repeal of the Corn Laws, and in 1903 the women's movement was born here. They may have been down but they weren't out. Even in 1819, when eleven were killed and 600 injured by the yeomanry at a peaceful demonstration for voting rights, the people continued to campaign. The massacre was named 'Peterloo', and when the Repeal Bill was passed in 1846, the Free Trade Hall was built on its site to celebrate the success of the Anti-Corn Law League.

The people also knew how to enjoy themselves, and after the passing of the Ten Hour Bill in 1847, they had the time to do this properly. Monday nights were concert nights at the Free Trade Hall with the new and crude Hallé Orchestra; Sundays were given over to day trips out to Cheshire to the extent that one frustrated minister told his dwindling congregation that the rest 'all went to Heaven or to Hallé'! The Ten Hour Act also gave people the opportunity to learn, and schools popped up left, right and centre. Elizabeth Gaskell was amazed at the avid reading habits of Mancunians, the ever-present desire to better themselves, while Angus Bethurne Reach, writing in 1849, remarked on the vibrancy of the area and the intelligent pupils in the schools.

The fervent interest in politics was one manifestation of this. The Trade Union movement grew rapidly here and the Labour party gained most of its momentum in 1906 thanks to the highly unionized cotton and mining industries. Political writers had their heydays in and around the city: Engels supported his friend Karl Marx here and George Orwell immortalized the political climate of the North in *The Road To Wigan Pier*. Politics were a major part of the lives of the working classes, and when the universal male franchise was granted in 1867, political clubs sprang up everywhere. Local people took elections seriously: they were a major form of bar-room debate, and during the deep depressions of the 1920s and 1930s were the source of hope for the thousands of poverty- stricken, unemployed families.

The Second World War pushed unemployment problems away as Manchester suffered heavily from the effects of the Blitz. On 22 and 23 December 1940, the city was devastatingly attacked. 1,300 people died and 30,000 homes were destroyed. Both the Free Trade Hall and the Royal Exchange were ruined while Manchester Cathedral was also damaged. Miraculously, the heavily industrialized area of Trafford Park, which surely must have been a target, remained unscathed. In Salford, 560 died and 8,000 homes were destroyed. Putting right the damage lent a new sense of purpose to the city: houses had to be rebuilt, and as many of the worst hangovers of the Industrial Revolution were now long gone, there was an opportunity to enhance the cities. This process went on well into the 1960s, the results ranging from the lovely authentic Free Trade Hall to the Arndale Centre – which brings us more or less up to date.

These days, politics are still important to the citizens of Manchester. The North/South divide in the city is most appropriately emphasized by the telly graphics during a general election. The blue splodge in the middle of the predominantly red North-West is Cheshire/South Manchester, although at times during the 1980s even some of the Labour party strongholds began to turn shades of purple. The poll-tax seems to have reversed this trend somewhat, but the southernmost parts of Manchester are still, and always will be, true blue – with a little yellow thrown in at times for contrast.

An avid local Lancastrian interest in politics is still evident, especially in areas out of the city. To the north, differences in areas very close together are stark. Ribble Valley boasted hard-right Home Secretary David Waddington until the Majorettes packed him off to the Lords (and lost the seat). Next door, in Blackburn, former NUS president and Shadow Minister for Education Jack Straw rules the roost. Rochdale, once a rampant red, was seduced in the early 1970s by-election by local Liberal heavyweight hero Cyril (now Sir Cyril) Smith, and the love affair has continued through the demise of his party, largely due to the enormous commitment he has to his local community.

Back in Manchester itself the Labour party rules, with its most famous MP being Gerald Kaufman, member for Gorton and the Shadow Foreign Secretary. Beyond the national scene, local government is very much a notable part of life in the city. The Labour-controlled city councils of Salford and Manchester have often been criticized for 'loony left' policies by the more paranoid quarters of the national press, but their tremendous effect on the growth and revival of the cities cannot be questioned. Salford's chief executive Roger Rees and Manchester's leader Graham Stringer are two of the most powerful men in Greater Manchester, and have a say in everything that goes on. Graham Stringer effectively rules the roost in the city and is both praised and criticized for his dominance; in spite of challenges from the right and middle, however, he remains firmly in control. Manchester City Council work very closely with Salford, the Metropolitan Borough Council of Tameside (and to a lesser extent Trafford) and the Central Manchester Development Corporation to bring investment and prosperity to the area.

Trafford has benefited tremendously from this, as has the city centre. Trafford's jurisdiction covers the industrial area of Trafford Park as well as the affluent blue areas of Sale and Altrincham, and operates, largely due to its politics, much more independently of the City Council than the other MBCs. Tameside has worked closely with Manchester City Council to develop housing to the east of the city, and Salford has joined forces to bring prosperity to the Salford Quays and Castlefield.

Salford City Council also led the way in 1990 to improving the 1960s housing hangovers by demolishing eight monstrous and largely ghettoized tower blocks, and rehousing the few remaining tenants in more human surroundings.

The Greater Manchester Police Force, the largest outside the Met, is an extremely powerful political force in Manchester. Led by James Anderton, it has been the focus of much controversy over the years. Mr Anderton is a high-profile public figure and runs the force with a firm hand, having a very large say in what goes on in the city. Along with Graham Stringer, he was a prominent member of Manchester's Olympic Bid Committee, and is a renowned religious heavyweight (he was awarded the Catholic cross, *pro ecclesia et pontifice*, in 1982). Even so, his 'hotline' to God did not stretch to swaying the IOC decision – presumably, even the Lord couldn't produce £35 million. The police are not popular with the lesbian and gay community, who have still not forgotten Anderton's charges of 'licentious dancing', and the Manchester Police are notably much less liberal than most other British police forces in their policy on minor soft drugs 'offences'.

Local Media

As with most things, Manchester is the second largest media centre outside of London. The newpaper beloved of all Hampstead residents, the *Guardian*, began its life as the *Manchester Guardian*, conceived by John Edward Taylor – who achieved fame and hence financial backing for his newspaper with his eyewitness account of the Peterloo Massacre in 1819. It is part of the group that owns the *Manchester Evening News*, Britain's largest regional newspaper, and *City Life*, the city's fortnightly listings magazine, as well as most of the local freebie papers. Quite a monopoly!

The city is also a power base for regional and national television; Granada, the self-proclaimed largest independent television network, has interests way beyond *Coronation Street* in areas as diverse as the satellite station BSB and motorway service stations. Manchester is also the headquarters of the mighty BBC's services in the North.

Reflecting the city's musical superiority are the radio stations, even if they are not so numerous as one might expect. Hopefully, with the proposed new broadcasting laws, more are sneaking up on the horizon.

In all sections of the media, the city is buzzing, and this section should help you to sort out what to read, watch or listen to and why.

PRESS: NEWSPAPERS AND MAGAZINES

The *Manchester Evening News* sells over 250,000 copies daily and claims to have over one million readers. In bygone days, it was a predictably right-wing rag, with a steady crop of biased news articles. Since the appointment of new editor Mike Unger, the paper has shifted more to the centre, and the once-endless Labour-bashing articles are now relatively rare. As a result, complaints of bias have inevitably come from other quarters: even in the new era of *MEN* perestroika, occasional questionable articles slip through the net.

The *Evening News* is undoubtedly the most comprehensive source of information and news within Greater Manchester and has an invaluable classified section. The daily Post Bag is a hysterical read (though not intended as such), representing the opinions of people like Disgruntled from Sale and providing an almost *Viz-Magazine*-style source of entertainment. More seriously, on Mondays the *MEN* produces an Information Section with details of transport developments, chemist opening times and other such indispensable snippets of information. The newspaper's influence within the city cannot be underestimated: without it the Olympic Bid would never have gained the momentum and support it did, and any charity or trust knows that once the paper champions its cause the ways ahead are paved with silver.

Out of the city, more independent towns such as Bolton, Oldham, Bury, Altrincham and Stockport have good local newspapers, and the smaller suburbs have free sources of local information stuffed weekly through the door.

The weekly classified newspaper *Loot*, famous in London, now publishes a North-West edition, which is excellent for cars, flats, and buying and selling pretty much anything.

Turning to magazines, *City Life* has to be the best source of 'what's on' and listings information in Manchester. Packed full of lively articles and columns (regular columnists include Jim Reeve and Henry Normal), the magazine is good for a read in its own right. The real treasure, however, lies in the abundance of reviews and detailed listings. Its critics accuse it of left-wing bias, which really only results from its youthful and exuberant views of life in the city, including a concern for so-called minority issues. *City Life* is published fortnightly at 90p an issue and is an essential asset to living in the city.

The nearest rival to *City Life* comes in the shape of two publications, *Avant* and *Uptown*. Both are owned by Uptown Publications, along with *Girl About Town*. Both *Uptown* and *Girl About Town* are freebies containing listings, reviews and articles. *Uptown* has often been disparaged by deadly enemies *City Life*, although it is in fact quite useful and pretty interesting. The war between the two magazines frequently spills over into their editorial pages. *Uptown* can be found in the Central Library, the Tourist Information Centre, or being handed out in town; *Girl About Town* is usually found in a white handbag on the dancefloor at Sacha's.

Avant, the North-West magazine from Uptown Publications, strives hard to be different. It's a glossy and seriously professional monthly, which is usually well worth the £1.25 cover price. *Avant* is not so much of a 'what's on' as a 'why it's on' magazine and is full of articles and interviews geared towards the North-West.

A radical political alternative to these is *Link-Up*, available bimonthly from alternative outlets for only 10p. There is a variety of good special interest magazines. The *Artful Reporter*, distributed monthly around theatres and galleries in the city, as well as libraries and information centres, is the region's most comprehensive guide to the arts. The magazine is full of reviews and articles of interest to those of an artistic temperament, and it also has its own listing section containing details of performances, exhibitions, access and facilities. Well worth digging out.

For minority interests, *Cahoots* and *Scene Out* are invaluable. The latter, very much like *City Life* in appearance, subtitles itself 'the Guide to the Lesbian and Gay North'. It contains thorough listings as well as a massive variety of articles of interest to lesbians and gay men. *Cahoots* deals with all forms of minority issues from vegetarianism to racism and is useful for the more unusual and marginal activities in the city, especially complementary medicine, alternative lifestyles and personal growth – with helpful listings. It may look like it has been thrown together in someone's front room, but funds are severely limited, and the people down at the *Cahoots* offices do a sterling job. With the closure of Grass Roots, the radical bookshop, any dedicated alternative form of media is a rare and precious thing.

RADIO

There are five local radio stations in the Greater Manchester area. The Beeb's effort is **GMR**, the snappily-named Greater Manchester Radio (FM: 95.1 MHz, AM: 1458kHz). GMR is a rather bland station with a seventy per cent speech bias. Occasionally, there are some specialist music programmes which can be worth twiddling your dial for, although the majority of the output has a tendency to float right through your head without ever connecting with any of your senses.

KFM (FM:104.9 MHz), on the other hand, has a major music bias, especially specialist jazz, blues, R'n'B, and soul. The station's DJs are actually animated and interesting when they do speak, and this, coupled with laudable intentions to promote local talent, makes KFM well worth gluing your ear to for a while. Unfortunately, based in Stockport, its transmission area is largely confined to southern Manchester.

Manchester's most famous independent radio station is **Piccadilly**, which is now split down the middle to suit different generations. **Piccadilly Gold** (AM: 1152 kHz) is perfect for the wrinklies and for those of you who secretly revere Val Doonican and the Drifters. More up-beat is Piccadilly's other half, **Key 103** (FM: 103 MHz), a solid local making brave attempts to be 'seriously happening'.

Sunset Radio (FM: 102 MHz) is a brilliant addition to Manchester's rather tired radio scene. It was formerly a pirate station, and was one of the few to be granted its legal status under recent laws. Sunset is a 24-hour ethnic station that features everything from jazz to bhangra, from Greek tavernas to ragga. It is the only radio station that concentrates fully on World Music. Listen in if you can't afford a holiday, and pretend that you're in Ireland, Africa or a Southern American Gospel Church followed by a Blues Bar, Asia, Kuwait or even Jerusalem. It's a pretty well-travelled station.

TELEVISION

After the BBC thankfully abandoned *Nationwide* in 1983, and replaced it with a beefed-up *Look North-West*, the old favourite *Granada Tonight* finally faced some stiff competition. Those who kept their tellies on at tea time gradually discovered that Granada had a more informal appeal than dear old Auntie, and that its common gaffs were really quite endearing. As with other independent stations, Granada has surged forward with a more exciting variety of local programmes such as *What's New*, an attempt at a visual equivalent of *City Life*, shown on Thursday nights and well worth watching if you're bored or baby-sitting.

Homespun celebrity Anthony H. Wilson (he of Factory Records, ex-*Granada Tonight* and the sadly missed Haçienda) is back on the air with Lucy Meacock presenting *Granada Upfront*. This is a stimulating issues programme that encourages loud and occasionally violent audience participation, which makes for riveting viewing.

3. MILK AND HONEY

Restaurants and Cafés

If looking at the number of Mancunian restaurants in the *Good Food Guide* were indicative of its citizens' eating habits, a stranger to the North could be forgiven for thinking that we must either be a city of starving waifs with no money to spend on eating out, or simply unimaginative folk with no interest in food beyond the realms of black pudding, tripe and Lancashire Hot Pot. Manchester was, er, lucky enough to be chosen for the country's first drive-in McDonald's (in Fallowfield). In reality, with areas like Chinatown and Rusholme tempting the taste buds, it is more surprising that Manchester's inhabitants are not twenty-stone, credit-blacklisted health hazards. A veritable hotchpotch of culinary delights ensures that there is something in the city to whet every appetite.

CHINATOWN

As you would expect from a city with the second largest Chinese population in the country, Manchester offers some of the best oriental cuisine outside of South-East Asia. Unfortunately, for the most part it would be cheaper to hop on a plane to Peking: you are expected to pay dearly for many meals. Still, Chinatown is a must, and there are a few cheap gems to be found in its streets. One of which is definitely not the **Yang Sing** on Princess Street (061-236 2200); widely regarded by many to be the best Chinese restaurant in the country, tables here are booked up for ages in advance (probably due to the fact that people have to save for so long in order to go). Once you've secured the loan, however, your stomach will never stop thanking you: the food is heavenly. The restaurant began life in a much smaller venue on George Street, which is now occupied by the **Little Yang Sing** (061-228 7722) – smaller, but no less expensive!

There are hundreds of restaurants in the area, but to find the cheaper ones, hunt down the back streets; if the locals are there, it's definitely a good sign. (Beware of machete-swinging Triad gang fighters, though – they tend to disturb a relaxed atmosphere!) The **Win Wah** on Portland Street, is a little cheaper than the other high-profile restaurants and is popular, so again, book in advance (061-236 2214).

Cheaper still is the **Happy Seasons** on Faulkner Street (061-236 7189). The restaurant serves **Singaporean** food as well as the more traditional Chinese dishes, and is a real treat: it isn't the smartest of places, but the food is delicious and the prices affordable. Further down the road at 56 Faulkner Street, is the **Penang Village** (061-236 2650), which serves **Malayan** food – a sort of mixture of all of the good Indian and Chinese dishes. Although the place isn't cheap, the food is delicious and offers a change from the standard menus of traditional Chinese restaurants.

INDIAN

Rusholme is the curry centre of the North-West. Dotted at regular intervals down the Wilmslow Road are dozens of restaurants ranging from the upmarket to the 'post-club curry crew' venues. As with Chinatown, it is difficult to choose a few, but unlike Chinatown, none of the meals will set you back too much, and all of them are of a high standard. The **Tandoori Kitchen**, 131 Wilmslow Road (061-224 2329), offers a brilliant combination of good grub and very cheap prices, which instead of including hidden extras seem to offer hidden refunds! Most people who go here don't realize that either nan bread or pilau rice is included in the cost of a main course and think they have to pay for the sundries. In addition, charges for popadums are for two and not for one as is more common in the area. The restaurant is unlicensed but you can take your own drink with you – which makes the whole experience even more cost-effective. One word of warning, however: don't assume that it's an after-club place because doors close at midnight.

A stone's throw away, but much more upmarket, is **Sanam** at 215 Wilmslow Road (061-224 8570). It is a little more pricey than the Tandoori Kitchen, although it still cannot be termed expensive, and the décor is more classy. There are several Sanams on this stretch, each one worth a nibble, so if you wander into the wrong one by mistake, it won't make a great deal of difference!

Moving into the city and hence into a higher price bracket, try the **Deansgate Indian Restaurant**, Longworth Street, off St John Street (061-835 1888). Although quite pricey at night-time, it has a brilliant lunchtime 'eat as much as you can for £6' menu (£5 for NUS card holders). You're unlikely to sniff a chapatti for that amount in the **Kathmandu** on Sackville Street, largely due to that rare honour, an entry in the *Good Food Guide*, but also admittedly due to its delicious and unusual **Nepalese** menu. Ring 061-236 4684 to book – and do book because it's popular.

Cheap food in the city centre is hard to find, but if you go to the **Everest**, 63 Whitworth Street (061-236 6286), you'll be pleasantly surprised: being primarily **Bangladeshi**, the dishes are more unusual. On Upper Brook Street, people snigger at the tatty front of the **Plaza** unless they've eaten there. The food is delicious and very cheap, and it is open until 0300. There isn't a phone: it's not really the sort of place you book anyway. Well worth hunting down. Undoubtedly, the cheapest sit-down meals in the centre are at the **Café Yaqoub** (2 Union Street), where you eat your curry with chapattis rather than a knife and fork, and **Cuckoo Chef**, 71 Oldham Street, both near Dry and Affleck's (see *Café Bars*).

VEGETARIAN

Thanks to champions of the veggie cause like Harold Bishop, non-meat eaters are no longer perceived by British society to be brainless hippies, and even the most conservative places now include decent herbivore hunger halters on the menu. Gone are the days when vegetarian alternatives were limited to cheese pizza or egg flan, and in Manchester in particular the choices are vast – though surprisingly there is no specialist vegetarian restaurant in the central shopping area.

At the cheapest end of the scale, near Manchester Poly on Oxford Road, is **On the Eighth Day** (061-273 4878). It may look like a transport caff from the outside, and it certainly isn't the place for a romantic *diner à deux*, but it is ideal for a cheap dinner-time face-stuff, and the food is tummy-rumblingly good. A little farther south in the same mode is **Café Paradise Lost**. Here you can get a good home-made bowl of soup for 60p (students get a ten per cent discount!), but you are hereby warned to go easy on the beans: the lavvy is outside!

Very popular and a little more on the classy side is the **Greenhouse** on Great Western Street in Rusholme (061-224 0730). It's a pretty and unusual place: it will cure the hunger pangs, but take your cheque-book – you'll be paying meaty prices. Cheaper, and also out of town, are **Greens**, Lapwing Lane, West Didsbury, and **Pie in the Sky** (it's on the first floor – which it shares with what is probably Manchester's best suburban bookshop, **The Book Loft**), Wellington Road, Withington.

Not exclusively vegetarian, but with menus extensive enough to appear so, are the **Lime Tree Café** (and its sister restaurant on Barlow Manor Road in Didsbury), at the Fallowfield end of the Wilmslow Road (061-225 7108), the **Howling Scream** on Oldham Street (see *American*) and the **Viceroy of India** on Whitworth Street (061-236 6268), which can rustle up over forty vegetarian dishes.

ITALIAN

Coco Ristorante Pizzeria on Fountain Street (061-832 6176) is the only restaurant in Manchester to have been given an entry in Courvoisier's *Best of the Best Handbook*. It is a playground for Manchester's rich and famous, and star-spotting is possible in more ways than one as fake stars twinkle in the fake branches of a fake tree above your head. There is a suitably swish and romantic atmosphere, however, so if you're trying to impress....

Seriously though, if you're not rich, grab some friends and eat at **Basta Pasta** on Mosley Street (061-228 1203). It's a very trendy eatery, but only really good value if there are a few of you, namely four, because then you qualify for the 'Basta Feast', where you can eat as much pasta as you like for a relatively nominal fee. It's also a bring-a-bottle place, and if you are a student you can claim a ten per cent discount. The clientele and the décor might not be as sophisticated as Coco's, but the crowd are younger and more fun.

Worth travelling to for sheer authenticity is **Pepe's** in Whitefield, 264 Bury New Road (061-766 2557). There are no fake Italian accents in this place; home may be Ramsbottom, but the heart is in Roma. The background music sounds like a compilation of the last twenty years of Italian Eurovision entries but the food and drink will raise Pavarotti-like passions in you. Unlike many Italian restaurants, a real bonus lies in the fact that the dedicated veggie is adequately and imaginatively catered for.

Elsewhere, a pizzeria is pretty much a pizzeria, and there isn't a great deal to distinguish one from the next. Seek out your local, or you could always patronize Pizza Hut or Pastificio if you get desperate, in which case there are numerous branches throughout the city.

AMERICAN

American-diner-type places look set to take over the world. Up-market McDonald's abound in the strangest of places, tending to inspire deep feelings of yankophobia, but in reality, some of them offer massively portioned, saliva-stimulating platters to keep all but the most rampant xenophobes quiet and happy.

On the other hand, **Dick's Last Resort**, marketed as 'The Ultimate

American Bar and Grill', is enough to make the less adventurous quail: it could generously be described as lively and loud. No doubt that will offend the hordes of people who patronize the place, so try it out for yourself and see: 76 Deansgate (061-839 1663).

Several steps up is **Tootsies**, Wilmslow Road, Didsbury Village (061-434 8252). Renowned especially for bargain two-litre jugs of Pimm's or Long Island Iced Tea, it's a perfect place for the liquid lunch. If you're just there to get sozzled, don't eat: the portions are enormous and very, very, very filling. Also keep your eyes open for free offers and student discounts. In town, the latest addition (at time of print) to the American scene was **Henry J. Bean's**, Blackfriars Street (061-832 8900). Famous in London's King's Road for cocktails, they have now opened a branch here. A standard American bar with plentiful food and cheap cocktails during 'Happy Hour' time (1730-2030).

If an exceptional 1950s-style American restaurant with a hint of Mexico, a really extensive menu and reasonable prices is what you desire, you would be mad to miss the **Howling Scream**. It's pretty trendy (as would be expected from its Oldham Street location) but there is no hint of an intimidating atmosphere; instead, a rather more laid-back, relaxed feel hovers over the restaurant, making you tempted to eat a little bit more to prolong the pleasure.

FRANGLAIS

Probably due to the fact that English food is kept mostly within the walls of the home, most restaurants add a few French dishes to the menu in an attempt to retain an element of street cred.

If you fancy rubbing shoulders with the cast of *Coronation Street*, gorge at the **Market Restaurant**, Edge Street (061-834 3743). They have a starters club here (for people who like starters) and a pudding club (no prizes...) that meet a couple of times each month to eat copious amounts of beginnings and ends for a mere £13 per session. The clubs are very popular, so book well in advance. If you prefer your meal, like a good story, to have a beginning, a middle and an end, this restaurant won't disappoint; although the prices may seem expensive, your stomach will send you love letters for the rest of your life.

Nearby, at the Manchester Craft Centre, 17 Oak Street, is the **Olive Branch**. The food is simple but seductive and sensibly priced. As the name would suggest, it's peaceful and there is a large vegetarian menu. Ring 061-832 8055 to book, but for a lunchtime shopping break it's unnecessary.

For a more truly French flavour, try **Café de Paris (La Crêpe Rit)** in Chorlton (Manchester Road, 061-881 6699). The crêpes are so delicious that the restaurant has won several awards – which, unusually, hasn't sent the prices into orbit. For the same with a more unusual setting, try its little sister floating in the city centre: **La Péniche** is a little boat moored at Paradise Wharf (Ducie Street, behind Piccadilly Station; 061-273 5553). The gentle lapping of the water while you eat adds a certain *je ne sais quoi* to the atmosphere, although the crêpes themselves are enough to make you drift away. Not for the seasick.

MORE UNUSUAL EATERIES

The **El Macho Mexican Restaurant** Portland Street (061-236 9626) provides a hot and tasty meal of enchiladas, tacos and salsa at a reasonable price. After washing this down with a mixture of tequila, Sol and marguerita you may feel an impulse to jump up and down on the table a lot, wearing a poncho and a ridiculous hat and pretending to be in Mexico. This is not really a good idea. The old-established **Casa Espana**, 100 Wilmslow Road, Rusholme (061-224 6826) is more traditional but sound.

If a good moussaka and dish-flinging fun is more your scene, there are two very good **Greek** restaurants. **Bouzouki By Night** (061-236 9282) can be found lurking on Princess Street, and **George's Taverna** is on Union Street (061-834 3857). Both are worth a visit if you're a Greek food freak, or want to reminisce about that wonderful holiday in Crete.... The **Kosmos**, 248 Wilmslow Road, Fallowfield (061-225 9106), near the Queen of Hearts (see *Pubs and Bars*), is good and very popular – but you must book. They try to get away from the Greek stereotype of lukewarm food – even the bill comes on a red-hot plate.

If you're feeling a little loaded and don't mind small portions of delectable food, try a **Japanese** restaurant. They are invariably impeccable but expensive. One of the better ones is **Mina Japana** in Chinatown on George Street (061-228 2598). Portland Street is a good place for the adventurous, boasting two **Thai**, one **Vietnamese** and one **Korean-cum-Japanese** eateries, none of them outrageously priced, within two or three blocks.

For a welcome and unusual change, you could try the **Armenian Restaurant** situated on Princess Street (061-834 9025). Don't be put off by exotic dishes, you don't have to eat the sheep's eyes (well, not unless you really want to...). It's certainly worth a bit of experimentation. There's ancther good Armenian restaurant – again imaginatively called the **Armenian Restaurant**, in Withington at 404 Wilmslow Road (061-434 3480), near Mulberry's.

For that special occasion try **That Café**, actually a smart restaurant, in otherwise unpromising Levenshulme, 1031 Stockport Road (061-432 4672). The walls are so hidden behind masses of 1930s knick-knacks, pictures and china that you'd think you were in an antique shop, were it not for the friendly candlelit atmosphere and the 1930s music playing in the background. There's nothing antique about the menu, which is interesting and original with a selection of 'country' wines alongside the expected château bottlings.

CAFE BARS

Café-bar culture has hit Manchester in a big way. Whatever the pros and cons, it is a fact that most café bars serve good food, excelling at lunchtimes, and are worth looking into. As mentioned in *Pubs and Bars*, Manchester City Council are keen to bring licensed cafés out on to the streets. 'English cities in general are behind the times', complains Graham Stringer, leader of Manchester City Council. Whether or not we will soon be able to munch away in the now-traditional warmth of an English summer rests in the hands of our benevolent police force -- so for the moment the plastic plants of the café bars will have to provide a poor substitute for the great outdoors. Not, of course, that you'll find a plastic plant anywhere near the more cool caffs.

Dry 201, on Oldham Street, in spite of its over-hyped image at night, is brilliant during the day for food – and is surprisingly reasonably priced. Likewise, the café upstairs in the **Cornerhouse** (Oxford Road) is pretty popular, although the tea would probably be more at home in a motorway service station. The **Green Room** (Whitworth Street West) and the **City Art Gallery** (Mosley Street) have arty little cafés where you can have a cup of tea, a slice of cake and discuss the meaning of life.

More 'foody', less 'arty' and very tasteful are **Greens** (1 York Street) and **Walcots** (Hanging Ditch). Greens may evoke visions of plastic plants, spritzers and yuppies, but nothing could be further from the truth. It stands in the grandiose setting of an old bank, and although the abundance of marble and mahogany is quite humbling, the atmosphere is by no means antiquated. Track suits mingle with pin-stripes and an air of informality prevails, helped along by the brilliant music. In addition, the beautiful staff are always ready with a smile and good service, unlike the narcissistic posse behind other bars. There is a servery offering hot and cold food between 1100 and 1500, and the menu changes regularly. The restaurant is upstairs and the well-stocked bar is on the ground floor. Walcots, another (though less majestic) wooden wonderland, is smaller and more intimate. The food is tasty, though not exotic, and varied enough to ensure a few visits that won't worry the bank manager unduly.

Although crowded with portable telephones and stilettos at night, the 'sophisticated' café collection of **Henry's** (Parsonage Gardens), **Muswells** (King Street West), **Courtneys** (Parsonage Gardens) and **Ronnies** (St Ann's Square) are all excellent for food during the day. The bars are pretty well stocked and the food not to be scoffed at.

One of the latest additions to the café-bar scene is the snazzy **Manto** (short for 'Manchester Today') **Café** (Canal Street, between the gay village and UMIST). Its bold blue façade *à la* Charles Rennie Mackintosh lends a welcome touch of style to a run-down area.

PUB GRUB

Most locals will serve a decent pub meal, and if suffering from that mandatory Sunday-morning hangover, when distant voyages are rarely relished, you may feel inclined to stay close to home. However, if you can stomach some exploring, the following are especially recommended; in addition, many of the pubs in the *Pubs* sections are mentioned for their quality food, so check there as well.

The **Vine** on Kennedy Street is recommended for light snacks and lunchtime fodder; joining it in the city centre, the **White Lion** on Liverpool Road (near the Air and Space Museum) is excellent for its grub, value and atmosphere.

In Chorlton-cum-Hardy on Rifle Road (walk down Hardy Lane from Barlow Moor Road – reached by buses 22, 46/7, 84-6, 270, or take Junction 8 off the M63), is **Jackson's Boat**. It is best during the summer, so you can take full advantage of the massive garden and local walks: Sale Water Park is nearby. In Didsbury, the **Royal Oak** on Wilmslow Road (buses 20, 40/2/5/9, 157, 170, 370) is famous for its massive cheese lunches, as is the **Mark Addy** on the waterfront in Salford (Stanley Street: bus 60-anything, walkable from city centre), which is particularly lively on Sundays. Also recommended in Salford is the **Prince of Wales** on Oakfield Road, off Regent Road: they'll throw a meal together for you at any time, and there is a little beer garden. The **Queen of Hearts** in Fallowfield (buses 40-anything – except 47 – 142, 143) is good for pub food, but if you want something more substantial, move next door to its restaurant the **Mock Turtle**. In Burnage (bus 169, Burnage BR), the **Sun** on

Burnage Lane is recommended, but it only serves pub food during the week and you can't drink outside – even though there are lovely gardens. Nearer the city in Rusholme on Victory Street, off Claremont Road, the **Osborne** will give you a decent meal for a couple of quid. Don't be put off by the seedy exterior: underneath beats the heart of a good old-fashioned pub.

Pubs and Bars

Pubs and bars *around* Manchester would probably be the right title for this section in view of the fact that since the 1970s the number of inner-city pubs has fallen so dramatically. CAMRA (Campaign for Real Ale) revealed in September 1990 that, compared to 445 pubs within one mile of St Peter's Square fifty years ago, there now stand only 150. Many old pubs are boarded up and many of the rest run down. This is not due to the much-publicized new teetotalling tendencies of the Mancunian population – the so-called 'Lucozade' crew – but more to the combined effects of an exodus of population from the centre to the suburbs and the yuppifying of the drinking scene throughout the 1980s. Many people now prefer spritzers in the plastic-planted wildernesses of the wine bars; others strut their stuff in café bars boasting huge stocks of bottled world lagers. This gentrification of the city centre pub scene has resulted in the closure of many of the more traditional pubs, or the total massacre of their interiors by large breweries desperate to become 'trendy'. The smaller independents have fled to the suburbs, where competition is not so tough – and to which people now seem prepared to travel in search of a good pint.

Whatever your tastes, don't lose heart: the picture is not one of total gloom. Even with the massive cuts, 150 pubs should be enough for a modest night out with the resultant immodest hangover. Even for the Real-Aler, there is still plenty of choice....

LOCAL BREWERIES AND BEERS

Although the big seven national breweries control eighty per cent of the market, some particularly brave or fortunate local breweries have clung on to their independence and continued to produce excellent beers. Manchester has somehow managed to avoid the sort of local monopoly syndrome often created by the larger breweries buying up and then ruining the best of the rest. Even so, Whitbread have moved in on Manchester in recent years – taking over Strangeways-based **Boddingtons** in 1989, and a year earlier **Chesters**, who used to brew at Salford. So far, they have tried to keep Boddies intact, heavily promoting its tarnished Real-Ale image ('If you don't get Boddies, you'll just get bitter...'). At Chesters, however, things definitely ain't what they used to be, and it remains to see whether or not Boddingtons will survive in its well-loved form.

Holts is the most popular family-run brewery in Manchester. Many claim it produces the best beer in the North, although CAMRA say that it is an acquired taste. Whatever the opinions on the beer, no one can deny that it's the cheapest pint money can buy. The brewery refuse to inflate their prices to suit demand and a pint of Holts will cost you half that of an inferior London pint. (Much of their profit, by the way, goes to cancer research at the famous Holts Institute at Christies.) There are 94 tied houses, the highest concentration of which you will find in Eccles (which boasts thirteen), Salford and North Manchester.

Hydes is the smallest of the independents, with only 49 tied houses. Small it may be, but it certainly isn't insignifcant. One of the few breweries in the country that brews without the use of artificial additives or preservatives, a pint of Hydes retains an image of purity. Don't be fooled, however: their strongest beer has a kick like a donkey in DMs, and no amount of careful brewing will avoid that hangover in the morning. Only having a handful of pubs, you may have to travel to sample their wares, but at least the reasonable prices should help reimburse your travelling costs.

Lees, based in Middleton, are another family-based brewery, and as most of their outlets are in Middleton, they are a rare and wonderful discovery elsewhere.

Robinsons, based in Stockport, have recently followed in the footsteps of the 'big seven' by refurbishing most of their pubs in modern, 'trendy' taste. This is a great shame because their beer is actually extremely palatable – try Old Tom.

There are two home-brew pubs in the area, both of which were once owned by the major breweries and sold off cheaply as unviable properties. Both bear testimony to the fact that if you sell decent stuff and provide a good atmosphere the punters will come to you. The **Lass o' Gowrie**, where you can see the brewery in the cellar from the pub, and **West Coast**, based at the **King's Arms**, sell some of the best booze in the country, and people travel a long, long way to wet their whistles with the ales on sale. Which leads us on to....

REAL-ALE PUBS

City Centre

The **Beerhouse** on Angel Street (off Rochdale Road) is as popular for its food as its beer. Selling Holts and Theakstons, as well as many guest beers and real ciders, it's a good all-rounder of a pub: pretty basic and often busy. The **Castle** on Oldham Street captures the old, solidly traditional aspects of Victorian grandiosity which were a feature before the likes of Dry and Affleck's moved into the neighbourhood. It is the only Robinsons pub in the city centre, and worth travelling to for the Old Tom.

Step into the **Circus Tavern** (Portland Street), and you'll begin to think you're in one of those reconstructed heritage places. There is no music, no pool table, video machine or one-armed bandit. You won't find a drop of lager within its walls; if you want to drink, there are two Tetley hand pumps – and noise is limited to a low buzz of conversation. It really is a one-in-a-million type of pub, and even more unusual for being so centrally positioned. The main doors will be locked on a Friday or Saturday night to keep out the rave contingent, but if you're keen there is a 'secret' entrance on Rayner Street.

The **City Arms** (40 Kennedy Street, off Cooper Street) is one of the city's most popular and genuine pubs. It's good for lunches and serves a wide range of beers, but being so prominent on the city circuit, it is full of 'after work' types. The **Jolly Angler** on Ducie Street doesn't fall into this unfortunate trap, and is worth visiting for a good quiet atmosphere and a tasty pint of Hydes. It is in a drab area, but very close to the Piccadilly eyesores about to be redeveloped, so things might change. At the time of writing it is popular with a wide range of people who have the love of a good pub in common, and is well worth a visit.

The **Marble Arch** on Rochdale Road (junction with Gould Street) celebrates its birthday each year with a modest beer festival. As it gets older, the festival gets less modest due to the fact that the number of beers on sale corresponds to the age of the pub. In 1990, there were 102! To ensure safety from alcohol poisoning, sample the substantial food. **Mr Thomas's Chop House** (52 Cross Street) is a gorgeous terracotta building, and inside is heaving with all sorts of people from all over the city. Being a free house, the beers change regularly and it is listed in CAMRA's *Good Pub Food Guide*.

In Shambles Square (behind Marks & Spencer) are the two most famous pubs in the city, the **Old Wellington** and **Sinclair's Oyster Bar**, which are both listed buildings dating back centuries – the only timber-based constructions still standing in the centre. When developers wanted to make way for new roads the pubs were moved one-and-a-half metres from their original site. They serve as tourist attractions and restaurants as well as pubs: very versatile! **Tommy Ducks** is another pub that has stood firm in the face of redevelopment, and now stands rather ludicrously alone in the midst of swirling roads and highways near G-Mex on East Street. A brave little vision, it is a popular pub, and even the Greenall's is palatable, though the famous collection of knickers and undies pinned to the ceiling is no more. The **Crown and Kettle** (2 Oldham Road, Ancoats, next to the all-glass printing building) is notable neither for the beer nor the clientele, but is well worth a look in for the décor – wrought-iron ceiling with hanging plants, lifesize plaster relief of Winston Churchill (who?) outside Number Ten, and panelling in one room taken from a wartime airship. The **Briton's Protection** (across the street from G-Mex) is a relatively unspoilt watering-hole with a wide stock.

West Manchester

The **Braziers Arms** is a boisterous backstreet Boddies pub on Hodson Street (off Blackfriars Road) in Salford and very much a beer drinker's pub: it has retained a traditional feel in spite of the loud telly and juke-box vying for attention. Joining in the singing is more or less obligatory unless you want to join the pensioners barricaded in the back room! Definitely one to go to when you've had a few. One of those bonuses in life, a good Greenall's pub, is to be found in Salford on Holland Street, just off Langley Road South. The **Beehive** has stayed pretty much the same in the face of redevelopment all around it, largely due to its general popularity, and is well worth seeking out. In the north of Salford – in Broughton's Back Hope Street, between Lower Broughton Street and Great Clowes Street – is one of those tiny locals that seems to have survived all forms of contact with the outside world since the beginning of the century. The **Star** is not quaint or oldie-worldy, but more the sort of place you would have called in to on the way home from the mill.

Eccles is somewhat of a beer drinker's paradise, boasting forty-six Real-Ale houses out of fifty-four pubs – so must be worth a crawl. The **Duke of York** in the town centre (Church Street) is very popular in spite of being quite pricey. It is especially lively on its many jazz, blues and folk nights – ring for details (061-707 5409). Further west, in Worsley, is the **Duke's Gate** (Clegg Lane, Little Hulton). Very much a local favourite, the pub boasts one regular who drinks a hundred-and-nineteen pints of Holts each week; the brewery seem to be unsure whether or not this is an endorsement of the quality of the beer or of their prices! Whichever, he is probably largely responsible for the pub's high sales record, and was still alive at the time of writing.

North Manchester

The **Old House at Home** in Crumpsall (Bottomly Side) is a village pub in an urban armpit. Pretty and traditional, it is another persistent surviver in the face of development – largely due to the campaigns of loyal locals. The mix makes the atmosphere lively but relaxed, and it's worth an evening's supping and winding down. Down the road in Cheetham Hill, the **Queen's Arms** is a gem for beer drinkers, food freaks and lager lovers alike. Lying low on Honey Street, just off Redbank, it offers some of the best food in the city, and a vast variety of drink makes the washing down of a meal little less than orgasmic. People travel a long way to come here and are never disappointed.

In Newton Heath, the **Railway** has become much loved for its authenticity and vibrancy, the latter especially at the weekends. It squats on Dean Lane, about two hundred yards from the Oldham Road. Actually on the Oldham Road, towards Miles Platting, is the recently opened **Bird In The Hand**, which is gaining a pretty good reputation as a free house. Worth a sip or two.

East Manchester

Opposite the Belle Vue Showcase on Hyde Road is the **Coach and Horses,** which used to be a real community pub, but now, due to the cinema, is a pop-in shop between films. The beer is still good – it serves Old Tom – so at least if the film is crap, you can console yourself with a decent pint. The **Railway** (oh, yes, another one) on Pottery Lane is reputed to be the best Real-Ale pub in East Manchester. Full of local character and overflowing with all the 'old' favourites (and not failing in the real cider department either) this is certainly a place to undo your belt by a notch and down a few pints. The whole of the Hyde Road is littered with good old pubs, and is well placed for a crawl as there are regular buses to carry you back home – if you can still remember where home is!

South Manchester

Moving south of the city towards Didsbury and Chorlton, you'll find copious numbers of bustling pubs, busy on every night of the week. Due to fervent patronization by the student population, pub life thrives. Many are featured in *Studentsville Suppin*, and the ones listed here are those which are also very popular with the local non-student community.

The **King's Arms** may be difficult to find, but squinting at your *A-Z* pays off when you get there. It is situated on Helmshore Walk, off Skerry Close, near Brunswick Street. It owes its considerable popularity to the fact that it is the other of Manchester's two home-brew pubs. It is simple and comfortable, and as well as brewing beer it excels in authentic lagers: at present, it is working on a special Chinese lager. On Wednesdays there is music from a lively Irish community, who know a good beer when they see one.

Somewhat off the beaten track of Manchester's intelligentsia is one of Holt's top three sellers, the **Claremont** (124 Claremont Road). It was built when Moss Side was affluent and certainly looks as though it has seen better days, but venture beyond the dilapidated exterior to the friendly, multi-cultural, multi-aged atmosphere within and you'll have a good night. Don't be put off by Moss Side's reputation: grab your sense of adventure and explore its many pubs.

Down in safer and posher Didsbury is the **Albert Inn**, on William Street, just off Wilmslow Road. It is a throbbing Hydes pub, handy for all the other pubs in the area, two of the best of which are the **Royal Oak** and the **Station** – which get so busy that the customers spill out on to the pavement.

IRISH AND FOLK PUBS

As well as the King's Arms mentioned above, there are a number of lively Irish pubs, noted for friendly atmosphere, folk music and very good beers. The **Salutation** on Higher Chatham Street, just off Oxford Road near the College of Music, is one of the favourites, and is as full of students making the most of the Irish ambience as of the Irish themselves. On Sundays there are floor music sessions, when all good players are welcome to join in and jam, and at other times during the week there are bands-a-jiggin' and feet-a-tappin'.

In West Gorton on Hyde Road, the **Traveller's Call** is one of the most unspoiled and authentic pubs in the city. Very popular with the Irish community and those seeking refuge from the onslaught of art-deco elsewhere, Irish musicians often get together and play at the back of the pub. In Chorlton, there is the celebrated **Chorlton Irish Club**, where music is ever-present and floor-jamming sessions take place on Mondays, as they do at the **32 Club** in Ardwick Green.

In the city centre, the **Jolly Angler** on Ducie Street is a lively Gaelic haunt (see *Real-Ale Pubs*), as is the **Moulders** in Ancoats. Out of the city, try the **Crown** on Wilmslow Road in Didsbury, the **Ducie Arms** on Cambridge Street in Hulme, or the **Gardener's Arms** on Victory Street, Rusholme for folk and blues specials. And the list goes on: there is much folk culture to be had in this dirty ol' town....

STUDENTSVILLE SUPPIN'

Many of the pubs listed in the above sections are favourites with the student population, but the ones below are positively dominated by them, and many gear their services to their faithful, youthful clientele.

One such place is the **Crescent**, on The Crescent in Salford, opposite the University. It is a reliable source of good beer and heavily patronized by students. Mini beer festivals are held here every June and October, suitably coinciding with the beginning and end of the academic year. Also popular with the Salford crew is the **Mark Addy** (Stanley Street, on the river Irwell – see *Pub Grub*), which is also being marketed very heavily by the people down at Salford Quays as a local favourite.

There are many other popular places in Salford, particularly around the area of The Crescent, but the real campus lies down on Oxford Road/Wilmslow Road, where the combined populations of Manchester University, Poly, College of Music and the Medical Schools rule.

The **Lass o' Gowrie** (see *Local Beers*) on Charles Street, behind the BBC on Oxford Road, would be a lot better if it weren't full of media types, although the students tend to counteract this influence a lot. (If you don't like either students or media types, you do have a bit of a problem, however.) The ales are excellent, although they are so eagerly downed that they don't always have the time to mature, and the best brew is only produced at the beginning and end of the academic year. It is perhaps optimistically called the Graduation Brew, and you needn't be told how well this goes down.

Near Manchester Poly's Mandela Building on Oxford Road is the **Flea and Firkin**. In the mode of other Firkin pubs in the country, it consists of a large open space with wooden floors and assorted paraphernalia; in traditional Firkin fashion, there are also some rather attractive stuffed fleas hanging around the place. A Real-Ale paradise, it is always full of Dogbolter-downing students from the halls across the way, and has an excellent atmosphere even if it's a little too boisterous at the weekends. On Thursdays there is jazz of sorts, and on Fridays a pub singer who sounds as drunk as the punters – but no one seems to notice. A flea's jump away is the popular **Old Steam Brewery**, with live music and cabaret some nights.

In Fallowfield (Wilmslow Road), the **Queen of Hearts** has benefited from the inhabitants of the massive Owens Park Halls. It is very lively, if way too crowded on a Friday. The beer and food are good here too, and the décor is better from the inside than the outside (it used to be a church hall) would suggest. Nearby is the **Friendship** (Wilmslow Road, corner of Egerton Road). Some way down the road to Didsbury, in Withington, is the **Red Lion**. Always full of students, but popular with the locals too, it has an excellent quiz on Mondays.

Continuing south into Didsbury, the **Royal Oak** and all the other pubs in the area are invariably buzzing with news of the day's non-existent lectures, and moans of non-existent funds as they pay for another pint. Ah... tough life!

BIJOU BARS AND BOTTLED BEERS

As observed in the introduction to this section, bars – as opposed to pubs – are taking over the city, and most of them boast the trendy, bottled, foreign beers. The images vary from 'fun pubs' to 'posing palaces', and even for the dyed in the wool bitter boffin there are places worth looking into. Manchester City Council have recognized this trend and are initiating talks with the Greater Manchester Police Force in an attempt to be able to bring café-bar culture out on to the streets. So far the answer has been negative, but perhaps if bread was served with wine, and bars undertook certain alterations, they would change their minds!

If you are wearing the trendiest of togs, trip on down to **Dry** on Oldham Street. The uncomfortable chairs and minimalist décor evoke memories of comprehensive school dining halls but this is, of course, the height of good taste. At night the place is buzzing, but beware of 'anti-normal' door policies: you need to riffle through your clothes drawer to find your most outrageous garments before contemplating a visit. For all its faults, Dry is a good place for a gawp and a gossip, and at least the 'doormen' are prepared to explain their subjective policies in comprehensible terms. That, in fact, sums up quite adequately: Dry – the bar with the thinking person's bouncer.

If you suffer from the 'goldfish syndrome', a desire to be seen, stroll on down to the **Cornerhouse** on Oxford Street. Here you can focus nonchalantly through an alcohol-induced haze on the 'Art In the Bar' exhibitions. More arty than trendy, it's full of right-on intellectuals waffling about some foreign film they've just seen at the cinema, when actually they didn't have a clue what went on because they didn't understand the lingo and couldn't see the subtitles properly. The bar staff are amazingly pleasant when taking into consideration the volume of pretentious crap they have to endure. Having said all this, the atmosphere in the bar is pleasant, and the cinema a rare and wonderful treasure (see *Cinema, Theatre and Classical Music*).

In town, on York Street, is **Greens**. Featured in *Pub Grub* for its food, the extensive bar is even more busy at night as folks flock in to ogle its sexy staff and applaud the head barman's expertise with glass tossin', cocktail shakin' circus tricks: eat your heart out Tom Cruise. Another goody is **Corbière's**, just off South King Street, but unfortunately, from here on in, pseudo-sophistication and spritzers start to take over in the form of the overcrowded haunts of Parsonage Gardens.

A little out of the city on Wilmslow Road, Fallowfield, in the basement of the Lansdowne Hotel, lurks **Severe**. The bar boasts the largest selection of foreign bottled beers in Manchester and little else – but if that's what you're after, you can't go far wrong. The place is too dark to be seriously posey, and the cavernous nooks and crannies are more suited to hiding away than grabbing the limelight. The music is excellent, the crowd is fun and relaxed, and the place itself is brilliant unless you are over five feet tall – in which case constant head banging on the ceiling can induce brain damage, or stooping will result in a slightly hunched back. Calling all Esmereldas....

Not all the best lagers are limited to the bars, of course: many pubs stock a good selection of the fizzies, and they are often cheaper. Several revered Real-Ale pubs also stock the best bottled and draught lagers. Try the **Flea and Firkin** and the **Queen's Arms** – see above – as well as most of the studenty pubs already mentioned.

If a lager-swilling, serious spilling night that leads up to dancing on tables (and ends up as you fall off them) appeals to you, you should be at the **Beerkeller** on Piccadilly. A firm favourite with birthday outings from all over the county, this is no place for the faint-hearted, the insipid-sipper, or the driver. Don't wear those 'dry-clean only' items – a towel would be more suitable. Admittedly tremendous fun, but don't admit that to your friends over in the Cornerhouse.

FLOOR SINGING PUBS

If you either want to laugh or to step on the road to stardom (while others laugh at you), an evening at a pub inviting floor singers is an experience not to be missed. Various Shirley Basseys and Frank Sinatras from Crumpsall or Stretford strut their stuff to the great delight of the sadistic spectators on most nights of the week in some corner of the city.

The **Jolly Angler** on Ducie Street offers an official night on Mondays, although the merry throngs in there are not averse to a good old singsong at other times. Most of the others are to be found out of the city: evidently the city types are too cool for such self-made entertainment. In Ashton-under-Lyne on Mondays, try the **Station** on Warrington Road. To the north of Oldham, the **Swan Inn** in Dobcross is good on Sundays, and if a Thursday is free, check out the **Nags Head**, Waters Green in Macclesfield, or the **Church Inn**, Millbrook in Stalybridge.

Gargle that salt water, belt out those scales, then sit and laugh yourself silly at everyone else.

4. JOY RIDES: DAYS OUT AND ABOUT

There are many ways to spend a wet afternoon in Manchester, and there are plenty of wet afternoons, believe me. Here are a few wonderful and wacky ways to kill time on those wild and windy days.

Museums and Galleries

THE 'BIG' ONES

Manchester Museum

- **Location:** Next to the University, Oxford Road, M13; 061-275 2634.
- **Transport:** Buses 5, 40-anything, 184/6, 143, 157, 159, P11, W2 from city centre to University precinct.
- **Times and cost**: Open Mon-Sat 1000-1700. Free.
- **Disabled access:** Limited slightly by some stairs. Telephone for details.

Housed in the attractive part of the University is this rambling and fascinating museum. It is noted for its Egyptology section, its fossils and skeletons – the latter of which includes an unfortunate elephant who moved here from Belle Vue Zoo after she passed on! In spite of all the 'ologies', even the most hyperactive and difficult child will love this place as the imagination can really run rampant.

Ideas for combined visits: Close to the Pankhurst Centre and a short bus ride from the Whitworth Art Gallery and Platt Fields Park.

Museum of Science and Industry

- **Location:** Liverpool Road, Castlefield; 061-832 2244.
- **Transport:** Deansgate BR or walk from city centre.
- **Times and cost:** Mon-Sat 1000-1700. £2.00 (£1.00 children).
- **Disabled access:** Extensive.

Winner of Museum of the Year 1990, this museum is one of the stars of Castlefield (see *Parks and Houses*). It is based on two sites, one of which used to be Liverpool Road Railway Station – the first commercial passenger railway station in the world. In the original engine sheds are the steam trains which on occasion will be noisily and smokily set loose. In the Air and Space Gallery (separate adjacent site, same ticket) there is a space simulator that you can try out for yourself or, if you prefer something more down to earth, you can wander around 'Underground Manchester': reconstructed sewers. Be warned, they are not very realistic: as well as smelling quite pleasant, you won't see even one Teenage Mutant Ninja Turtle! Even so, children will be considerably more entertained in this museum than you ever were when science consisted of sitting hopefully over a Bunsen burner waiting for the bell to go.

Ideas for combined visits: The Granada Studios tour is nearby, as is the rest of Castlefield.

Manchester Jewish Museum

- **Location:** 190 Cheetham Hill Road; 061-834 9879.
- **Transport:** Buses 79, 135, 137 from city.
- **Times and cost:** Mon-Thurs 1030-1600; Sun 1030-1700. Closed Jewish holidays. £1.00 (50p children).
- **Disabled access:** Limited.

Housed in a grand old Spanish and Portuguese synagogue, the museum gives a detailed and interesting account of Jewish life and traditions. The Holocaust is of course chronicled, but the museum is careful not to let it overshadow the many other aspects of Jewish history and tradition. It is an excellent and valuable source of cultural education, but not really suitable for young children unless they're the angelic Shirley Temple types: they will be bored. Otherwise, well worth a visit.

Ideas for combined visits: The Museum of Transport – see below.

Manchester Museum of Transport

- **Location:** Boyle Street, Cheetham Hill; 061-205 2122.
- **Transport:** Buses 79, 135/7.
- **Times and cost:** Weds, Sat, Sun, Bank Holidays 1000-1700. 70p (30p children).
- **Disabled access:** Extensive.

The museum represents over one hundred years of transport history with lots of old vehicles on show. There are also extensive archives depicting the development of transport in the city. Each spring the museum holds a festival weekend with extra exhibits: a model railway and a rally with the old cars and buses. It's not the most enthralling of places unless you're a transport buff, and probably holds more appeal for children than for adults.

SMALLER MUSEUMS AND ART GALLERIES

Gallery of English Costume

- **Location:** Platt Fields, Rusholme, Wilmslow Road; 061-224 5217.
- **Transport:** 40-anything bus (not 47), 157, 159, P11, W2.
- **Times and cost:** Summer: Mon-Sat (not Tues) 1000-1745; Sun 1400-1745. Winter: As above, closing at 1600. Free.
- **Disabled access:** Limited.

The gallery exhibits clothing from the seventeenth century to the 1960s. It's a fabulous museum for all ages with a certain element of banality added by the exhibit of the staff uniforms at the Midland Bank. Otherwise, it's brilliant, and you can spend the afternoon imagining yourself dressed in every period of history from Mary Queen of Scots to Mary Quant.

Ideas for combined visits: The museum is part of Platt Fields Park (see *Parks and Houses*), and a short bus ride from both Manchester Museum and Whitworth Gallery; it's also within walking distance of Maine Road, Manchester City's football ground.

Greater Manchester Police Museum

- **Location:** Newton Street, Manchester; 061-855 3290.
- **Transport:** Walking distance from Piccadilly.
- **Times and cost:** By appointment only. Free.
- **Disabled access:** Difficult.

An absolutely fascinating museum. Naturally morbid kids with heads full of dungeons, dragons, cops and robbers will adore the police cells (the officer showing you around may be bribed to lock them away for you). Adults may be more fascinated by the forgery den. There are illustrations of the Peterloo Massacre of 1819 (see *ROOTS*) and other exhibits charting the development of a police force which owes its origins to a local lad, Robert Peel.

Ideas for other visits: The museum is well placed for all the other city centre attractions listed.

Lancashire County Cricket Museum

- **Location:** Warwick Road, Old Trafford. 061-848 7021.
- **Transport:** Warwick Road (not Old Trafford) BR from Piccadilly, or buses 230, 253-7, 259, A63/4.
- **Times and cost:** Open only on match days. Free.
- **Disabled access:** On request.

The Cricket Museum is more a mass of members' memorabilia than a museum, charting the success of one of the country's best teams. A must for young and old cricket buffs alike, but otherwise pretty dull.

Ideas for combined visits: Manchester United Football Museum.

Manchester United Football Museum

- **Location:** Warwick Road, Old Trafford; 061-872 1661.
- **Transport:** As above plus buses 115, 250.
- **Times and cost:** Daily, (not Sat) 1000-1600. £1.50.
- **Disabled access:** On request.

The first football museum in Britain at the world's most supported club (if not the best). It charts the progress of United since 1878 and is a shrine for all those pilgrims that travel here to see their beloved team. There isn't much else to say about the place.

National Museum of Labour History

- **Location:** 103 Princess Street; 061-228 7212.
- **Transport:** City centre.
- **Times and cost:** Wed-Sat and Bank Holidays 1000-1700; Sun 1400-1700. Free.
- **Disabled access:** Limited – telephone first.

There is a second site due to open at the Upper Campfield Market in Castlefield in 1991. The Princess Street site is the very place at which the

TUC first met in 1868, and the museum occupied the building after relocating from London. It charts the history of the Labour Movement up to modern times, and exhibitions change regularly. In 1990 they ranged from visions of Elizabeth Gaskell's Manchester to the Ambulance Men's Strike of 1989 – so there is a big variety. It will probably bore the children to death, but it's a class museum for adults.

The Pankhurst Centre

- **Location:** 60-62 Nelson Street, Chorlton-on-Medlock; 061-273 5673.
- **Transport:** Off Oxford Road, buses as for Manchester Museum.
- **Times and cost:** Mon-Fri 1100-1500. First Sunday of every month 1400-1700. Otherwise by appointment. Free.
- **Disabled access:** Extensive.

See *Women* in *THE MORAL MAJORITY* for details of other functions at the Pankhurst Centre. The actual museum bears testament to the efforts of Emmeline Pankhurst and her daughters, who set up the Women's Social and Political Union in 1903: the ensuing suffragette movement is chronicled in detail. You can wander round the lively Women's Centre afterwards, and grab a coffee or a veggie snack at the restaurant.

Ideas for combined visits: Close to Whitworth Art Gallery and walking distance from Manchester Museum.

Working-Class Movement Museum and Library

- **Location:** 51 The Crescent, Salford; 061-736 3601.
- **Transport:** Salford Crescent BR or 60-anything bus.
- **Times and cost:** Tues, Weds, Fri 1000-1700; Thurs 1000-1700; Sun 1400-1700. Free.
- **Disabled access**: Limited.

Again, not really for the children but interesting for adults, this museum is the product of the love and dedication of Ruth and Eddie Frow, who, over the years, have collected 20,000 books and many pieces of working-class interest. Both the library and museum are a must for any student interested in Britain's social history.

Ideas for combined visits: Round the corner from Salford Museum.

Salford Museum and Art Gallery

- **Location:** Peel Park, The Crescent, Salford; 061-736 2649.
- **Transport:** Salford Crescent BR or bus 60-anything.
- **Times and cost:** Mon, Weds, Thurs 1000-1700; Tues, Fri 1000-1900; Sat 0900-1300; Sun 1400-1700. Free.
- **Disabled access:** Reasonable.

This museum is another must. It boasts the Lowry Heritage Centre, housing the largest collection of famous matchstick men and matchstick cats and dogs in the world. There is also an excellent local history library.

Every child in Manchester at some point or another must have been taken to Lark Hill Place, the reconstructed 1900s street at the museum. Everything is as it was: little shops, a leech doctor's surgery, a pub, cottages, a middle-class parlour, cobbled streets and those curiously trendy lanterns that are springing up all over Castlefield.

Salford Mining Museum

- **Location:** Eccles Old Road, Salford; 061-736 1832.
- **Transport:** Bus 60-anything bus to Buile Hill Park.
- **Times and cost**: Mon-Fri 1000-1230 and 1330-1700; Sun 1400-1700. Free.
- **Disabled access**: Limited.

The museum also contains the Gallery of Mining Art (and you thought they just dug coal down there...) depicting life down t'pit, along with doomed canaries, disasters and so on – all from the miners' point of view. The rest of the museum contains a Buile Hill Number One pit and a 1930s Buile Hill Number One drift. Yes, well, the videos and pictures will explain all. It really is an ideal way to capture those elements of heritage which are often ignored and forgotten, but which were a major part of the city's strength.

Portland Basin Industrial Heritage Centre

- **Location:** Portland Place, Portland Street, South Ashton-under-Lyne; 061-308 3374.
- **Transport:** Several buses including 216/8/9, 236/7.
- **Times and cost:** Tues-Sat 1000-1700; Sun 1300-1700. Free.
- **Disabled access:** Limited.

The museum is one of the best out of the city and charts Tameside's social and industrial history – including a regional love of fish and chips! There are sections on Class and Community depicting the marked differences between the working and middle classes last century and at the beginning of this one, and on Education and Local Government. A real education for everyone except the very young – who will be constantly whining about how boring family outings have become.

City Art Gallery

- **Location:** Two sites: Mosley Street and Princess Street; 061-236 9422.
- **Transport:** Walking distance from Piccadilly.
- **Times and cost:** Mon-Sat 1000-1800 Sunday 1400-1800. Free.
- **Disabled access:** Reasonable.

The extensive collections of the City Gallery are housed on two sites. The Mosley Street Gallery is the more traditional: there is a reconstruction of L. S. Lowry's sitting room, one glance at which will send you over to Salford to paint a few smoky chimney pots, no doubt. The rest of the gallery, recently redecorated in authentically heavy nineteenth-century splendour, boasts an extensive collection of pre-Raphaelites, Turners, Stubbs and a Dutch Collection. The most expensive acquisition was *The Crucifixion* (attributed!) by Duccio di Buoninsegnia, peanuts at £8.1 million. It is doubtful whether this forms a part of the innovative 'rent a picture for as little as nine pounds' scheme. Still, there's always hope.

The extension into the old Athenaeum Gentleman's Club in Princess Street was intended to provide space for showing the (actually quite good) modern collection, but the regular (imaginative and varied) short-term exhibitions have elbowed that out – a pity. Check with *City Life* for details of exhibitions and events. The **café** is thought by some to be the best (if not the cheapest) lunch spot in town.

Whitworth Art Gallery

- **Location:** Oxford Road (opposite St Mary's Hospital); 061-273 4865.
- **Transport:** Bus 40-anything (not 47), or 157, 159, P11, W2.
- **Times and cost:** Mon-Sat 1000-1700. Open until 2100 on Thurs. Free.
- **Disabled access:** Extensive.

The University's art collection is housed in a lovely large building standing on the edge of picnic-inducing parkland. It is famed for its permanent collection of watercolours, textiles and wallpapers, as well as an ever-changing exhibition of contemporary art. There is also a café and a shop.

Ideas for combined visits: The collection is close to the Pankhurst Centre, Manchester Museum and Platt Fields Park, so a day could easily be spent visiting all four – if you can stand the culture shock.

Chinese Arts Centre

- **Location:** 36 Charlotte Street; 061-236 9251.
- **Transport:** City centre.
- **Times and cost:** Tues-Fri 1030-1700; Sat and Sun 1400-1700. Free.
- **Disabled access:** Difficult.

The centre opened in 1989 to celebrate Chinese arts, crafts and customs, which were hitherto largely ignored in the city despite its extensive Chinese population. It's a fine place to browse: the exhibitions change regularly, and there is an atmosphere that seems to create its own little timewarp. The café and craft shop contribute to the general unhassled mood of the centre. Certainly cheaper than a massage for winding down, and heartily recommended.

CONTEMPORARY ART

The main venues are the **Cornerhouse** (top of Oxford Road), with three floors of challenging up-to-the-minute shows (galleries open Tuesday-Saturday 1200-2000), the **Holden Gallery** and **Righton Gallery**, both in the Poly buildings around All Saints on Oxford Road. The **Castlefield Gallery**, Liverpool Road (Tuesday-Saturday 1030-1700, Sunday 1200-1600), has a good mix of big names and local artists – and is a good place to pick up cheap originals. For photography exhibitions, visit the **Viewpoint Gallery**, Old Fire Station, The Crescent, Salford, opposite Salford Museum and the University (Tuesday-Friday 1000-1700, Sunday 1400-1700). Out of town, the **Turnpike Gallery**, Leigh (above the Public Library, buses from Arndale Bus Station) is particularly adventurous.

Check *City Life* for details of other exhibitions. From time to time, community centres and theatres hold special exhibitions in a historical or cultural vein – keep your eyes on the local press for details. The outlying towns contain some fine galleries and museums as well. Details of these in *DALES, HILLS AND DARK SATANIC MILLS*.

LIBRARIES OF SPECIAL INTEREST

Don your duffel coat and your Hush Puppies, and search out some of the city's excellent special interest libraries. The most magnificent is the **John Rylands Library**, part of Manchester University, which holds more than five million books, some dating back to the third millenium BC. To get your sticky mitts on many of the books you will need academic permission, but the building alone is worth a good look, and there are always exhibitions of many of the older books anyway. It was built as a tribute to John Rylands by his wife, who had it modelled on Mansfield College in Oxford. The happy pair are immortalized in marble in the main reading room – don't mistake them for a couple of amorous librarians. Open Monday-Friday 1000-1730, Saturday 1000-1300. Details on 061-834 5343. The **Portico Library and Gallery** on Mosley Street (entrance on Charlotte Street) is a restored Georgian private library containing over 40,000 volumes, focused mainly on nineteenth-century works of fiction, travel and writing. If you're looking for a Jackie Collins, I'm afraid you'll be a teensy bit disappointed. Open Monday-Friday 0930-1630. Details on 061-236 6785. **Chetham's Library**, where Engels did much of his work, has an outstanding local history collection housed in the superb medieval buildings of Chetham's School of Music – see below.

Tours and Walks

There are a number of guided walks and tours operated by Manchester City Council and the Tourist Information Centre. These operate mostly through the summer months, and are detailed in a leaflet imaginatively entitled *Guided Walks and Events.* Especially interesting are the following walks: **Mysteries of Haunted Manchester**; the **Manchester Meander**, a sort of 'get to know the city' tour; all of the ethnic community tours, which show the areas and traditions focused on Jewish, Asian, Italian and Chinese quarters of the city; **Pubs of Character** and the **Real-Ale Tour**, both over-eighteens only, and pretty obvious why. You might feel a bit of a prat traipsing around the city in a group of tweedy women, but grit your teeth as they are well worth attending. There are some other strange tours, as well as some very bland-sounding ones that nobody ever claims to have been on, so set off on such delights as **A Boxing Day Stroll**, and **Canals Under the City Streets** at your peril. For bookworms, there is an excellent 'book trail' that will take you in and out of the city's lesser known bookshops. All the tours cost £1.50 (£1.00 concessions) and details are available from the Tourist Information Centre, St Peter's Square (061-234 3157/8). They also arrange special tours for people with disabilities if seven days' notice is given.

By far the best way of getting to know the city centre at your own pace is by walking around it. Such a walk could take a whole day or more if you're tempted in and out of the shops, museums and galleries, or it could be a quick sprint around the more obvious sights. The best place to start is probably St Peter's Square, at the back of the **Town Hall**; this itself is worth far more than a passing glance – a fabulous Neo-Gothic building with an interior that lives up to its tantalizing outside features. Tours do take place around the Town Hall, usually on Wednesdays, but check with the Tourist Information Centre first as they are subject to change due to the political machinations in the council chambers. Next to the Town Hall is the **Central Library**, which looks like it would be more at home in Rome. Deep within its bowels is the excellent Library Theatre, details of which can be found in the *Theatre* section in *THE TWILIGHT ZONE*.

In front of the Town Hall in Albert Square, is the **Albert Memorial**, which is the original of the upstart in London's Hyde Park. Gilbert Scott, the designer of the London memorial, claimed that it was all his own work, but it bears too great a resemblance to Worthington's Manchester design to be a coincidence. Tut, tut! If you look carefully at the floor in front of the Town Hall – in amongst the McDonald's wrappers – you will find a mosaic of a cotton plant flower to remind the good folk of Manchester of the source of the city's wealth. Around the statue are four other flowers: the rose, the thistle, the shamrock and the leek, which the astute among you will have worked out represent the four countries of the United Kingdom.

Crossing over from Albert Square down Mulberry Street, you'll stumble across the delicate little Roman Catholic Church of St Mary's, better known as the **Hidden Gem**. The name comes from a quotation attributed to a bishop of Salford: 'No matter on what side of the church you look, you behold a hidden gem'. Its particular attraction is its lost and alien appearance in the midst of towering office blocks.

Doubling back to Albert Square, if you turn to look at the right of the Town Hall your eye will rest on a huge, black, semi-circular building: **G-Mex** (The Greater Manchester Exhibition Centre), built from the hollowed-out remains of the old Central Station. G-Mex forms the southern part of the grandly titled **Castlefield Urban Heritage Park** (see

Parks and Houses). Castlefield can be incorporated into this city walk, or if your pins are not likely to last very long, you can keep it for a trip in its own right. Whatever your choice, make your eventual way down to Deansgate via Peter Street, past the **Free Trade Hall**, the site of the 1819 Peterloo Massacre. On Deansgate you will see the spectacularly ornate John Rylands Library. By turning right at **King Street** you'll enter the more salubrious parts of the shopping zone. King Street is best in the spring and summer when it is full of fauna and flora as well as plenty of talented buskers belting out Vivaldi's *Four Seasons*. If all you want to do is flash your credit cards around, King Street is good all year round as all of the upmarket chains and designer shops are in this area.

If you walk halfway up King Street and take a left through St Ann's Passage, you will arrive at **St Ann's Church** (hideous on the outside since the stone facing was stripped away, but with a grand eighteenth-century interior) and **St Ann's Square**. This is another potential spot for street cafés and already teeming with buskers – it's the Mancunian equivalent of Covent Garden (except that it's enjoyable). To the right is the resurgent **Royal Exchange** and to the left the **Barton Arcade**, the glass domes of which were modelled on Crystal Palace. A shame it's so hidden by surrounding buildings. Turn left down St Mary's Gate and then right on to Deansgate where, after a short walk (probably at this stage, hobble), you'll come to **Manchester Cathedral**, which was built in the fifteenth century and modified extensively by the Germans in 1940. Now restored, it plays host to many classical concerts. If you want to attend one of the cathedral's services, they take place at 1030 and 1530 on Sundays and 1730 during the week: they are really quite humbling experiences – whatever your religious leanings. For details of the classical concerts, see *Classical Music* in *THE TWILIGHT ZONE*.

Adjacent, on Long Millgate, is **Chetham's School of Music**, housed in fine and well-preserved medieval buildings, together with a famous library. There are fascinating regular tours – details on 061-834 9644. Over the road is the river Irwell, which serves as the boundary between Manchester and Salford. This area is being 'redeveloped' (which is a euphemism for being tarted up with fresh cobbles and fake gas lamps), and walks are planned for the district. The Castlefield Information Centre will give more details.

Walking back along Cathedral Street through the Market Place, you will come to **Shambles Square**. Two pubs in the square date back hundreds of years: they were physically uprooted and moved during redevelopment. From here, go up Market Street as quickly as possible in order to minimize the impact of the Arndale Centre. From the far corner of Piccadilly Gardens, turn right down Portland Street towards **Chinatown**, the centrepiece of which is the impressive Chinese Imperial Arch on Faulkner Street. This arch is the largest of its kind in Europe; it was designed in China and built by an imported workforce of experts from Beijing. The art and culture of Chinatown are impressively displayed in the Chinese Arts Centre in Charlotte Street (see *Museums*), and the whole area, of course, comes dramatically to life during the Chinese New Year celebrations at the end of January.

At the end of Charlotte Street is the Portico Library (see above); if you then turn left down Mosley Street, you can pass the City Art Gallery on the way back to St Peter's Square. And lo! you're back where you started. As from 1991 Metrolink will be up and running through the city centre, which may well make parts of this walk a little easier on your throbbing feet.

GUARDIAN *AND* MANCHESTER EVENING NEWS *TOURS*

These newspapers' offices are on the site of an eighteenth-century poorhouse, next to the John Rylands Library at 164 Deansgate. Both newspapers offer tours around their departments, which are especially interesting for anyone who is fascinated by the inner workings of the fourth estate. The *MEN* tours take place at 1330 Monday to Friday (presumably when the many of the staff are down at the pub). Details on 061-832 7200, extension 2313. The *Guardian*'s production tour starts at 1945 going right through to around 2300. If you can do without an evening in the pub, it's well worth watching Manchester's biggest gift to the national newspaper scene roll off the presses. Details on 061-832 7200, extension 2418.

GRANADA STUDIOS TOUR

- **Location:** Granada Studios – entrance Water Street off Quay Street; 061-833 0880.
- **Transport:** Walk from city centre or Deansgate B.R.
- **Times and cost:** Mon/Tues, Fri-Sun 0945-1900 (last tour 1630); Weds/Thurs 0945-2300 (last tour 2100). Wait for it... £6.95 or a bargain £21.00 for a family ticket.
- **Disabled access:** Extensive.

The tour takes about ninety minutes, but you should allow three hours' browsing to make sure you squeeze every last drop out of your entrance fee. Unless you slip into a state of uncontrolled ecstasy at the sound of the *Coronation Street* theme tune, the tour really is a bit of a rip-off. The *Coronation Street* set is by no means the whole tour, as you are also taken around a complete mock-up of the House of Commons (where they filmed Jeffrey Archer's *First Amongst Equals* among other things), as well as The Giant's Room, which the kids will love and which will make you feel positively Lilliputian.

The studios are the sort of place you feel obliged to take visitors, and because it's such a tourist trap, very few locals ever bother to go: another indication of Mancunian common sense. Incidentally, if you slip around the back and peer over the wall, you can see the back of Coronation Street, the viaduct, the Kabin and the corner of Alf's Mini Mart without even paying. However, if your life's ambition is to sit in the snug of the Rovers Return and sip a pint of Newton and Ridley's, then you'll just have to fork out. The rest of Castlefield is nearby.

WATERWAYS AND BOAT TRIPS ON THE CANAL

The **Bridgewater Packet Boat Service** operate boat trips up and down the canal basins in Castlefield and Salford; they use traditional narrow barges pulled by the horses you see in the bitter ads. Details on 061-748 2680.

Parks and Houses

CASTLEFIELD URBAN HERITAGE PARK

One of the grottiest, grimiest areas of the city has been the beneficiary of vast amounts of planning, time and especially money, and is beginning to emerge as an unusual centre for tourists and locals alike. Much work is yet to be done, as can be seen from the still-putrid canals lapping at the newly pedestrianized walkways, which appear a little self-conscious with their spruced-up lamps and incongruous tourist signs. On a quiet day the atmosphere is surreal – rather like an abandoned film set – yet there is evidently a great deal of potential in this area, and the signs are that this is going to become one of the hubs of Manchester city life.

Already, the **Museum of Science and Industry** (see *Museums* above) has won the Museum of the Year Award, and the 1990 Castlefield Carnival has provided a taste of how things could be. Markets, hotels and bars and a major classical concert venue are planned in an area that already has G-Mex and Granada Studios. There is also an underwhelming Roman fort, an intimate art gallery and an excellent information centre, from which staff organize walks and tours in the district. Details on 061-832 4244.

Every Bank Holiday Monday there is a brilliant street market on Liverpool Road, bringing the district sharply to life. The whole reclamation process and its commitment to the area's heritage is breathtaking, and is the most obvious testimony to Manchester's determination to grow and develop without losing touch with its past. Ten Brownie points.

HEATON PARK AND HALL

Take a train to Heaton Park Station and spend a day at the largest municipal park in Western Europe. Within it is a beautiful Neo-Classical country house which you can view – but telephone first for details because opening times are erratic (061-236 9422, extension 237). In the park there is a boating lake, a pets' corner and a model garden centre, as well as a ghost laid on for your delectation. In these days of global warming, it's a wonderful way to accumulate radiation poisoning. Top up your tan, and then hop on the tram to Crumpsall. The **farm centre** is open Tuesday-Friday 1030-1530 and at weekends 1100-1530. The **model garden centre** opens daily 1000-1500, and the **tramway** (which costs 20p) Sundays and bank holidays 1200-1700 and Wednesdays 1030-1500. Although the park is open in winter, many of its attractions are not. Further details on 061-773 1085.

PLATT FIELDS PARK

This park in Rusholme is home to the Gallery of English Costume (see *Museums*, above). A large and beautiful rose garden and boating lake (which fills up in the summer with boozy students), it is within walking distance of the Whitworth Art Gallery, the Manchester Museum and some of the tastiest curries in the country. What more could anyone ask? Take bus 40- anything (not 47), 157/9, W2, P11, or any other bus with Fallowfield or Wilmslow Road as its destination.

TRAFFORD ECOLOGY PARK

If you thought that Trafford Park was a large and terminally unattractive industrial estate, you would be right. However, did you know that until the turn of this century the area was preserved as a large country estate? Then the lake was filled and became a car park, and the surrounding area degenerated into a dump. In 1979 Esso offloaded the eyesore on to Trafford Borough Council, to be used for nature conservation as the country's first ecological park in an industrial area. A decade on, the park is now home to an abundance of wildlife, and the car park has reverted to a lake once more. The major intention beyond that of mere conservation has been to educate. To this end the park hosts many exhibitions, events, a study area, an experiment area and an amphitheatre. Details on 061-873 7182. Public transport around here is complicated: train to Trafford Park from Piccadilly and then a walk or bus ride along Trafford Park Road is probably the easiest. Open 0900-1630 weekdays.

FLETCHER MOSS GARDENS

Though it looks dingy from the road, this park (named after a local worthy) is the pride and joy of the City Parks Department. Hidden behind the tennis courts is a huge rock garden on a slope, with streams, winding paths and many unusual plants and shrubs. It is well maintained, with something attractive to see at almost any time of year. There are woods, extensive walks and lots of good spots for snogging in the long grass in the meadows stretching way out towards the River Mersey (when they're not flooded, that is). You can walk along the river for miles, if you're so inclined, with good riverside pubs at Northenden and Chorlton. Buses 40/2/5, 157 to East Didsbury: alight at the Didsbury and Old Cock pubs. In the corner between the pubs is the entrance to the **Parsonage Gardens** – much smaller but still interesting with its museum of local history.

One of the distinctive features of the North-West architecturally is the black-and-white half-timbered Elizabethan house; several of these are dotted around Manchester and are open to the public. To the south, **Bramhall Hall** in Bramhall and **Wythenshawe Hall** in Northenden both have extensive parks (good for picnics), while **Ordsall Hall Museum** is a surprising find in the middle of grimy Salford, (Taylorson Street), walkable from city centre (061-872 0251).

Kids' Stuff

Many of the places listed throughout this book are ideal for younger members of the family. Especially notable are the Museum of Science and Industry, Heaton and Trafford Parks and the Manchester United Museum. One of the guided walks available from the Tourist Information Centre is geared towards youngsters, enlivening the life and history of the city with storytelling, mystery and ghost tales. The children have to be accompanied on this tour – which is no great shame, as it is a great deal more fun than many of those aimed at the adults! 061-234 3157/8 for details.

Greater Manchester Play Resources Unit (GRUMPY), Grumpy House, Vaughan Street M12 (061-223 9730) supply play/arts/crafts materials – including an Aladdin's cave of junk material from industry. Individuals as well as groups can be members, but resources (and information on activities and books) are available to anyone working with children and young people.

Both the **Cornerhouse** and the **Green Room** offer children's events at the weekend. At the former, it's usually in the form of a film on Saturday afternoons. The Green Room has a **Sunday Funday**, which is a more imaginative children's cabaret and theatre workshop. Kids (and lots of adults) love it; activities vary greatly. For details of the Saturday Club at the Cornerhouse ring 061-228 2463 and for information on Sunday Funday 061-236 1677. Saturday painting and fun sessions are held at Castlefield Gallery (061-832 8034). Many leisure centres have special facilities for children: the Gorton Tub and Tameside Leisure Park in particular are paradise for kiddies though useless for actual swimming. Details of these and places for roller skating, ten-pin bowling, etc, in *SPORT AND LEISURE*. Lots of other community events are geared towards children: check the *City Life* Kids Listing section for one-off events

On Whitworth Street West, there is a Star Wars offshoot called the ***Laser Quest Labyrinth***. It's not suitable for those under seven (or small children over seven) as the equipment is too bulky. The object of the game is to disarm your opponent by scoring a direct hit with your laser beam. Great intergalactic fun, if a little pricey at £3.00 for fifteen minutes (£2.00 for children). Maybe for that special treat....

For details of crèche facilities, see *Women* in *THE MORAL MAJORITY*.

Special Events

Spring and summer mark the onslaught of merry festivals from every section of the community. Some are laughably naff and badly attended, some atmospheric and brilliantly organized. The following are some of the more successful and deserving of the annual offerings.

- In **Chinatown** there are vibrant celebrations of **Chinese New Year** at the end of January; during the second week of September each year, there is a **Moon Festival**.
- The **Castlefield Carnival** (in September) was born in 1990, and was a resounding success. On Bank Holiday Mondays there are also markets and festivities in the area.
- June marks the month of the **Arts Festival** in Manchester. The best ever took place in 1990, all over the city, in every theatre, on every street corner and in the depths of every cellar – in celebration of Manchester's Olympic Bid. Even though the bid failed, the festival alone was worth the effort, and hopefully those high standards will remain for all future June festivities.
- Wigan Pier is the unlikely centre for an **International Jazz Festival** in June, and Buxton also jumps on the June Jazz bandwagon with an annual festival – though not on the same scale.
- G-Mex plays host to countless annual conferences and events but among the more notable is the **Guinness Soccer Six Championships** in December.
- For the more politically minded there is a massive international **Socialist Conference** in November with speakers and delegates from all over the world.
- There are many community festivals around the city throughout the year. Chorlton Park plays host to the **South Manchester Music Festival** with a credible crowd of trendy bands, and in November the **Community Festival** in Crumpsall draws them in from all over the city.

In addition, there are annual sports events, comedy fairs, special interest days, anti-everything weeks, pro-everything-else weeks, and countless community projects. Out of the city are some excellent fêtes and carnivals – *City Life* will keep you posted.

5. THE TWILIGHT ZONE

Nightlife and Music

Variety is the spice of nightlife, and Manchester offers up a vindaloo on this particular menu. More bars than Strangeways, more clubs than Jacobs and more culture than a student kitchen: a myriad of entertainment awaits your leisurely perusal. Making it even more appealing is the fact that most entertainment won't invoke stormy letters from an irate bank manager, and many of the venues are well within walking distance of each other. Even the slightly outlying areas are easily accessible by bus, train or taxi (try Ancoats for a dirt cheap journey home). Many areas outside the city centre have developed a thriving nightlife – so whatever your area of town, your budget or your taste, there's no great excuse for being bored.

NIGHTCLUBS – CITY CENTRE

Dance, Hip-Hop, Indie

The pride and joy of Manchester's club scene was the **Haçienda** in Whitworth Street West – until it was closed in January 1991 due to increased incidence of violence, and pressure from the police eager to calm public jitters over drug abuse. Whether it reopens under a different name or passes into folklore remains to be seen – so watch the listings in *City Life*.

Similar pressures have been brought to bear on **Precinct 13** (South King Street) and **Konspiracy** (Fennel Street). As with the Haçienda, the circumstances surrounding these closures largely serve to demonstrate a failure to get to grips with some of the more serious problems of organized crime within the city. Don't despair, however: there are still plenty of places to enjoy....

First port of call is **Dry 201** on Oldham Street (061-236 5920). The minimalist décor is firmly in tune with contemporary tastes, and it's important for *you* to look stridently trendy, or you won't be allowed in. It's worth trying out – if only to see what the fuss is about.

If you want to get an idea of the Haçienda style in its heyday, get yourself along to **Man Alive**, Grosvenor Street (061-273 4110).

Wednesday is a notoriously good night here, as it is at the **Number One** club, Central Street (061-834 1292), when it's their mixed night. New on the scene is the **Soundgarden**, 8 Back Piccadilly (061-839 4289). Although it only opened in October 1990, it has gained a mega-reputation so fast that you have to queue on Saturday nights well before doors open to get in. £3 before 2300 and not a cat in hell's chance of reaching the door after that to pay the increased £4 admittance; it's close enough to Dry to attract the trendy posse, and good enough not to rely on it.

A welcome innovation in 1990, combining clubs with culture, was **Awareness '90**, held at the Mechanics' Institute (home to the National Museum of Labour History), Princess Street. The concept was to create a rave with visual stimulation and without the aid of Ecstasy. At the door, a would-be Nigel Kennedy (or someone similar, *i.e.* with a violin) would greet you before you wafted airily into the Gallery, where sounds from a Sunset Radio DJ enveloped your aural senses. The eyes would focus on the art while the heart rejoiced in the opportunity to appreciate an exhibition without having to search through the mind's store of arty terminology in order to appear knowledgeable. Taking place on Friday evenings throughout the summer, it was a wonderful way to be cool without busting a gut on the dance floor. May there be an Awareness '91, '92, '93....

Mainstream Discos

If a good night out consists of donning a shirt and tie, or skirt and heels, and then downing some lagers or spritzers, watch this space. Strutting your stuff to the latest Jive Bunny is the speciality of **Sacha's** in Tib Street (061-228 1234) – look out for the stuffed polar bear – which hosts the terrifyingly named 'Frantic Fran's Hen Night' on Thursdays. A little more upmarket is the popular **21 Piccadilly** (061-236 7825), situated on Piccadilly Square in the strange black-and-blue building that looks like an ornament shop, but which is, in fact, an amusement arcade. A weekend boogie here after 1030 will set you back £5, although there have been rumblings of controversy in *City Life* magazine about the place's door policy.

Continuing upmarket is **Discothèque Royale**, Peter Street (061-839 1112), a converted theatre with tier upon tier of ornate balconies. *Hit Man and Her* has been filmed here several times giving the place an inflated ego, so expect to pay accordingly.

Very mainstream, but much cheaper and without a dress code, is the **New Continental Club**, 2 Harter Street, off Princess Street, (061-236 5521); it may remind you of a sweaty college disco, but it can be good fun, especially if you're with a few friends and you're skint.

Alternative

The **Banshee** in Oxford Street (061-228 7728) is the Goth centre of the city. Wednesdays are free Rock Nights and Thursdays the free 'Goths grab grebos gotta grind go grungeful' nights – hold yourself back if you can! The rest of the time sees general alternative/rock music, with Saturday night setting you back only £2. The **Ritz** (Whitworth Street West, 061-236 7515) has excellent and popular Gothic/alternative nights on Mondays, while **5th Avenue** (121 Princess Street) plays alternative on Thursdays for £1.75.

NIGHTCLUBS – BEYOND THE CITY CENTRE

Should your feet be tapping on a Tuesday, go and find 'Life' at **International 2**, 210 Plymouth Grove, M13 (061-273 8834). It's cheap (£2), plays excellent music, is very popular – and the evening is broadcast by KFM. A little farther south, in Didsbury, try **Fridays** in Palatine Road (061-434 4986), deservedly popular, especially on Mondays. Hidden in Hulme, however, is the real gem of the club scene, **PSV** in Clayburn Road (061-226 7526). Split into two levels, it will relieve itchy feet with funk and hip-hop downstairs, and soothe and relax you with reggae and soul upstairs. It's free during the week and only £2 at the week-end, so you'd be daft to miss it. One small word of warning, however: Hulme isn't the most bijou of areas, and it's probably easiest to get a taxi from the nearby city centre. If you do walk, make sure there are no holes in your shoes and avoid stepping on used syringes!

Good on any night is **Severe** (formerly Granville's), on Wilmslow Road underneath the Lansdowne Hotel (061-224 6244). It's a cosy yet cavernous place, with Manchester's largest stock of bottled beer. Entry is usually free unless something special is going on, in which case there is some small admission charge.

For a night out with all the garish trimmings, try **Heartlands** in Trafford Park (Ashburton Road East, 061-872 3010). Friday nights are particularly well worth the £3 entry fee – just to visit a club that has been featured in the *Sunday Sport*!

Friday nights at the **Academy**, Manchester University, Oxford Road (061-275 2930), are rapidly gaining deserved popularity. Admission costs only £2, and student ID is not necessary unless it's getting very full, but get there early if you don't have an NUS card. You do have to have one (or know someone who will sign you in) to get into the celebrated **Poly Bop** (Manchester Polytechnic, Mandela Building, Oxford Road at All Saints) on a Friday.

It is impossible to cover the sheer range of the hundreds of clubs that exist in and around the city. New clubs are opening all the time (and many older ones closing or changing names and altering images), so experimentation is really the only way – not too much of a drag in these hedonistic times.

VENUES

Manchester wouldn't have achieved its present success in the music industry if it weren't for the strong base of support for live bands in the city. Manchester looks after its own: its venues and clubs actively promote local music, and a passion for home-grown talent is displayed in crowded venues on every night of the week.

The major indoor touring venue is the **Apollo** in Ardwick Green (061-273 3775), seating 2,800. Its biggest drawback is in fact its seating, since many bands prefer to play to wildly active and dancing crowds. The Apollo restricts this freedom as your feet tend to get stuck down the back of your chair – although for the bigger and more sedate 'artistes', such as Suzanne Vega, Belinda Carlisle *et al.*, the venue is just fine. Some solution to the seating problem has been found in the form of **G-Mex** in Windmill Street (061-832 9000 or 061-834 2700). Used for everything from the Northern Secretarial Exhibition to soccer, G-Mex is versatile to say the least. Both the Happy Mondays and James chose to play here in 1990 because of the large open space offered, with the resulting buzz that you simply don't get in an all-seater. Unfortunately, the costs involved in playing the old converted railway station are pretty high, which is reflected in expensive ticket prices.

If Paul Coombes, owner of the **International 2** (210 Plymouth Grove, 061-273 8834), goes ahead with plans to extend his 1,500-capacity venue, there will be a cheaper alternative for the bigger names in a place that already has a tremendous reputation. It boasts an excellent seedy atmosphere and a huge variety of music, as does its little sister, the **International** (47 Anson Road, 061-256 2793). Renowned for smaller gigs, the International actively promotes local talent and the under-represented bands of the world music scene. On Mondays there is a showcase for up-and-coming local hopefuls – a sort of indie

Opportunity Knocks. Its capacity of 800 is ideal for such events, and at some point during the year there is bound to be something here that you feel you absolutely must see. Be warned, however, about the toilets, which at the time of writing certainly do not merit five stars in anybody's 'Good Loo Guide'. Watch that liquid intake!

The traditional place to see a 'we're-almost-there-and-aren't- you-going-to-be-glad-you-saw-us-first-when-we-make-it' band in Manchester is the **Ritz** (Whitworth Street West, 061-236 4355). The gigs are so lively and so loud that the dance floor feels more like a trampoline – so if someone comes up to you and tells you they were walking on air at the Ritz, they were not necessarily tripping. The Ritz is still, in spite of unprecedented competition, one of the best places both to watch and to play. The balconies afford good views of performers and springy dancers alike, and the atmosphere is good, hot and sweaty. New competition came in 1990 from Manchester University's new venue, the **Academy** (061-275 2930). Its 1,500 capacity and supposedly £100,000 light show have already secured it a formidable reputation as one of the better venues, although the atmosphere isn't quite as good as some. In spite of being housed within the University, the Academy is anxious to promote itself as a public, and not merely a student, venue; the bar is not subsidized, although it is still cheaper than most clubs. Gigs are advertised widely in the local press.

In addition to the larger venues, there are hundreds of smaller places dotted in and around the city. **Band on the Wall** in Swan Street, Ancoats (061-832 6625) is one of the best. If yous likes yo blues, reggae or jazz, look no further. Reggae generally struts its stuff on Friday, and Saturdays are given over to R'n'B. The programme is varied, and whenever you go, you are guaranteed a good time. The place itself looks rather jaded – so much so that you could be forgiven for thinking it had closed down before you arrived. You actually have to knock on the door and only then do the bouncers let you in. Once within its walls, the customers are varied: a wider cross-section of the community you will not encounter elsewhere. Students rub shoulders with middle-aged locals, and the only thing they have in common is a love of the place and the music.

Nearly as popular is the **Boardwalk** (Little Peter Street, 061-228 3555). Almost all of Manchester's biggest bands have played some of their earliest gigs here. Very much a locals' place, it was, according to Sarah Champion (mild and objective author of *And God Created Manchester*), the scene of the most popular gigs of the 1980s. At present its capacity is only 300, but an extension is to increase that to

700, and with a new veggie diner to be installed upstairs, the place seems to be going upmarket. Definitely worth a visit, especially to check out new indie bands and to keep your street cred intact.

In addition to these, most of the clubs at some point or another have gigs on their premises, and many of the venues listed have club nights. Again, as always, check *City Life* for updated information. If it was a quiet evening after which you hankered, with some unknown musician like Bowie or Prince, rumours abound that their sort can often be found hanging around Manchester City's **Maine Road** ground. (Probably busking for enough cash to watch a game!)

JAZZ

In addition to the numerous little jazz bars and pubs around the city, major jazz jamborees take place regularly at such venues as the **Internationals**, the **Academy** and **Band on the Wall** (see above). The **Royal Northern College of Music** (Booth Street West) and the **Free Trade Hall** (Peter Street) also put on frequent jazz concerts, though these tend to be calmer and more sophisticated affairs than the gigs at the above (see *Classical Music* for their addresses).There are many pubs with jazz residencies. On Oak Street (just off Tib Street), you will find the **Wheatsheaf**. Here they have a Jazz Society on Thursday nights, as well as other gigs and folk evenings throughout the week.

Out of the city, at the **Fleece** in Glossop (Bernard Street, buses 211/4/5, 236/7), jazz and blues are performed on Thursday and Saturday nights. Still in the east, but nearer to the city in Ashton-under-Lyne, the **Witchwood** is famed for regular jazz (Old Street, buses 216/8/9, 236/7). To the south, on Wilmslow Road, Withington, underneath the Barbican Hotel, **Mulberry's** offers jazz and blues on most nights, except when the Comedy Cellar is on (see *Cabaret*). Admittance is usually free to all of the above unless a special act is performing. The standards are high and the atmosphere lively: well worth a nosey. Again, the list is by no means exhaustive – check *City Life* for details.

CABARET

Venues for cabaret vary as much as the content. From the satirized, tuneless pub singer to excellent fringe comedy, the cabaret scene is diverse but nearly always entertaining. The **Green Room, Cornerhouse** and **Contact** (see *Theatre* and *Cinema*) sometimes play host to comedy acts and unusual performers, usually of the fringe or alternative type. Out of trendy theatreland though, the most consistent venue is **Buzz**, upstairs at the Southern, Nell Lane, Chorlton (061-881 7048). A session usually costs around £3, but the quality is worth paying for as the place has an excellent reputation. Over in Crumpsall, the **Abraham Moss Centre** (again, see *Theatre*) is a popular cabaret venue, with local and cultural acts given priority. The Comedy Cellar at **Mulberry's** (see above) takes place on Saturday nights; its stamp of approval lies in the fact that the *City Life* Comedian of the Year 1990 competition was held there. In addition, many community centres and pubs host cabaret events intermittently throughout the year, which are usually advertised well in advance.

Cinema, Theatre and Classical Music

There has been a great commitment given over to the arts in this city. In an age where culture has been systematically ignored, or even attacked through reductions in funding, Manchester's interest has been something of an anomaly. The development of the North-West, and Manchester in particular, as a major cultural centre has owed its success to close working relationships between the city and metropolitan borough councils, arts organizations and various patrons, most notably (again!), Bob Scott.

North-West Arts will, by the time you read this, have become a board with responsibilities for many theatres and organizations such as the Hallé, previously funded directly by the Arts Council. There is speculation that the changes are in fact a form of delegation, and a shirking of responsibilities on behalf of the government (surely not!), but many believe that the changes are a good thing and that the new Arts Board (North-West) will be more accessible and sympathetic than a centralized body.

The reality of such hopes remains to be seen, but at least with such a strong base of support, a proven record and an uncanny ability to create much out of very little, Manchester is setting out on to its new cultural pathway with secure walking boots.

CINEMA

Strangely enough, although Manchester has a wide proliferation of cinemas, there is only one deep within the heart of the city. This syndrome graphically exhibits the history of British cinema – its rapid decline throughout the 1970s in our town centres, and its astonishing revival in out-of-town mega multi-screened film palaces (of which there are three in Greater Manchester). Still, the city-centre **Odeon**, Oxford Street (061-236 8264), has survived and is running successfully on its standard quota of box-office smash hits; an evening show will cost you £3 (£2 concessions).

Of the three multiplex complexes, the **Belle Vue Showcase** (Hyde Road, 061-220 8765) is the biggest (and most expensive: £3.25/£2.25 concessions). Get there on the train from Piccadilly to Belle Vue, or buses 209-15 or 224-9 along Hyde Road. Their evening shows usually start quite late (around 2130), so a taxi home may be necessary. The **Warner Multiplex** in Bury (Pilsworth Road) has twelve screens and costs only £2.95 (£2.50 concessions). It is, however, more than a little inaccessible, being situated on the Heywood Pilsworth Industrial Estate (just off Junction 3 on the M66). Buses 488 and 495 go from Bury town centre to the cinema, as does the 136 from Manchester Piccadilly bus station. Details on 061-766 1121. Nearest to the city centre is the eight-screen **Cannon** at Salford Quays, Trafford Park Road (061-873 7155). At £3 for an evening show, it boasts that it is cheaper than the Belle Vue, although there are no concessions. Take the 174/5 Salford Enterprise Zone Bus or buses 52, 71, 84, 92 along Trafford Park Road: GMPTE will give you details (see *Travel and Transport*). Whether or not you enjoy the Multiplex experience is a matter of preference. Such cinemas do offer very comfortable seats, a sound system devoid of scratches and crackles, uninterrupted enjoyment of the film without annoying intermissions and a plentiful supply of popcorn and sweets to guarantee a chomping good time.

Some people, however, prefer the intimacy of the good old-fashioned flea-pit, complete with a supply of naff adverts for the local curry house and second-hand car showroom. There are many such small locals in the suburbs that have successfully survived the squeeze and are now regaining their popularity:

Old Street, Ashton-under-Lyne (061-330 1993)
Kingsway, Burnage (061-443 1004)
Buxton Road, Davenport (061-483 3801)
Gatley Road, Gatley (061-491 0711/428 2133)
Heaton Moor Road, Heaton Moor (061-432 2114)
Hollins Road, Hollinwood (061-681 1441)
Corporation Street, Hyde (061-368 2206)
Stockport Road, Marple (061-427 5951)

Manchester Old Road, Middleton (061-643 2852)
Market Street, Stalybridge (061-338 2156)
Princess Road, Urmston (061-748 2929)
Bury Old Road, Whitefield (061-766 2369)
Wilmslow Road, Withington (061-445 3301)
Bolton Road, Worsley (061-790 9432)

For artier or more avant-garde films, the **Cornerhouse**, Oxford Street (061-228 2463), is the major venue. There is a three-screen cinema, as well as a bar, café and art gallery in this highly trendy complex. Many of the old cult, art, minority and foreign films are shown here: get your sticky hands on one of their monthly programmes for details – you should be able to find one in the local library, the Tourist Information Centre or the Cornerhouse itself.

The **Manchester and Salford Film Society** (meetings in Fallowfield, enquiries on 061-224 1243) is less lively and trendy than the Cornerhouse, but offers historic and continental films you're unlikely to see elsewhere; it is notable as the country's oldest film society. The **University** and the **Green Room** both show offbeat films occasionally (see *Theatre* for details). Check *City Life/Uptown* for updated listings.

THEATRE

From classical to radical, from *Chess* to Chekhov – Manchester's theatreland will satisfy most appetites. Tickets for all performances can be booked at the **Manchester Ticket Shop**, Town Hall Extension, St Peter's Square (061-236 7076). They deal with everything from the Pogues to pantomime – everything, in fact, for which you need a ticket (buses and trains not included). Their service doesn't end in Manchester: tickets for shows in many other parts of the country can be bought and booked through them.

The **Royal Exchange**, at St Ann's Square and Cross Street (061-833 9833), is the icing on Manchester's cultural cake and one of the most prestigious theatres in the country. It looks like some futuristic time machine that has landed in the ornate Victorian building that houses the theatre. Most of the repertoire is classical, but the occasional British and world première gives a contemporary respectability to the place. Prices are varied and discounts are often available. For many performances, there are cheap tickets on offer right at the front on floor level. If you don't mind craning your neck slightly these can be excellent value. The top tier of seating (of three) is where they stick the schoolkids, so unless you want amorous fourth-formers snogging through soliloquies sit elsewhere. Wheelchair access to the theatre is good, and there is an induction hearing loop.

The **Palace Theatre** – also in Oxford Street (061-236 9922) – and the **Opera House** in Quay Street (061-831 7766) are the more conventional face of theatreland: Lloyd-Webber and Jeffrey Archer addicts flock here in their hundreds. This is not to say, however, that they don't produce some occasional flashes of brilliance, and not all of the mainstream theatre is too trashy. They both seat around 2,000 people, although the Palace's auditorium is considerably larger. The Palace plays host to some notable touring companies (including Glyndebourne Opera, the Royal Shakespeare Company and the National Ballet), as well as some good musicals and a huge panto at Christmas. The Opera House is committed to long-running musicals and the odd thriller to draw in the punters. It was rescued from a future as a Bingo Hall by Bob Scott (who also revamped the Palace and created the Royal Exchange) – and even *Evita* is preferable to that fate! Disabled access is limited to wheelchairs, and is not extensive. Telephone for details.

Within the Library Theatre Group are the eponymous **Library Theatre**, surprisingly enough situated underneath the Central Library in St Peter's Square (061-236 7110), and the **Wythenshawe Forum** (061-437 9663) at the Civic Centre, Wythenshawe (buses 5 or 43). The Library relies for all of its funding on box office takings and dwindling local government finance: there is no Arts Council grant. However, the theatre seems to manage very well without it, receiving rave reviews all round. Most of the plays here are contemporary, with some excellent musicals, and usually offer a more profound message than is readily available in most mainstream theatre. With its strong repertory reputation, the Library succeeds in bringing many world premières to its stage.

The Forum also has an excellent reputation for musicals, although they tend to be a little more traditional. Like the Library Theatre, it has good facilities for people with disabilities: the visually impaired and hard of hearing are well catered for, as are those in wheelchairs. Both theatres offer a 'two for the price of one' discount for accompanied disabled people.

The **Green Room** (061-236 1677) is situated underneath two railway arches on Whitworth Street West. Seating only 165 people, it is one of the smallest yet most explosive theatres in the city. Blink and you will have missed a production, so it is worth keeping a very close eye on the listings: there are bound to be things on that you will want to see. Even the more traditional plays performed here will be given a new lease of life: reviews overflow with fulsome adjectives such as 'experimental', 'innovative', 'fresh' and 'inventive'. The place is necessarily full of languid youths posing happily away, most of them blissfully unaware of the events occurring on stage. The Green Room also puts on regular meetings, films, exhibitions and a Sunday Funday for the younger clientele. Wheelchair access and provision for guide-dogs are available: no induction loop.

The **Contact Theatre** (061-274 4400/4747), situated just off Oxford Road on Manchester University campus, is committed to making theatre accessible to young people. There is a youth theatre, as well as a whole host of workshops and exhibitions designed to beckon you in through the door and to promote a greater understanding of the plays and authors. Some productions offer 'theatre days', with an opportunity to gaze meaningfully at the text with the members of the company in a socially interactive kinda way. Many plays have after-show discussions – not of the 'fancy a pint, then?' variety. All of this could so easily become dogmatic, but the Contact usually succeeds in keeping the discussions lively, often funny, and always interesting. It's a good deal more fun than buying a lorry-load of *York Notes* on your chosen texts. The theatre is a twenty-minute walk from Oxford Road Station, or a short bus ride from the centre (buses 40/2/3/4/5/6/9, 50, 143, 157/8, P11, P15 or W2). There are many generous concessions, including cheap tickets for people with disabilities and their companions. Wheelchair access, induction hearing loop and provision for guide-dogs. There is also a Saturday Club for kids (see *Kids' Stuff* in *JOY RIDES*).

The **Bolton Octagon** currently has Jim Cartwright as its writer-in-residence, and so his brilliant plays get their first airing here. Even *Brookside*'s Shea and Billy first performed their two-hander *To* here before it transferred to London and a nationwide tour. Much of the North-West's brightest acting talent struts its precocious stuff across this versatile stage. An unusual design allows the stage to be moved so that performances can take place in any way from theatre in the round through to the traditional proscenium arch production. Bolton is most easily reached from Manchester by train from Victoria Station, and the theatre is on Howell Croft, behind the library and art gallery on Le Mans Crescent. Details on 0204-20661. Disabled access is varied, so check first with the box office.

Oldham Coliseum succeeds in balancing all acts from *Richard III* to *Dick Whittington* without resorting to the tack of some of the city centre theatres. Train from Victoria Station to the prosaically named Mumps station, or take bus 51 or 82 from Manchester. The theatre is a five-minute walk from both train and bus stations on Fairbottom Street, just off Yorkshire Street. 061-624 2829 for details. There is an induction hearing loop and wheelchair access but only three spaces for wheelchairs, so book well in advance.

The **Abraham Moss Centre**, on Crescent Road in Crumpsall, has been unusually successful in creating a reputable theatre group (Up the Hill) while retaining a strong cultural community base. The theatre is fully accessible to the disabled and can be reached from the city centre by buses 78/9, 135/7 or by walking from Woodlands Road Railway Station for five minutes. The first Crumpsall and Cheetham Hill Community Arts Festival was held at the centre in November 1990, and is planned to be an annual event. The theatre booking office can be reached on 061-795 9308.

CLASSICAL MUSIC

Manchester is home to two major British Orchestras: the **Hallé** and the **BBC Philharmonic**. The former had humble origins in the nineteenth century, when Charles Hallé came from Paris to Manchester to teach music and started a series of concerts for the workers on Monday nights. From these small beginnings a great orchestra developed, which has managed to weather various more recent commercial storms with the help of local support, and which now has a bright future. The Hallé plays mostly at the Free Trade Hall on Peter Street (061-834 0943) and at G-Mex, Windmill Street (061-832 9000 or 061-834 2700), the latter being the venue for their more commercial concerts such as the popular 'pop classics'; oh well, they gotta make a livin', man. A new and bigger home is presently being sought for Manchester's most beloved orchestra. The other Mancunian band, the BBC Philharmonic, also play at the Free Trade Hall and often use the Royal Northern College of Music in Booth Street West, off Oxford Road (061-273 4504) as a venue. They actively encourage a wide cross-section of the community to attend their concerts and offer excellent discounts, most notably their standby student tickets for as little as £2.50.

The **RNCM** itself offers a wealth of musical talent, not only from its own renowned students but from a wide variety of guest orchestras and performers. Along with **Chetham's School of Music** in Long Millgate, next to Manchester Cathedral (061-834 9644), the college has enhanced Manchester's musical and cultural reputation and produced world-famous artists. Several distinctly non-classical types are numbered among RNCM's former guests (for example Courtney Pine), so the repertoires evidently vary. Check them out.

In the **Cathedral** itself concerts are often performed, while the **Royal Exchange Theatre** plays host to the Manchester Midday Concerts and other excellent and intimate classical concerts – usually chamber or soloists – during afternoons when there isn't a drama matinée performance.

The **University Music Department** (in Denmark Road, off Oxford Road by the Whitworth Gallery, 061-275 4982) offers a wide range of orchestral concerts, recitals, early and contemporary music, and particularly series of chamber concerts by the resident world-famous Lindsay String Quartet.

Out of the city, **Buxton Opera House** (0298-72190) puts on some pretty excellent concerts, as do the **Albert** and **Victoria Halls** in Bolton (0204-364333). **Christchurch** in Didsbury (061-456 9037) and **Peel Hall** at the University of Salford (061-745 5288) are also popular and have a good reputation. Tickets for all the above-mentioned venues, can be bought and booked at the Manchester Ticket Shop (see above).

TOURING COMPANIES

The major touring opera and ballet companies usually play to a fully booked Palace Theatre (see *Theatre*). The 1990 season included the English National Ballet, Opera North and the Glyndebourne Opera Group. Such performances are advertised well in advance, and are not on for very long as a rule, so be sure to take full advantage of them.

Out of the city, the Buxton Opera House is a popular touring venue with many companies, and some of the stuff here is not to be missed. See above for details.

6. DALES, HILLS AND DARK SATANIC MILLS

No other city in Britain lies in such close proximity to an incredibly varied concentration of countryside. To the east and south-east lies the last wilderness area in England, handily packaged as the **Peak District National Park**. To the north, rugged and rambling **Lancashire** joins forces with the Brontës' beloved **West Yorkshire**, drawing the tourist or visitor inexorably on to the majestic (if somewhat over-exposed) **Lake District**, home of Lakeside poetry, hoary mountains, silent waters and endless tea shops. Meanwhile, down to the south-west, you can explore pretty and affluent **Cheshire**. The differences between the regions are extraordinary: within an hour's travelling time, twee English villages, large old industrial towns, imposing mountains and lakes, moody moors and green and pleasant lands can be reached. An escape from the city is never far away, and the countryside surrounding Manchester is such that you will always be able to find something new to gasp at.

Within fifty miles are many of the other major northern cities: Sheffield, Liverpool, Leeds and Bradford. Each one is easily accessible by public transport, and they are all worth some serious exploration in their own right. However, this book does not cover these major conurbations; instead, it looks at some of the more rural and lesser-known nooks of the North. Whether it's a rustic ramble you crave or simply a change of scenery, you'll find some small corner that will bring out the poet or the painter in you. (Or, of course, the rural lager lout, as you wind down in front of that almost mythical roaring log fire in some far-flung Dales hostelry.) Don the flat cap, leash up the family whippet, and explore....

Lancashire, West Yorkshire and up to the Lakes

On her visit to Lancashire in the full flush of the Industrial Revolution, Ann Radcliffe noted 'the cheerful populousness of the rich towns and villages' of the county. Her sentiments are just as relevant today, and are evident in the friendly people and the vast range of things to do. Lancashire itself is a county of surprising contrasts. To the south are the old mill towns of Bolton and Bury, leading up through the valleys to Burnley and Pendle (home of the Lancashire Witches) and to Blackburn (home of Blackburn Rovers). From here, if you branch to the west, you reach the seaside, crowned by the supremely tacky, brash and dirty resort of Blackpool – which combines rivers of beer, mountains of chips and a constant barrage of bingo. (But, boy, is it fun.) In sharp contrast, if you head east you'll reach solid and ancient towns and villages nestling at the feet of swelling hills.

From East Lancashire you cross over into West Yorkshire, home of the wool industry, a revitalized – and often unlikely – tourist trade, as well as those Three Sisters. The towns and villages of Lancashire generally seem to belong together more than do their counterparts over the ancient divide in Yorkshire. In the county of the white rose, the towns and villages seem to operate more independently of each other, giving a stronger feeling of isolation. This is largely explained by the fact that in Lancashire everything is geographically much closer together, meaning that the atmosphere is quite different. However, the isolated feeling in parts of Yorkshire is one of its most appealing characteristics, with remote and tiny villages shivering stoically on the edges of bleak moors. Even in these highly populated times, it is possible to stray into the wild, leaving civilization far behind, until your eye sees only 'the outline of swell and sweep – on the wild colouring communicated to ridge and dell by moss, by heathbell, by flower-sprinkled turf, by brilliant bracken, and mellow granite crag'. (*Jane Eyre*)

The Lancashire hills and Yorkshire moors have some of the most spectacularly unspoilt scenery in the country; Yorkshire in particular has managed to retain a genuine 'James Herriot' appeal – despite concerted attempts by the local tourist boards to package it all up and market it. As you travel farther north, the hills get higher and the valleys deeper, and you enter the southern Lake District. The area is really out of the jurisdiction of this book, but do make it a priority visit – out of season, if possible. (One recent summer bank holiday saw road blocks on approaches to the Lakes: the inevitable had happened and a 'No Vacancies' sign was slapped on the whole great outdoors.) However, if you're prepared to search out and explore off the most beaten of tracks, real gems of beauty without the omnipresent George and Margery from Dorking can still be found. A car, a solid thirty-gear mountain bike, some good boots and willing feet (or a raised thumb) are really the only ways to steer clear of the most overcrowded crannies of the district. Simply because it is a little farther afield, it is really best to think about spending a few days at a time in this area.

WIGAN, BOLTON AND BEYOND

■ Tourist
Information: Trencherfield Mill, Wigan Pier, **Wigan**; 0942-825677.
Town Hall, **Bolton**; 0204-364333.
Charnock Richard Service Area, M6 (north-bound); 0257-793773 and 791925 (accommodation).
112 Lord Street, **Southport**; 0704-33133 and 500175 (accommodation).

You can either take a train out to **Wigan** from Manchester Victoria, or bus 32 or 33. If you travel on bus 33 or by car, it is worth stopping off at **Worsley** on your way. (Take the A6 from Manchester, then the A577 to Wigan, detouring on to the A572 for Worsley.) The village demands a quick stop for its pretty canal walks and boat trips from outside the Packet House. Due to a concentration of iron ore from the old coal mines, the water is coloured a vivid and psychedelic orange, which fits rather startlingly into this delightful rural setting – in great contrast to to the canal development at Castlefield, which is altogether more forlornly industrial.

Wigan itself boasts several attractions. The town's Central Park is home to Wigan's **Rugby League** team, winners of the 1989 Challenge Cup. Go on a Saturday to see a game that more closely resembles a religious rally in its fervour; visit on any weekday to have a mooch around the shopping centre and **market**, and perhaps venture along to that notorious butt of music-hall jokes turned self-proclaimed attraction, **Wigan Pier**. After years of being a dowdy, run-down canal-side wharf, the Pier has striven to become the slick and natural heir to all things cultural in the town; as if to prove its new-found credentials, it plays host to the annual **International Jazz Festival** in July. All year round at the Pier, there is the obligatory heritage centre on the waterfront with the awesomely awful name of **The Way We Were**. The browbeaten, honest folks of yesteryear are portrayed by a motley crew of aspiring Equity members, whose only brief seems to be that they should live out every cliché in existence. We can only wish them luck in their next job. During the summer there is a water-bus service, and throughout the year the **Mill at the Pier** is both a nightclub and on Sundays a jazz club (0942-44888 for details).

In the parish church, back in the town centre, is the **altar tomb of Sir William Bradshaw**, who was a fourteenth-century knight. He and his wife, the fair-named Mabel, lived in Haigh Hall. In 1314, after the brave knight had gone to war in Scotland, his wife heard that he had been slain. Unfortunately, this report turned out to be untrue: on his triumphant return home ten years later he found that she had remarried. In those pre-Marriage Guidance Council days he took the only option known to him: skewering the new hubby and ordering Mabel to walk barefoot from Haigh Hall to Wigan Cross once a week for the rest of her life. Where's a New Man when you need one?

Haigh Country Park lies three miles north of Wigan, and these days you can take a bus from the centre (with your shoes on). There are 250 acres of parkland, a small zoo, a model village and, of course, Haigh Hall. On Bank Holiday Mondays the park plays host to a country fair, complete with medieval jousts, jeep rides and all kinds of equally historically compatible delights.

To the south of the town are two famous race grounds. See the horses at **Haydock** (0942-725963 – train from Manchester or bus from Wigan to Newton-le-Willows, or by car along the A58) and the kart racing at **Three Sisters**. The latter has a karting school as well as putting on professional races (0942-270230 – bus from Wigan, or either A58 or M6 to Junction 25).

If you continue out to the north-west of Wigan, either on the train, local bus or along the M58 then A570, you will come to **Southport**, a lively seaside town where the sea is about two miles from the sea front at low tide. Plenty of sandy beaches, a funfair and a decent shopping centre. It's not as tacky as Blackpool; in fact, it's really rather posh – but then again, it's not so much fun.

Bolton is reached by train from Manchester Victoria, or by car via the M61. In the town centre itself is the excellent theatre, the **Octagon** (see *Cinema, Theatre and Classical Music*), as well as the **Museum, Art Gallery and Aquarium**, situated immediately opposite in gorgeous Le Mans Crescent, behind the civic centre on Newport Street. The town has a pretty good shopping centre, crowned by its superb markets chartered in 1251. For the more adventurous and sporty, there is the **Water Park**, Great Moor Street. This place allows you to bask in tropical heat, wrestle with rugged rapids and lose every ounce of dignity on slides and other rides. Although worth a visit in its own right, many of the best things about Bolton are just out of the town.

If you continue north on the train from Victoria, get off at **Hall i' th' Wood** and visit the house where Samuel Crompton invented his Mule. The house is lovely, and the village and countryside surrounding it are well worth an amble as well. Less than a mile to the north, at Bromley Cross, is **The Last Drop Village**. A busy little place, especially on Sunday afternoons, it has been developed as a heritage centre. If you're itching for a shop there is an excellent **flea market** held here as well as a lively pub and café.

Just to the north of Bromley Cross Station is **Jumbles Country Park**, another 250-acre park with all the usual attractions. It's good for picnics, and there is a lovely village nearby called Turton Bottoms, where a good pint can be had.

If the mention there of a pub has captured your interest, get back on the train and travel a little farther up to **Entwistle**. A Real-Ale pub like no other, stuck in the middle of nowhere but right next to the station, the **Strawberry Duck** has character, good beer, good food and a lively clientele who travel from all over Lancashire. It is definitely worth taking the train: the beers are too good to be avoided if you're driving, and in any case, it takes a very dedicated navigator to find the place by road.

A short hop by bus along the Chorley New Road, in Queens Park, is **Butterfly World** (summer only, 0204-363528). Most certainly not for the squeamish, there are thousands of butterflies and moths at various stages of metamorphosis and in free flight (though the pupae and caterpillars don't tend to fly very far) – and that's the pleasant bit! You can then go and have a peep at tarantulas, scorpions, locusts, stick insects, centipedes and silk moths ... do you get the picture?

To the north-west of Bolton is the **Camelot Theme Park**. Situated at Chorley, just off the M6 if you're coming from Wigan, or the M61 from Manchester or Bolton, it is a sort of second-class Alton Towers, but still brilliant for the children and the childish. The park has a medieval theme, with funfair rides, a 'wild wood', an indoor playland and a tournament arena for jousts and chivalric tests. All over the place are worthy folk dressed up as jesters, knights and damsels, and there is a good atmosphere – albeit a bit naff. Even the cool and trendy will have a good time, although they'll probably pretend not to! If the weather is good, don't forget your swimming togs, as there is a splash pool and a water slide. When hunger pangs set in, there are the usual fast-food joints like the **Round Table Burger Bar** or **Lancelot's Plaice Fish and Chip Shop**. Good grief, King Arthur must be turning in his grave.

OLDHAM, BURY, ROCHDALE

- Tourist Information: Derby Hall, Market Street, **Bury**; 061-705 5112.
  84 Union Street, **Oldham**; 061-678 4654.

The Clock Tower, Town Hall, **Rochdale**; 0706-356592.
Museum, High Street, Uppermill, **Saddleworth**; 0457-874093.
41/45 Kay Street, **Rawtenstall**; 0706-217777.

Travelling north on the train from Victoria to **Bury**, stop off at **Heaton Park** (see *JOY RIDES*). Once in Bury town centre, you can browse around the famous market, stuff your gut with black pud, or hop on a bus to the Multiplex Cinema and Megabowl Alley (featured in *Cinema* and *Sport* respectively). As well as the above, Bury also boasts the **East Lancashire Railway** chugging up the Irwell valley to **Ramsbottom**. The line dates back to the old cotton days, and was closed in 1972 when it was considered no longer viable. Campaigners complained that it was a valuable part of the area's heritage, and it was eventually reopened for visitors in 1987. The steam trains run at weekends and bank holidays, and there are views of rugged countryside, curiously interspersed with the old mill villages that sprung up during the years of the Industrial Revolution. Alighting at Ramsbottom, you can take a short bus trip to the **Helmshore Textile Museum** (open weekends and bank holidays 1100-1600) and to **Holcombe Hill**, where the **Peel Tower** stands. The tower was built to commemorate the death of Sir Robert Peel, best known as the founder of the Bobby brigade. He was also the Prime Minister who repealed the Corn Laws (see *ROOTS*), putting bread into the bellies of his fellow Bury folk, so he was pretty popular up this way. Every year, on Good Friday, there is a pilgrimage to the tower, and thousands of people walk there for a service. At other times you can walk up a hundred-and-fifty steps to the top of the tower, and see for miles across Greater Manchester to the south and over to Pendle to the north.

There is a train from Victoria to take you through **Oldham** to **Rochdale**. In both these hilly areas there are dry ski-slopes (see *Sport*). Oldham boasts its **Local Interest Museum**, which for the past two years has exhibited a display of 'Shopping – the way it was' complete with a reconstructed street. Oldham is surrounded by lovely villages, the prettiest of which lie to the north-east, huddling around **Saddleworth Moor** (see *Peak District*). Buses leave regularly to **Uppermill**, **Dobcross** and **Delph**, where on Whit Sunday there are processions and street shows, with brass bands and all-day opening in the pubs.

Rochdale is one of those attractive towns that nobody really seems to bother visiting – which is quite good because it isn't full of day-trippers. The river Roch runs through the middle of the town and the widest river bridge in the world, **The Esplanade**, runs over it. The world-famous **Co-op** chain of stores and funeral services started life in the town in 1844, and there is the **Rochdale Pioneers Museum** (061-832 4300; Tuesday-Saturday 1000-1200 and 1400-1600, Sunday 1400-1600) in the tiny house where this great empire began. The memorably Gothic **town hall** dates back to 1871; it is magnificent inside and can be visited on a guided tour (0706-47474, extension 4775). If you yearn for the great outdoors, the Esplanade is surrounded by parks – the most pleasant being **Broadfield Park**, which rises steeply up to **St Chad's Church**. It's worth the haul to the top as the views are superb, and the church itself (dating back to the thirteenth century) is a sight worthy of the severe exertion.

Heading north, just off the A58 (buses from Rochdale), is the village of **Wardle**. It isn't far from Rochdale, yet it appears to have been lost in some sociological time-warp. The two lanes that lead into the village go no farther, making it a remote cul-de-sac in the hills. There is a large village square, where you can almost imagine the stocks once stood, two big stone chapels, a couple of really good pubs, and that's about it. It's a serene and beautiful place to retreat into, with the moors and hills surrounding it making for some frighteningly healthy walks.

Eastbound from Rochdale off the A58 (Rochdale Road East) is the **Chamber House Urban Farm**. Especially brilliant for children, you can see the maids-a-milkin' (well almost – the ruddy cheeks and three-legged stools having been replaced by yards of clanking machinery), the lambs-a-friskin', and meet the farmer-a-farmin'. It is also a conservation area with lots of wild flowers, trees and shrubs. There is disabled access and the farm is open 1300-1600 daily.

PENDLE AND CALDERDALE

■ Tourist Information:

Burnley Mechanics, Manchester Road, **Burnley**; 0282-30055.
Ribble Valley Borough Council, Church Walk, **Clitheroe**; 0200-25566.
20a Scotland Road, **Nelson**; 0282-692890.
15 Burnley Road, **Todmorden**; 0706-818181.
1 Bridge Gate, **Hebden Bridge**; 0422-843831.
2-4 West Lane, **Haworth**; 0535-42329.
Piece Hall, **Halifax**; 0422-368725.

A day here just simply ain't enough; the area demands several weekends, and if you can wangle the use of a car, all the better. Calderdale and Pendle together, stretching from the northern tip of the Peak District to the Yorkshire Dales, form the central chunk of the Pennine Way. The scenery is absolutely breathtaking, and the area steeped in fascinating history. And the pubs. Oh boy, the pubs....

Shooting north through Lancashire up the M66, by train from Manchester Victoria (change at Blackburn), or by bus from Chorlton Street Station, head (like Sir Gawayne) for **Clitheroe**. The town clusters around the old castle on the hill, and each autumn a solemn torchlit procession culminates here in a sizzling firework display. The town comes to life on this night (telephone the Tourist Information Centre for details), the pubs overflow and the streets are full of folks stuffing their faces and having fun. It is reputed to be the town in which Malory's Sir Gawayne rests, in 'the comeliest castle that ever a knight owned'. For the rest of the year it is quieter: it has a quaint shopping centre and acts as a good centre from which to explore the west side of Pendle.

A bus rattle away is the village of **Whalley**, with a lovely ruined abbey resting peacefully by the stream. Fresh garlic grows in abundance around the abbey and the smell hangs in the air, keeping away the vampire developers. Whalley is really popular at night with the bright young things of Lancashire: its many pubs are lively, and round the corner from the Whalley Arms, it is blessed with a nightclub that has to be seen to be believed.

To the west of Clitheroe is the village of **Waddington**, reached by local bus. Smaller than Whalley, less accessible and quieter, it is what dreamy Lancashire villages are made of. A tiny brook dutifully babbles its way through the centre of the village, a cosy little tea room serves home-made cakes, and most importantly, there are more pubs than houses. These, particularly the **Higher Buck** and the **Lower Buck**, get deservedly busy at night.

Clitheroe lies to the west of **Pendle Hill**, the highest in the Pennines, giving breathtaking views of both Lancashire and Yorkshire. For the enthusiastic walker Pendle Hill can be assailed on foot, either at a more leisurely pace from **Sabden**, or via a steep walk up the 'Big End', beginning in **Barley**. Once at the top, on a clear day (and if you're not short-sighted), you can see Blackpool Tower, forty miles away. The many villages nestling around the foot of Pendle are worth visiting: all are quaint, small and invariably offer at least one good pub with brilliant food. In **Newchurch-in-Pendle** (bus from Burnley – see below – to **Fence** and then a one-mile walk), there is a beautiful church, perched on the hill and overlooking a pretty, grassy churchyard. On the side of the tower, carved into the stone, is a strange shape which is, in fact, an eye to guard the village from the evil spirits and the witches associated with the area. The witches are not merely legend, nor just an advertising executive's dream promotion: the last women in England recorded as being executed on the charge of witchcraft practised at Pendle. The most famous was Alice Nutter, whose home still stands in **Roughlee**, a further mile away from Newchurch. You can saunter back to Fence from Roughlee in about twenty minutes, and once you are back in the village, reward yourself with a drink and tasty bar snack at the lively and picturesque **Sparrow Hawk**, or a pint of Pendle Witches (yep, 'fraid so) at the **White Swan**.

Burnley, like Clitheroe, can be reached by train from Victoria changing at Blackburn, or by zapping up the M66 on a bus from Chorlton Bus Station; as the Leeds and Liverpool canal runs through its centre, you could also hop on a barge heading in the right direction. Although one of the 'little Manchesters' of the Industrial Revolution, it actually had a mill as early as the thirteenth century, and was manufacturing textiles before the cotton industry took hold. By the end of the nineteenth century, Burnley was the leading cotton-producing town in the world. With most of its 100,000 population working in cotton (as nylon made them sweat too much) or in mining, the town was very severely thwacked by the recessions of the twentieth century, not to mention the spectacular demise of its first-class football team, now bravely battling in the fourth division.

The town – like so many others – is trying to balance the need to retain its proud heritage while developing towards a brighter economic and social future. One such combination is the inevitable **Queen Street Mill Museum** (0282-412555), the only steam-powered cotton mill in Britain. Once inside, prepare to be deafened by over 300 looms, producing cotton with the help of staff dressed in the regulation Victorian costumes. Strolling around **Weaver's Triangle**, you can pretend you're off t' mill as you explore spinning mills and weaving sheds, workers' houses and a Victorian school. In the Visitors' Centre on Manchester Road there are displays and exhibitions.

In July each year there is a one-week **Pot Fair**, where you can barter for a cheap dinner set on the open market, followed by the town's **summer fair** on Fulledge Ground (near BFC's Turf Moor). Here you can eat copious amounts of popcorn, candyfloss and toffee apples, then throw up on someone's head on a stomach-churning ride. At **Towneley Park** (a bus ride from centre) there is an impressive Elizabethan Hall, woods, a golf course, a craft museum, bowling green and tennis courts, as well as cultivated gardens. There are fairs and events throughout the year.

From Burnley take a bus, or the A646 if by car, to **Hebden Bridge**. (There is a train straight through from Manchester Victoria if you want to 'do Calderdale' direct.) West Yorkshire is most quickly reached by car via the M62, but for a scenic route follow the country roads through Rochdale (A58) up to Hebden Bridge. The town itself is a surprising centre for alternative lifestyles, with shops and facilities to match. It's pleasant rather than spectacular, although much has been done to spruce it up, and as a result it now boasts a little marina and a shopping centre which is excellent for 'antique' gifts and general browsing. Also, unfortunately, it has become a little too touristy – though the older parts of the town still capture the real atmosphere of old Yorkshire, and if you can drag yourself up the steep hill to **Heptonstall**, with its hexagonal Methodist chapel, you could almost be stepping back in time.

Out of the village, there are some riveting rambles to be had. In the distance, purple heather clings to the moorland, while below, the river gurgles its way down to drops like **Lumb Falls** at Crimsworth Beck. Hebden Bridge does tend to get just a bit too busy in the summer, with tourists clutching hold of their pictorial copies of *Wuthering Heights*. It doesn't matter too much though, because if you use your nous and travel a few miles away from the village, you won't even be able to hear the ready click of Instamatics. The whole **Hebden Water** area is worth a wander: it is a steep-sided gorge covered with loads of trees, contrasting dramatically with the barren moorlands. It was christened 'the Switzerland of the North' by the people who used to retreat here at weekends from neighbouring Halifax after a hard week at the mill.

A few miles north of Hebden Bridge is **Haworth**, Stratford of the North, celebrating all things Brontë. If Charlotte, Anne and Emily could but have foreseen the mass prettification of their village that has taken place, they would probably have burned their books. West Yorkshire is not a classically pretty place: if you are after pretty villages and pleasantly undulating countryside, travel south to Cheshire. Instead, this part of Yorkshire is overwhelming and majestic, but it is also harsh and occasionally bleak, as the Brontë sisters well understood. Their passionate words would not have been inspired by the insipid touristy atmosphere and clutch of twee shops that now make up their home village. This is not to say that the village isn't worth a visit, but you should be well steeled and prepared for the onslaught of Wildfell Hall Tea Shoppes, Heathcliffe Emporiums and the odd Villette B&B. To really feel the power that motivated those three isolated and imaginative young women, step out of the village and take to the moors. The stretches of heather cut short by jutting crags, and the strong winds that seem to blow even when the rest of the country is sweltering, isolate and exhilarate; then you can appreciate those old texts you were forced to read at school.

Two miles south-west of Haworth lie **Ponden Hall and reservoir**. Walk from Haworth through the village of Stanbury until you come to the reservoir, which is situated right on the **Pennine Way**. The whole area is beautiful, and Ponden Hall is the Thrushcross Grange of *Wuthering Heights*. To the north lies **Keighley Moor**, to the west the **Forest of Trawden**, and there are some wild and wonderful walks to be had.

To the east of Hebden Bridge, back on the Manchester-Leeds railway, is **Halifax**. Like the industrial cotton towns of Lancashire, Halifax was very active during the Industrial Revolution; after a slump, it has turned itself into a thriving town, marketing its heritage with fervour. In **Piece Hall** (0422-368725) there are two museums: the Pre-Industrial and the Industrial. There is also an art gallery, shops and a café. The real attraction is the craft market though, which used to be an old cloth market (well actually, the cloth was new; it is the market that's old, dating from 1779). Halifax is a busy and friendly town that has some excellent pubs, shops and clubs, and which certainly merits some considerable exploration.

In Dobbins Yard there is the **National Museum of Working Horses** (0422-346835), where you'll find out about the history of the old Webster's Bitter horses from the telly. It's a brilliantly innovative heritage museum: most other places seem blinkered to the trusty old form of transport.

Further afield in Lancashire, Yorkshire and Cumbria, there is much to be seen that this book can't hope to cover. For more information, contact the following Tourist Information Centres:

The Lakes

Cumbria Tourist Board, Ashleigh, Holly Road, Windermere LA23 2AQ (09662-4444).

Lancashire

Blackburn	0254-53277
Blackpool	0253-216232
Garstang	09952-4430
Lancaster	0524-32878
Preston	0772-53731

Yorkshire

Bradford	0274-753678
Ingleton (Water Falls)	05242-41049
Knaresborough	0423-866886
Leeds	0532-462454
Settle	07292-5192
Skipton	0756-792809
York	0904-621756

The Peak District

■ Tourist
Information: Museum, High Street, Uppermill, **Saddleworth**; 0457-874093 or 870336 (accommodation).
The Crescent, **Buxton**; 0298-25106 or 77889 (accommodation).
Station Forecourt, Norfolk Street, **Glossop**; 04574-5920.

The Peak District was Britain's first National Park – nothing if not an obvious choice. To the north are wild and barren moors, leading down to boggy bits with lots of hills; then into some beautiful wooded glens, and, as it flattens out, into villages and farmland. The Pennine Way erupts halfway up and rises continuously to the north, right through Yorkshire and Northumberland into the Scottish borders. The variety of the landscape is astounding: industrial towns at the edges stand juxtaposed with picturesque villages and isolated plains.

To the north, you can approach the Peak District via Oldham to **Saddleworth Moor**. You can get a bus from Oldham to **Uppermill**, where the **Saddleworth Museum** is found. It is the museum of an old Pennine parish and you'll find it in an old mill, on the bank of the Huddersfield Canal (High Street, 0457-874093). The Moor forms the northernmost tip of the Peak District National Park, and there are some healthy and heartening walks over to the Pennine Way, running right the way down the centre of the district.

In between Uppermill and Meltham lies **Wessenden**, with reservoirs, a waterfall, a stream and a play area. Grub can be grabbed at Wessenden House, and the area is relatively undiscovered outside of the local vicinity so that you'll not feel too crowded out by the millions systematically trampling other parts of the region.

To the south of here (where the A635 crosses the moor), if you're really morbid, you can see where the Moors Murders took place. There is an eerie atmosphere and the moorland is barren: not the most pleasant of experiences, given its history.

For the central Peak District, take either the train from Manchester Piccadilly or buses 211, 214, 215, 236, 237 to **Glossop**. As well as a great pub – the **Fleece** (see *Jazz* in *THE TWILIGHT ZONE*) – Glossop has a genuinely pleasant shopping centre and a brilliant market. The area to the north and east of Glossop is peaty, mossy and a potential leg breaker in places. Don't be fooled into trekking to places like Moss Castle -- there is plenty of moss, but no castle! Instead, head south along the A624 (buses from Glossop) to **Hayfield**. The village has the **Sett Valley Trail** – in other words an easy walk – to the west. If you follow the trail to New Mills, you can hop on the train back to Manchester, although this will, no doubt, invalidate your British Rail super-awayday-off-peak day return.

If you're feeling a little more ambitious, however, don the hiking boots and set off east for the **Kinder Plateau**. The River Kinder carves its way through to the plateau where the **Kinder Downfall** is. It's a massive natural amphitheatre of rock, making it excellent for endless bouts of hide and seek. Oh – and don't forget the almost obligatory spectacular views too, of course. Also from Glossop, take a southbound bus along the A57 to **Derwent Dams** in **Fairholmes**. At the dams, there are the three huge Ladybower, Derwent and Howden reservoirs where members of the Dambuster squadron were trained. You can hire bikes at Fairholmes, or take the same bus on its route to Castleton and Buxton (see below).

The best parts of the district, however, are most easily reached from **Buxton**. Take a train from Piccadilly (or join the line at New Mills). The town itself is worth a day, and the **Buxton Opera House** (not much opera) is an excellent theatre if you decide to be down this way at night. In fact, the theatre is worth a special trip if there is something you fancy seeing – it has a very good reputation. They perform everything here from the English National Ballet to Old-Time Music Hall, and in 1990 they had a series of signed shows for the deaf. Details on 0298-72190.

Although renowned for its natural spring mineral water (which is actually owned by Perrier!), Buxton has plenty of pubs for the hardened drinker. If you are also a wizened jazz fan, try the **Cheshire Cheese** in the High Street for some serious jamming. Each summer, there is an **Arts Festival** offering a fairly impressive menu of tourist-inducing happenings of the arty kind all over the town, with main events centred around the

Opera House. Adjacent to the railway station is the **Steam Centre**, funnily enough displaying steam locos.

Heading out east on the A6 and then A619 (buses from Buxton), you can see **Chatsworth House**. It's one of the loveliest and most famous stately homes in the country, built between 1686 and 1707. There are extensive gardens, galleries and all of the usual trimmings associated with such places. Open daily from Easter to September 1100-1600. For the kids, there's a farmyard and an adventure playground. Open daily from Easter to the end of October. Details and prices on 0246-582204.

Lying north via the A6, and then the A625 (bus service from Buxton), is **Castleton**. The village itself appears to resemble an English Tourist Board 1000-piece jigsaw, stuffed to the gunwales with Quainte Olde Tea Shoppes charging anything but quainte olde prices. Just out of the village are the caves that originally made the area a tourist attraction. The main cavern is actually an old lead mine, through which you can sail along an underground canal.

If you don't fancy travelling so far out of Buxton itself, just to the south of the town is the **Buxton Country Park**. There are woods and glens and, at Poole's cavern, some more caves. Caves are a pretty regular feature of much of the Peak District: this results from the porous limestone hills.

Within easy distance are some of the more traditional and unspoiled villages and towns, walks and parks of the Peak District. It is possible to hire a bike in Buxton and travel at your leisure, and some schemes offer the chance to leave the bike in a different centre from the one you started out at so you can travel further afield and save face if you're lost or too tired to ride back! For details of this and of accommodation/ youth hostels in the area, contact the Tourist Information Centre above.

Cheshire

■ Tourist Information: Stamford New Road, **Altrincham**; 061-926 8336.
M6 service area (northbound), **Sandbach**; 0270-760460 or 761879 (accommodation).
Council offices, Toft Road, **Knutsford**; 0565-2611.
Visitor Centre, Vicars Lane, **Chester**; 0244-351609.
Town Hall, Northgate Street, **Chester**; 0244-324324 or 317962 (accommodation).
Town Hall, Market Place, **Macclesfield**; 0625-21955, extension 114/5.

Cheshire is the sort of county that American tourists think England consists of entirely. With its little villages nestling among green fields and bluebell woods, it's the kind of place that the Secret Seven and all other remnants of a child's bygone era must have hailed from. Even Rupert's Nutwood must surely be in Cheshire. It has been described as 'a little piece of Surrey that got lost on the M6', and this is made more apparent by the fact that the vast majority of people who move from the South to the North-West settle in Cheshire: it evidently reminds them of home. People from Cheshire have little local identity (most of them have moved from elsewhere) and so the villages lack the appealing local idiosyncrasies of those in Lancashire, Yorkshire and some parts of the Peak District.

While the Industrial Revolution was raging all around, Cheshire concentrated on agriculture, and managed to keep the mills away. Only Macclesfield can be thought of as being vaguely industrial in the sense that the Lancashire towns are, and even here the old mills are separated from the rest of the town. It is well summed up by the fact that while Lancashire was producing cotton, Macclesfield primarily produced silk! In the nineteenth century, Cheshire was where you went for your picnics at the weekend. In the twentieth century, it's where you shoot home after a hard day at your £50,000-plus job in the city.

Nowhere in the county will you find the rugged majesty of the North, but you will find some extremely eye-catching countryside, thankfully coupled with numerous picturesque village pubs (usually bursting with the youths of the Cheshire Set, resplendent in their Barbour jackets and green wellies). Practise the accent with a couple of plums in your mouth and set off from **Altrincham**. To get there, take a train from Manchester Piccadilly.

On the way down on the train you pass **Sale**, proud possessor of a large **Water Park** (see *SPORT AND LEISURE*). If the urge for a quick windsurf or sail grabs you, stop off here. If not, there are plenty of other park areas with more attractions further south. Once in the town of Altrincham, there is a popular shopping centre and market (see *Shopping*), and Manchester's only **ice rink** (see *SPORT AND LEISURE*).

To the west of the town (buses 38, H50, WX2 from Altrincham) lies **Dunham Park**, with **Dunham Massey Hall**. During the summer there is a riveting chance to 'meet the gardener' at 2100 on Thursdays. A fairly specific kind of attraction, that.... Generally more agreeable is to meander down through the grounds and see the deer in action in the deer park. In the house itself, which is otherwise pretty much like numerous others, there are often chamber concerts, which can be magical in such a setting. Disabled access is limited: even the restaurant is upstairs, although they will offer to bring you a tray down to eat on your lap in the hallway! As for the rest, it's very pretty: a wonderful place to have a picnic and wander around, but like many country parks and houses a little too geared towards the older and more genteel middle classes. (This may well remind you all-too-dreadfully of those afternoons of your youth, being dragged reluctantly around stately homes under the pretence of 'a family treat'.) Open from March until October, Saturday through to Thursday 1300-1700 (1200 Sundays and bank holidays). Details on 061-941 1025.

Bigger and better, and conveniently placed on the same bus route from Altrincham, is **Tatton Park**, which offers another stately home, an old hall, a 1930s farm, gardens and the mandatory deer park. What makes Tatton more attractive is that the grounds are so much more extensive, and you can escape that tourist herd feeling. To the south of the grounds there is a superb lake next to some enchanting woods that conjure up images of every sweet little fairy story in the book. You can also hire a bike here to get you around a little quicker; if you do so, you will receive a map of the area to make sure you manage to navigate your way back to base. The park and gardens are open all year, with the hall and farm open from April through to November and some off-season Sundays (0565-54822).

To the east of the southern end of Tatton Park is the village of **Mobberley**, next to which (on Beech Hill) is the **Hillside Ornamental Fowl Park**. You will find only attractive birds here – any Ugly Duckling would most certainly not pass the dress code. There are peacocks, flamingos, pelicans and very unfoul fowl, all strutting their eminently superior stuff in delightful grounds. You can take a picnic and feed the birds if you like. Caviar and smoked salmon only, please! Open 1130-1700 on Sundays, Wednesdays and Bank Holiday Mondays from Easter until the end of September (0565-873282).

The Altrincham train carries on down to **Chester**, which really is the classic historic, cameras-ready city. It was recently discovered that the medieval front above the shops in the main street was more of a front than people realized: it was too young to be genuine. Still, who hasn't worn a fake from time to time? The town is brilliant for shopping: upmarket, but much more substantial than Altrincham. It is also handy as a gateway (both by train and road) into the spectacular countryside of North Wales.

If you approach Cheshire via **Wilmslow**, step off the train first at **Styal**. Yes, another country park – but this one is also the site of a nineteenth-century mill village, by far and away the most genuine and well-preserved example in the country. The village can be seen as it was then (if you close your eyes to the ice-cream kiosks and parked coaches): there are the mill boys' dormitories, the old mills and houses and a heritage centre detailing the history of the village (Quarry Bank Mill, 0625-527468). Surrounding Styal is some eminently strollable countryside, well worth taking in before you get back on the train for Wilmslow. Again, like Altrincham, Wilmslow is a popular centre for the discerning (and wealthy) shopper.

From Piccadilly you can also get a train to **Macclesfield**; as the town has the highest concentration of things to do and is less twee and more lively than the others, it is advisable to do so. In the centre you can visit the **Silk Museum** (0625-613210) and dig up some of the history on the material and the town; then, shoot off to the **Paradise Mill** (0625-618228), where the stuff is still woven, before spending your hard-earned money on goods in the silk shop that would actually cost less elsewhere!

From either Wilmslow or Macclesfield, you can take a bus to **Jodrell Bank Science Centre**, a name which used to make every schoolboy's heart tremble with raw excitement. By car, come off the M6 at Junction 18 and follow the A535 for about five miles. Forget the crusty old school science lessons, and if possible, drag some children along: you might be responsible for a brilliant career! You can sit in the **gyro chair** and be made giddy if that's the sort of thing you like; or, if you really want to give yourself a headache, look in the **infinity mirrors** – and don't bother trying to count your reflections: you can't, that's the point of the exercise. This might seem obvious but, judging from the amount of people standing mumbling '982, 983', it's sound advice. There is also a **light table** where you can make a rainbow (no pot of gold though, folks), and a **gravity hollow** where you can send a world around a sun (they try to kid you into thinking it's our world – sheesh). Every forty-five minutes you can see an exhibition in the planetarium and come out feeling very small and insignificant. If that has whetted your appetite for astronomy, there are telescopes that you can get to grips with before gaping at the enormous **Lovell** (radio-) **Telescope**, and trying to understand how it works. The square-eyed can watch satellite TV (no scantily clad Italian housewives), or if the absurd tickles your fancy, laugh in disbelief at Isaac Newton's head telling you all about gravity. (Bet you never knew apples were that lethal!) The whole place is amazing – but as it gets popular, try to avoid Sundays and holidays. During the winter, it is open only at weekends. The **Granada Arboretum** on the same site and ticket is excellent for tranquil strolls. Details on 0477-71339.

North of Macclesfield, on the A523 (buses E7, 8, 10), is the village of **Bollington**. Pop into the **Waggon and Horses** for a swift half, but don't have too much because you can hire a bike from here to explore some of the Peak District and Cheshire countryside. If wheels don't grab you, you can canoe up the Macclesfield Canal. Details from **Adelphi Mill Gate Lodge** (0625-572681). Continuing north, either by bus, bike or boat, call into **Adlington Hall**. (The latter form of transport makes this a little difficult as there is no canoe park.) The hall is a lovely Manor House set within Capability Brown-style gardens. The Courtyard is built in black-and-white Tudor style and is twinkily pretty, while the front is more in the style of redbrick Barratt Homes (in the higher price bracket).

On the Buxton train route, south of Stockport, is a village/suburb called **Disley** (A6). Just to the south of Disley is the **Lyme Country Park** (0663-762023, buses 198, 199 from Stockport and occasional summer buses from Manchester pass the gate), which is well worth visiting and geared very much to young people as well as the usual Saga Holidays subscribers. The park itself offers a brilliant playground hidden in a woody dell, so that you can do your utmost to lose the kids if you want to explore the Hall. Each year, in August, there is a big festival held in the park, comprising the regular assortment of country fair attractions that are guaranteed Fun (not to mention expense) For All The Family.

We could fill the book with attractions in Cheshire: **Little Moreton Hall** is one of the prettiest Tudor houses; **Capesthorne Hall**; **Beeston Castle**; **Delamere Forest**, perfect for shady strolls; **Redesmere**, paradise for birdwatchers. For all these and more, contact the Tourist Information Centres.

7. SPORT AND LEISURE

Shopping

IN THE CITY

Manchester's city centre has been criticized by many (most notably the London press on a quick day-trip) for its marked lack of beauty. True, having stepped off the train at Piccadilly station the sight is not an especially pretty one. Piccadilly Square is the armpit of the city centre and leaps out to greet the eye and nose, eager to disappoint. The resultant first impression, swiftly followed by a stroll down Market Street (proud possessor of an award for the dirtiest street in England – did the judges ever visit the capital?), can be a lasting and unfavourable one. It would appear that this conception, borne out by many of the periodic pieces appearing in national newspapers, has become the established image of the city.

But what of the great abundance of magnificent Victorian, Edwardian and Gothic architecture strewn liberally around the city centre? Look at Chinatown, St Ann's Square, King Street or Albert Square: here you'll find charismatic and genuinely charming areas ripe with their own individual charm. Many of the old Victorian buildings and warehouses have metamorphosed into the best and most interesting of the new and unique shopping areas. In many other northern cities, old buildings are systematically razed in favour of the usual faceless modern shopping complexes. Not so in Manchester, which appears to have learned from past errors – namely the Arndale Centre – and is instead turning to its heritage to provide the base for its new image. Prime examples of Victorian emporia-cum-new-shopping-complexes include the **Corn Exchange** (Cathedral Street, off Corporation Street), the **Royal Exchange** (St Ann's Square), **Affleck's Palace** (Oldham/ Church Streets) and the **Craft Centre** (Oak/Tib Streets).

Each of these centres is within a stone's throw of the **Arndale Centre**, although, in terms of style, you could be a million miles away. The **Corn Exchange** (its origins fairly self-evident) specializes in anything fairly unusual: prepare to be fascinated. A bookshop concentrating on the occult, a clothes shop called **Cod Almighty** and a military paraphernalia shop rub shoulders here. **Scorpion's Nest**, stockists of the unconventional, claim to 'stimulate people to look at things with new eyes ... stretch the boundaries of the acceptable': aims which could just as easily apply to the Corn Exchange as a whole.

The **Royal Exchange**, fashioned out of the old cotton exchange, where the last day's closing prices can still be seen on the trading board in the theatre foyer, is a shopping centre for the flush. There are three floors, all with a coffee bar and a different emphasis on style, housing some excellent shops within. In the basement there are some superb antique shops, and **Arsenic and Old Lace** – with its grand selection of intricate and original wedding dresses tempting just about anyone to step up the aisle, if only to wear one of their creations. On the ground floor, the more conventional and upmarket chains thrive (**Benetton**, **Body Shop** and **Knickerbox** among others). This is where you begin to feel that you've entered the Arndale Centre on a higher social plane. Quickly ascend to the seriously trendy top floor, which is given over to high fashion and hair design (see *Clothes*). The image of the Royal Exchange, in keeping with that of St Ann's Square and King Street, is that of elegance and affluence: window-shopping around here is a real pleasure (if you've managed to chain your wallet down).

For fashion-conscious Manchester youth, **Affleck's Palace** is a godsend. Housed within a three-storey Victorian warehouse on Oldham/Church Streets, and conveniently close to **Dry** (see *Pubs and Bars*), Affleck's is more of a posing palace than a shopping centre, with the shops offering all the best selection of chic wear. There have been a number of unfortunate fires here, but they have – so far – been insubstantial enough to bring the place to a grinding halt. Affleck's could easily be featured in a television *Survival Special*; the place is indestructible, and the secret of its immortality lies in its rapid changing with the times. Many of the designers who originally pitched their stall in the Royal Exchange have moved to Affleck's, opting for its lively and streetwise image in preference to the crafted elegance of their former abode. Their fashions are affordable and accessible – an asset common to all of the stalls in Affleck's. This centre pulses to the same beat as the rest of the Manchester youth culture, giving it a vibrancy unmatched outside the pubs and clubs.

The **Manchester Craft Centre** on Oak Street is a fine place to browse or to search for some of those unusual and dinky gifts. Within its twenty-one studios, you will find a vast array of original craftwork at pretty ordinary prices. An excellent restaurant also helps to ensure that you spend a ridiculous amount of time – and money – here.

However much you dodge around it, however far we pretend that there are other shops, the **Arndale Centre** dominates the centre from its position slap in the heart of the city. It's a big yellow 1960s hallucinatory nightmare that you will need an oxygen tank and a compass to navigate through. Unfortunately, for those who slobber and drool at designer fashions but whose chequebook pushes them into Miss Selfridge or Top Man, the Arndale cannot be avoided. Shopping here could be described as a character-building experience, verging on a thorough training for the SAS. The Arndale Centre is a compulsive prison for all those whose only crime is to be not very rich. Some of the large chain stores – bless 'em – have maintained a safe distance across the road, and rumours abound that this whole area, including Piccadilly Square, is earmarked for an overhaul and face-lift. It's certainly to be hoped: it's a great shame that the most eye-catching feature of the centre is the city's biggest eyesore.

In any one of the above centres, you will find pretty much anything that you need. If you're after something specific, here's a guide to the things that you can expect.

Clothes

Most of the major clothing chains can be found in Manchester's city centre. In the Arndale, the ordinary and cheaper clothing companies vie for attention and hard-earned pennies. Thankfully situated on the outside of the centre is the large **Top Shop/Top Man**. Having taken over some smaller outlets – namely Radius, Gallery and Coppernob – there is actually some decent stuff in here. In close proximity you can find **Chelsea Girl/Concept Man** (at present metamorphosing into **River Island**), **Miss Selfridge**, **Stolen from Ivor** (especially good for jeans), **Next**, **C&A** and many others. For the more upmarket chain stores such as **Oasis** (a new outpost of the exciting chain from London), **Warehouse**, **Laura Ashley**, **Monsoon**, **Blazer**, **Liberty** and yet more **Next**, King Street is the place to flex your plastic. Deansgate boasts **In Wear/Matinique**, while **Benetton**, **French Connection** and **Knickerbox** can be found in and around the Royal Exchange. The commercial apartheid caused by hiving off the posh shopping areas around the Royal Exchange from the socially deprived Arndale becomes increasingly obvious, especially when you see that (oh-so-true to its solid middle-of-the-road reputation) the main **Marks & Spencer** stands equidistant between the two in Market Street.

For designer labels, or younger and trendier fashion, **Affleck's** and the **Design Centre** in the **Royal Exchange** are paradise. The most famous of the small designer chains in the city **Red or Dead** has two stalls in Affleck's and one in the Exchange. For the most part, in both of these places the fashions are fun, eminently wearable and fairly inexpensive. They make designer gear readily accessible to young people, which is surely what the fashion industry should be aiming for. If, however, money is no object and it's South Molton Street originals that you desire, there are several very exclusive designer shops in and around **St Ann's Square**, especially in Police Street and King Street. Browse and spend; but try to bear in mind those letters that will come winging their merry way from your less-than-delighted bank manager.

Some excellent **second-hand** stalls can be found in Affleck's Palace, one of which provides many authentic costumes from the Manchester theatres: especially good for 1950s originals. Out of Affleck's, try **Humana** on Oldham Street or the **Jive Hive** on Oxford Road, which sell everything from a nice sensible cardy to a fine selection of wafty wall-hangings for that bijou little room you dream about. As ever, keep your eyes peeled for a fine run-down of broken electricals and 1970s lamps at the weekend **jumble sales** and **nearly news** – details from your local weekly paper or the *Manchester Evening News*. An exciting wardrobe and a low budget can make a good team.

Books

RIP **Grass Roots**, the most radical and exciting of Manchester's bookshops, which closed in 1990 owing to a simple lack of money. The local book scene had looked stark as a result of the loss, but the baton has thankfully been picked up by **Frontline**, which you will find on Newton Street (off Piccadilly Gardens).

The major bookstores in the city centre are hardly likely to suffer from any lack of funds, especially given the vast student population. **Waterstones** (Deansgate), **Dillons** (Cross Street), **Willshaws** (John Dalton Street) and **Sherratt & Hughes** (St Ann's Square) are the authoritatively big stores, offering the occasional celeb signings and literary discussions in among the more pedestrian pot-pourri of book tokens and Jeffrey Archers. For the best second-hand bargains, there are some good shops in the studenty areas around Oxford Road and Wilmslow Road. The **Paramount Book Exchange** in Shude Hill (opposite the Arndale Bus Station) is worth investigating, and it's very easy to do so as it's open seven days a week until 1900.

If you're after textbooks and specialist academic books, **Haigh and**

Hochland, in the University Precinct Centre, Oxford Road, will make your every DNA chain quiver. If you're a student, however, do not be fooled into eagerly and faithfully buying all of your textbooks before you wave the parental Volvo goodbye: wait until Freshers' Week and pick up bargains from all the graduates desperate to pay off a small part of the interest on their overdraft.

For a bookshop with a very different slant on life, try the **Golden Dawn** in the Corn Exchange (see above). They specialize in the occult and the supernatural. Not for the faint-hearted – or the strict Catholic.

Records

Hundreds of small and specialist music shops exist throughout the city, often far outstripping the megastore **Our Price** and **HMV** (both on Market Street) both in terms of price and sheer variety. The **Vinyl Exchange** on Oldham Street is probably the best in the city. It stocks rare and precious vinyl alongside the mainstream selection, which makes for fascinating and unhassled browsing and listening. There's also a wee hint in their name, in that they will also buy or exchange your Womble faves for the Fall, or your Nolans' *Christmas Party Time* for New Order. Affleck's also houses a couple of good record shops: don't be put off by the seriously trendy image as the staff are very helpful and friendly. If you're in the area, **Sifters Records** on Fog Lane in Didsbury is excellent for buying and selling, and will even come and collect your box full of K-Tel compilations if necessary. Heavy Metal enthusiasts should follow the grease trail to **Power Cuts** (Chepstow Street, off Oxford Street), and any old trendy should pose a while in **Piccadilly Records** (Brown Street, off Market Street). Browse and bop till you drop.

Crafts and Gifts

You know the occasion.... You're dashing around like a blue-arsed fly to lay your sticky mitts on that oh-so-special gift that you just haven't been able to find in any of the Sunday supplements. Well, look no further....

For those frustrated smock-wearing souls, the **Craft Centre** (Oak Street) is your own personal nirvana. Here, each of the stalls displays and sells work from different craftspeople, many of whom have pretty blatant talent. Everything from ceramics to fabrics is made here, and you can usually find something to suit that difficult sister. Fear not if you're expecting to have to pay through the nose for such delights: most of the goods on sale here are very reasonably priced, especially when you consider how much time, skill and effort goes into the work. Similar stuff can often be found in the occasional craft fair in the foyer of the **Royal Exchange**.

The exotic plumage of this industrial city can be seen in **Oasis** in the High Street. This is no clothing chain but is, in fact, a garden centre. Yet it is not the kind of place that fills up with Allegros on a Sunday afternoon: the bent here is strictly tropical. They offer lizards, snakes, tarantulas and other ideal alternatives to the family pooch, as well as bonsai at a snip, cacti and all kinds of other off-beat botanical wonders.

If shopping for gifts gets you a little grizzly, Police Street has the ideal antidote. Situated in the basement of **Harriet and Dee** is the Teddy Bear Shop, peopled by every cuddly little fella from Paddington to Pooh. Bears here cost anything between a couple of quid for Pooh paraphernalia to hundreds for a Stein. Even if you don't put your pennies into fur, it's a great place to drift back to the soft, cuddly days of childhood, just before returning to that nasty old world outside.

Shopping in **Chinatown** can provide you with a whole load more than just oriental food. On and off Charlotte Street are some superb Chinese art and craft shops, including a Chinese market for that essential wok. Desert Habitat: they are cheaper and more authentic here.

Markets

Manchester boasts seven markets, although one of them is in the Arndale Centre which doesn't really qualify in strict terms. **Gorton** (Gorton Cross Street), **Wythenshawe** (Rowlands Way) and **Harpurhey** (Church Lane) markets have antique and junk stalls, the first two on Mondays and the latter on Thursdays, which are brilliant browsing grounds for useless gifts. These three markets also have food halls open Monday to Saturday (except Wednesdays), and open markets on Tuesdays, Fridays and Saturdays.

The others are especially good for fresh fruit and miscellaneous claptrap, and are found in **Longsight**, (Dickenson Road) on Wednesdays, Fridays and Saturdays; in **Bradford** at Grey Mare Lane on Mondays, Wednesdays, Fridays and Saturdays; at **Moss Side** on Denhill Road daily except Wednesday and Sunday – this one also has a flea market on Tuesdays. The best and most lively market in the city centre takes place at Liverpool Road, Castlefield on Bank Holiday Mondays, and is well worth a rummage.

OUT OF THE CENTRE

Many of the suburbs and towns around Manchester have become renowned for their characteristic shopping centres. In general, for chintzy character and expensive tastes, head south. For value and a more down to earth appeal, head on oop north. Having said this, because of Manchester's massive appeal to shoppers, the surrounding towns don't have much to offer that you wouldn't find in the city centre. Their markets, however, are usually better than any you'll find in the grand metropolis, and are featured almost exclusively in this section.

Altrincham (train from Piccadilly, buses 234/6) is a pretty town to the south of Manchester, and is a real favourite with the 'Cheshire Set' due to its classy boutiques and twee tea shops. Not really a must for bargain hunters, it is nevertheless a good place to take a visitor, and is close to the lovely villages, pubs and countryside featured in *Cheshire* in *DALES, HILLS AND DARK SATANIC MILLS.*

Bolton (train from Victoria or bus 8/9, 28) has the usual chain-store-type shopping centre, but the stores are the most varied outside Manchester city centre itself. Making it even more worthwhile is the fact that Bolton is a lovely town to spend some time in, even if you're not on a shopping frenzy. Its Market Hall has won prizes, and for real bargains try the Ashbourne Street Open Market (Tuesdays, Thursdays and Saturdays), which is renowned for fruit and fish as well as an assortment of what could only be described as miscellaneous stalls. There are loads of other things to do in Bolton – in fact, it's well worth a day-trip (see *DALES, HILLS AND DARK SATANIC MILLS*).

Bury (buses 90, 135) has an excellent open-air market on Wednesdays, Fridays and Saturdays, which draws bargain hunters from miles around (not, of course, that Northerners are a bit tight with the pennies – just careful). The town itself is famed for black puddings, so don't leave without several samples of coagulated pig's blood in your stomach – unless, of course, you're a veggie. As with Altrincham and Bolton, there is more to see than the shopping centre, so check the section on *Lancashire* before you leave.

Oldham (train from Victoria, buses 82, 170, 180/3/4) is the home of the famous Tommyfields market on Mondays, Fridays and Saturdays, with a flea market in which to scratch around on Wednesdays. Just out of the town there is a market in Chadderton on Wednesdays, and in Shaw, Hollinwood and Royton on Thursdays. All of the above markets are reached by a short bus ride from Oldham town centre, and combine the pleasures of bargain hunting with a traditional village-market atmosphere.

Stockport (train from Piccadilly, buses 189-192). The shopping centre itself is bland and boring, but the market is worth a visit for its fruit, veg and farm produce. It is open on Tuesdays, Fridays and Saturdays and, being protected by a charter dating from the thirteenth century, is unlikely to disappear in the near future.

Wilmslow, like Altrincham, is the sort of pretty town in which you're unlikely to do much more than window-shop. There are trains from Piccadilly and buses from Stockport, and again, it's a lovely place from which to step forward and see Cheshire.

Sport

Being a lively and energetic bunch, Mancunians have long excelled in all areas of sporting life. Even the garrulous cheers and jeers of those who merely spectate could almost be called a sport – in view of the vast amounts of energy exuberantly spent in supporting the home side. Manchester has a wide cross-section of participatory and spectator sporting facilities to accommodate this enthusiasm. With plans for an international stadium at Barton Cross, where the Olympics would have been held (sob), the already impressive sports stage looks set to dominate. Even excluding this ambitious project, new centres are popping up all over the city at an encouraging rate to replace other somewhat dilapidated facilities in the suburbs. As in the areas of tourism and business, leisure is high on the priority list for redevelopment.

Famed for internationally renowned soccer, Rugby League, American football, cricket and athletics teams, as well as individual stars such as Alex 'Hurricane' Higgins, Manchester has fair claims as a major world sports centre. Its grounds at Old Trafford play host to Test Matches and international Rugby League – as well as being home to the world's most supported football club, Manchester United. This area alone provides more than enough material for a sports freak's wet dream. It doesn't end here though: much more is on offer, and whether you want to play or to watch, there is no excuse for not getting involved.

SPORT AS A PARTICIPANT

This section can only scratch the surface of the wide variety of facilities available in the city, but it should at least provoke a few ideas and provide some inspiration for light exercise, pure pleasure or downright aggressive competition.

The easiest way to find out about local sports facilities is to check the various councils' leisure listings in the telephone directory, or to pick up a leaflet from the Town Hall. Manchester City Council provide a fully comprehensive list of centres and facilities in their *A-Z Guide to Council Services*, and Salford, Tameside and Trafford councils also produce sports information. Such centres provide numerous and diverse facilities for sports, as well as special groups and classes for everything from aerobics to karate. Check with individual centres for details, or with local papers/*City Life* for advance notice of classes and events.

If you're the winter-sports type and love slipping and sliding on snow and ice, there is an **ice-skating rink** at Altrincham in Devonshire Road (061-928 1360), within walking distance from Navigation Road Station, or by bus from Manchester (263/4). To the north of the city, in the Lancashire hills, you can ski on one of the best dry slopes in the country at Rawtenstall, or on a smaller version in Oldham. **Ski Rossendale** on Haslingden Old Road in Rawtenstall (0706-228844) offers hire and coaching (as well as a café), and is worth the trek out of the city. Bus 90 goes to Rawtenstall from Manchester, and from there you can catch a local bus to the ski centre; or take bus 170 to Moorside. Obviously, the trip is easier if you have a car – M66 to Rawtenstall and signposted clearly from there. For convenience, and especially if you are limited to public transport, try the **Counthill Centre** in Counthill Road, Oldham (061-678 4054). There is a direct bus from Manchester (407), or get a train to Mumps Station from Victoria and then one of buses 404/5/6/7, 413/4, 556.

If you prefer the water to have melted by the time you hit it, there are plenty of facilities for water sports in and around the city. For the more adventurous (and wealthy), windsurfing and other water sports are amply provided for at the **Sale Water Park** (061-905 1100), just off the Rifle Road. A town with a name like this was simply begging for sailing facilities. The place is supervised by life-guards to prevent accidents, and there are walks around the park as well as a bar, café and restaurant for those who don't want to get wet. Best reached by taking Junction 8 off the M63, or on foot from Dane Road Station. In the same area and slightly to the south is the **Chorlton Water Park** (Maitland Avenue, 061-881 5639). It is smaller than Sale, and reached by a pleasant walk from the former across the golf course. Sailing facilities are also provided at **Debdale Park**, along with **trout fishing** and **sailing for disabled people**. Debdale (Hyde Road, Gorton, 061-223 0816) is best reached by train to Denton or to Fairfield. There is much more besides to do here: for a comprehensive list, see *JOY RIDES*.

If your needs are a little less ambitious, but still water-orientated, there are numerous **swimming** facilities and pools in the city. Again, for a comprehensive list contact the local council. If you like to liven up your dips a little, try one of the wild and wet type complexes in the city. At the **Tameside Leisure Park** (061-368 4057; Walker Lane, buses 204, 210/1/4/5), there is an 80-metre giant waterslide, a wave machine, a white-water rapids channel, water cannon and fountains, all housed within a pseudo-tropical environment with controlled temperature and palm trees. Oh goodness, you could almost think you were in Florida! Slightly more down-to-earth is the **Gorton Tub** (061-230 7867) with an overhead rain-shower (this is more akin to an English environment!), two converging rapids, a flume, a whirlpool, an infant pool and an unpolluted beach. An additional godsend to mums is a crèche facility. The Tub is situated on Garrett Way, very near to Belle Vue Station, and close enough to Debdale Park to make a day outing.

Fore (ahem) golf fanatics, there are numerous facilities, both in the municipal parks and in private clubs. The more serious eighteen-hole contenders might enjoy a trek to the **Altrincham Municipal Golf Course** on Stockport Road in Timperley (061-938 0769), within walking distance from Altrincham Rail Interchange. A shorter, nine-hole course can be found in Worsley at the **Brackley Golf Course** on Highfield Road (061-790 6076) – and as there are courses all over the suburbs, it is probably best to check with the trusty old telephone directory for details. **Driving practice** is on offer at the **Kearsley Golf Range**, Moss Lane, Bolton (0204-75726). Take a train to Bolton, then a 126, 518 or 519 bus to Doffcocker and walk north for a couple of minutes. For those participants of lesser ability, the municipal parks often offer pitch-and-putt, mini-golf or Crazy Golf facilities. Check with each one individually for details.

With Lancashire County Cricket Club's ground based in the city, cricket is a popular participatory sport, especially among the young 'uns. There is an **indoor cricket centre** on Dell Road, Shawclough, Rochdale (0706 534266), or nearer to the city in the **Stockport Indoor Pavilion**, Didsbury Road (061-480 9810), near central Stockport; buses 20 or 197 from Manchester help combat the effects of the wet weather. Out of doors, there are hundreds of cricket grounds, especially in the suburbs, and many have junior and senior amateur teams.

If you are a **cycling** fan, and want to feel the wind in your hair (or on your crash helmet) without running the risk of losing a few limbs under a car, there are cycle speedway tracks at Debdale Park (see the paragraph on water sports above), Heaton Park (see *JOY RIDES*) and Broadhurst Park in Moston (a five- or ten-minute stroll from Moston Station on Lightbrowne Road). If it's a more sedate ride you're after, contact the Greater Manchester Cycling Project for details of rustic routes (details of the many different ways that the Project can aid the beleaguered cyclist can be found in *Travel and Transport* in *ORIENTATION*).

Still on wheels, but of the **roller skating** variety, there are two rinks. One is at Levenshulme: the Arcadia Sports Hall, Yew Tree Avenue near Levenshulme Station (061-224 0938); the other is Rollers, Holdsworth Street, Reddish (061-431 0261), a short 7, 104/5, 203 bus ride from Piccadilly Station. Rollers also has a mini skate-ramp, but if you're really into the **skateboard** scene, it's worth travelling up to Bury to the Goshen Sports Centre, off Manchester Road (buses 90/135 from Manchester – ask for Goshen Lane).

Should you want to take advantage of the renascent **ten-pin bowling** fad, it shouldn't be too difficult – with massive modern centres mushrooming all over the place. Like the multiplex cinemas, they tend to be located just out of the city in industrial parks – so if you go to Bury's **Megabowl** or Belle Vue's **Granada Bowl**, you can catch a few flicks at the same time. Great! The Granada Bowl (061-223 4161) is on the Hyde Road, and the Megabowl (061-767 9150) is right next to the Multiplex in Pilsworth (see *Cinema, Theatre and Classical Music* for directions). Out to the west, there is the **GX Superbowl** on Shield Drive in Worsley (061-794 3374), just off the East Lancashire Road (buses 30/1/2/4); in Bolton there is the **Hollywood Bowl** (0204 380270) on Carlton Street, very near to the station. All of the above are huge, modern, Americanized places with computerized scoring, eateries, drinkeries, bouncy slides for kids and snazzy bowling shoes. Great fun, and not bad value.

Back into the summery outdoors, and into strawberry-tinted images of **tennis**. Not to be outdone by Wimbledon, Manchester has many courts, most commonly in the municipal parks and sports centres, though these can be full of molehills or pot-holes; pretty frustrating for the Becker types, but adequate for the rest of us. If you are serious about tennis and need practice in all weathers, try the Puma Wigan Sports Complex on Robin Park Road, Newtown, Wigan (0942-45212). Nearer to Manchester, there are indoor courts at the Abraham Moss Leisure Centre on Crescent Road in Crumpsall (buses 78/9, 135/7, 061-795 7277 for further information). Private clubs are pricey, but details can be obtained from the Regional Sports Council (see later).

For all the budding Flo-Jos out there, the best **athletics** facilities are at the Belle Vue Athletics Centre on Pink Bank Lane in Longsight (061-231 1507) – get off at Belle Vue Station). Here, there is a 400-metre synthetic track, as well as field facilities, all of which are floodlit at night. Use of the track is free between 1000 and 1200, Monday to Friday.

In addition, there are many **snooker** halls; and most pubs have darts boards if that is where your sporting ambitions end!

There's a club called **Spice** that organizes parachute jumps, balloon rides, caving and the like, as well as more sedate pursuits; it's a good place to make friends if you're new to the area (details on 061-872 2213).

If there is a particular sport you are interested in, and you would like to follow it further, the **Regional Sports Council** (061-834 0338) can put you in contact with centres, clubs and facilities for whatever it may be. Most of the sports not mentioned in this section have been left out simply because most of the council sports centres deal with them, and they are too numerous to mention. For details of special facilities for women and the disabled, see *THE MORAL MAJORITY*.

SPORT AS SPECTATOR

Manchester offers the spectator a feast of entertainment, hosting top British and international competitions in a variety of sports. Almost every night of the week some high-profile event is taking place; if your throat can stand the pressure, see as many as you can – there's nothing like a Mancunian crowd to create an atmosphere.

Although renowned for many sports, Manchester is most particularly famous for its footie. Its two major teams both play in the top English division: **Manchester City** and **Manchester United**. Surprisingly enough, the latter (although said to be 'the most famous football team in the world') is not as popular with the Mancunian population as arch-rival, City. Despite their high spending during the eighties, United never quite managed to achieve the league success that many expected and demanded, nor fully succeeded in recreating the special magic of the Best/Charlton era. Nevertheless, they did win the FA Cup in 1990, making them the most frequent holders of the cup in the past twenty years. United play at **Old Trafford** (train from Piccadilly to Warwick Road – *not* Old Trafford – Station, or buses 230, 252/7, 259), a 50,000-capacity ground which is often full of fans from all over the country – and even the world. Their base of support stretches as far afield as the USA and South America, making them a popular choice as the first team allowed back into European competition since the Heysel Stadium tragedy in 1985.

Manchester City, based at **Maine Road** in Moss Side, are much more of a local side, and their supporters are some of the noisiest and most jovial in the country. Many would see the departure of Howard Kendall to Everton in 1990 as a betrayal, but the jilted fans are not ones to lose heart: instead, they have taken to selling traitor teeshirts around the ground! In the 1989/90 season, there was a massive pitch invasion when City played Crystal Palace. Dressed as the Blues Brothers, City fans went forward to meet their rivals – not in battle but to exchange scarves, hats and shades and to sing against arch-enemies, Manchester United. This camaraderie is what makes a City game such fun to see, especially when seen from the Kippax end – and whether you are a United or a City fan, a derby game is an event not to be missed. In 1989 City won 5-1; in 1990 there was a 3-3 draw. Having set precedents for six-goal derbies, there are few who will want to miss the next few seasons' battles of the Manchesters.

Manchester United are the proud possessors of the first-ever British Football Museum (see *JOY RIDES*). Poorer neighbours City offer tours around their ground for free from Tuesday to Thursday between 1030 and 1330, but disabled access is limited. The ground is located just off Claremont Road in Moss Side (buses from centre, 5, 15, 99, P11). More details can be obtained on 061-226 1191.

When the Football League was first started in 1888, neither of the Manchester teams was among the original twelve. Six, however, were from Lancashire, dominated by the mill towns of the North: Accrington Stanley, Burnley, Blackburn Rovers, Preston North End, Bolton Wanderers and Everton. Perhaps the predominantly northern roots of the football scene help to explain the fervent atmosphere of a game at a northern ground. These teams still play (not all, sadly, in the Football League!), and all are within easy reach of Manchester. Nearer both to the city and to the first division are **Oldham Athletic**, who play at Boundary Park (numerous buses from Oldham – train to Oldham Mumps from Victoria). Under the successful management of Joe Royle, who led them breathtakingly close to both the FA and Littlewoods Cups in 1989-90, they look set in the coming seasons to provide the first division with another Manchester team, and although their plastic pitch has been criticized for giving an unfair advantage at home matches, it would seem that there is an element of sour grapes to be detected among its detractors: Oldham have played as competently away as they have on their home ground.

In December each year, there is a lively **six-a-side soccer** tournament held at the G-Mex centre (Windmill Street, 061-832 9000 or 061-834 2700). All the major club sides are represented in the tournament, and the games are fast and competitive. For information on this and the many other sporting events put on at G-Mex (the place was even turned into an ice-rink for Torville and Dean), give them a ring on 061-832 9000.

Manchester provides a focus for **Rugby League**, which has a large body of support in the North-West, much of it congregating for important matches and internationals (notably in 1990, the second Test against Australia) at **Old Trafford**. First used for the sport in 1986, the ground has been filled to capacity at many matches by cheering fans, come rain or shine. Rugby League is the rougher northern version of Rugby Union. Because of its base of support, the game has been surrounded by an image of cloth caps and whippets, but it is in fact much more closely related, in terms of aggression and excitement, to American football (without the pads). First division sides **Oldham, Wigan** and **Warrington** compete weekly, and a live game is a spectacle not to be missed. Check *City Life* or the local press for details of fixtures.

Manchester also has a couple of notable **Rugby Union** teams that, although not currently in the Courage first division, have prestigious pasts. Worth a visit on a Saturday afternoon are former England captain Steve Smith's **Sale Rugby Football Club**, who play at Brooklands Road (061-973 6348) – train to Brooklands Station. Such a trip can bring enjoyment or despair depending on whether or not a hard-fought game results in victory over the high-profile, money-flashing, sexist-song-singing southern teams.

In the **Spartans**, Manchester has one of the finest European **American football** teams, and by far the best of the British. In spite of a bad season in 1987, they have been a formidable team for years, and are set to challenge America with the help of their coach Terry Smith. He reckons that Manchester's superiority in the field is due to a northern attitude and the fact that 'people who come from Manchester have a bit of a front – they expect to succeed'. They do indeed succeed: visit a Spartans game and witness this strange form of sado-masochism at Hyde United's ground in Ewenfield, Grange Road, Hyde (061-368 1031) – walking distance from Godley Station. The other Manchester side of note, the **All Saints**, play at Boundary Park (see above).

Another sport, hugely popular in the States and gaining momentum over here, is **ice hockey**. Each year, at the end of August, a tournament takes place at the Altrincham Ice-Rink (details above). Here, the

Trafford Metros, Manchester's best (and only) team play host to seven of the UK's top sides in a pre-season competition.

For a slightly more refined, traditionally English spectator sport, head back on down to **Old Trafford**, to the ground of the **Lancashire County Cricket Club** (transport as for Old Trafford United ground, see above, or buses 115, 250). Matches can be seen throughout the summer as Lancashire whip the daylights out of the rest of the counties. The ground also plays host to hotly contested Test Matches (well, the England team usually get hot under the collar), and if that's not exciting enough, you can always browse around the **Lancashire County Cricket Museum** (see *JOY RIDES*).

Greyhound racing at the **Belle Vue Greyhound Race Course** provides an ideal opportunity for a flutter on the dogs. Belle Vue has recently opened a £1.5 million extension and is now the best centre in the North. An action-packed evening is guaranteed, although whatever it is that makes those poor dogs believe they are chasing a real hare is a mystery. The stadium is situated on Hulme Lane, just off the Hyde Road (Belle Vue B.R.).

Back in American mode, Manchester's **basketball** hopes lie with the **Giants**; **cycling** credentials rest on the **Wheelers**, and **athletics** achievers come charging out of **Stretford Athletics Club** at an alarming rate. Over at **Belle Vue**, on Hyde Road, you can often see **speedway** zipping around the track. For this and all the above, check with the regional HQ of the Sports Council for details (061-834 0338).

8. THE MORAL MAJORITY

This chapter is designed, as the title would suggest, for the majority of the community who are still forced to live under the misapprehension that white, male, middle-aged, able-bodied, straight people are the overwhelming majority of our population – just because they are the ones who make the laws.

It isn't enough that this established society adopts an air of indifferent acceptance, calling it broad-mindedness, while steadfastly refusing to acknowledge and celebrate the diverse and essentially unique contributions that each section of its community makes.

Of course, virtually everything else in the book is relevant to 'the moral majority'; this chapter only hopes to highlight the pertinent facts and contacts for the many different groups that make up the cosmopolitan whole.

Women

There is a wide and intricate network of support for women in Manchester. In spite of limited funds, the council and voluntary organizations have succeeded in providing many facilities which, although insufficient in terms of demand, are welcome and comparatively extensive when seen alongside those of other cities and towns. This is not to say, however, that the entire Mancunian population hold women in high regard; as is the case almost everywhere else, there are the usual macho crowds who think that wolf-whistles and profanities are effective chat-up lines, and who think that shouting 'Lesbians' at two girls is actually an insult. Women the world over have learned to rise above this mentality, but at least in Manchester the pressing concerns of child care, abuse, discrimination and social needs are catered for as best they can be in the present political and economic climate.

Within the **Equal Opportunities** department at Manchester City Council are women's officers who can advise and offer practical support for women suffering from **discrimination**. Details on 061-234 3353. They are also a good starting place for any information that you may need on the vast network of groups and amenities for women in the city.

For those suffering from more than discrimination, the **Women's Aid**

Centre (061-236 6540) offers advice, support and refuge for victims of **physical and mental abuse**, and, if necessary, their children too. They are open daily 1000-1600. The city council also offers shelter for women and children who have been made **homeless** because of violence (061-234 4744). Women who suffered sexual abuse as children and need to talk can call the 24-hour helpline, **Taboo** on 061-236 1712. Those who have experienced rape or sexual assault will find sympathetic advice and support at the **Rape Crisis Centre** (061-228 3602), where the helpline is open Tuesday-Friday 1400-1700 and Wednesday-Sunday 1800-2100. At other times, there is an answerphone service. At the **St Mary's Centre** at St Mary's Hospital on Oxford Road (061-276 6515), there is a 24-hour immediate help service for women who have been raped or sexually assaulted. Forget the horror stories of doctors' attitudes towards rape victims: here you will receive nothing but the most generous and sensitive sources of support and help.

There are extensive **health** and **family planning centres** in the city, and most of them provide crèche facilities. Their hours vary and it is always best to telephone first for opening times and, if necessary, appointments. They are:

The Well Women Resource Centre:	1 Pilling Street, Newton Heath; 061-205 1257.
Beswick Women's Health Clinic:	Ranworth Close, Grey Mare's Lane; 061-223 6385.
Cheetham Well Women's Health Centre:	Old Library, Cheetham Hill Road – corner of Heath Street; 061-740 9973.
Cheetham Women's Health Clinic:	Smedley Street, Cheetham Hill; 061-205 1704.
South Manchester Well Women Clinic:	Wythenshawe Health Care Centre Stancliffe Road, Sharston; 061-946 0065.
Palatine Women's Centre (Withington/Didsbury):	63-5 Palatine Road; 061-434 3555.

For independent pregnancy advice from Monday to Friday 0900-1700, call at the **British Pregnancy Advisory Service**, Suite F, 57 Hilton Street (061-236 7777). As well as pregnancy advice, they can sort you out before the event with family planning, and also give infertility advice.

Many women, in particular **single parents**, face tremendous difficulties when trying to balance budgets with baby care. The dilemma is for the most part ignored by a government unrealistically obsessed with the traditional 'family unit' philosophy. In Manchester there is a **One-Parent Advice Centre** at Levenhulme, and they will be able to put you in touch with other organizations in the city. The centre is open Monday to Friday 1000-1500, and is situated on Chapel Street (061-248 6739). In Stockport, there is a self-help group called **Pulse** for young single parents. Details on 061-474 7393.

Manchester City Council operates a variety of **crèche facilities** and **day nurseries** for young children. The opening hours vary, and for the best advice you should contact the **Day Care Team** (North Manchester 061-205 7321; Central 061-226 8131; South 061-881 0911). They can also provide details of child-minders. Although on paper it might look as though there are many centres, most of them have long waiting-lists, and in some cases, you'd have to book a place before you conceived to get in! Those listed are not exhaustive – telephone Manchester, Trafford, Tameside and Salford councils (see *GREATER MANCHESTER POTTED DIRECTORY*) for further details.

For mothers working or living within the city centre catchment area, children between six months and eleven years can attend the **St Peter's Children's Centre** at the back of the Town Hall. It's a bright-looking place; judging from the amount of noise (and, unfortunately, the waiting-list), it's certainly a popular one. The centre provides holiday play schemes; evening and weekend crèche facilities can also be booked. Alternatively, if you are merely visiting the Town Hall or Central Library, you can unload the kids for a short while. For further information, contact the centre co-ordinator, St Peter's Children's Centre on 061-234 3246, or the **Under-Fives Unit** on 061-234 7231.

In South Manchester there are also four children's centres offering full-time and part-time care at: **Benchill** (061-946 0425), **Burnage** (061-443 1668), **Rusholme** (061-257 2542) and **Withington** (061-446 2131). A fifth is planned in **Moss Side** for 1991. The beauty of these centres is that they are fully accessible to disabled children, and integration is actively encouraged.

For mothers taking **educational courses**, the following colleges offer crèche facilities:

Manchester College of Arts and Technology

Moston Centre:	061-205 7525
Openshaw Centre:	061-223 8282

St John's Centre:	061-831 7791
South Manchester College	
Fielden Park Centre:	061-434 4821
Wythenshawe Centre:	061-902 0131
Adult Education Centres	
Abraham Moss Centre:	061-746 1491
Birley Centre:	061-226 1416
Birtles Centre:	061-499 1455
Collyhurst CE Centre:	061-205 1067
Daisy Bank CE Centre:	061-224 9464
Ducie CE Centre:	061-226 0428
Plant Hill Centre:	061-795 6010

There are also crèche facilities at the following sports centres:

Chorlton Leisure Centre:	061-881 2130
Gorton Tub Leisure Pool:	061-230 7867
Harphurhey Baths:	061-205 2013
Moss Side Leisure Centre:	061-226 0515
Sharston Baths:	061-998 4142

For some ideas on where to take children for that perfect day out, consult *JOY RIDES, DALES, HILLS AND DARK SATANIC MILLS* and *Sport*.

There are numerous **women's groups** in Manchester, the contact point for most events being the **Pankhurst Centre** on Nelson Street, Chorlton-on-Medlock. As mentioned in a previous chapter, it was at this site that Emmeline Pankhurst and her daughters launched the Women's Social and Political Union to campaign for women's rights. Though the centre of the suffragette movement subsequently moved to London, don't forget that it started right here! The present Pankhurst Centre has been running for three years, and co-ordinates the women's network in the city. Groups such as **Womenkind** are based here, and on offer are workshops on a range of subjects from self-assertiveness to self-defence, plus classes as diverse as rug-weaving and creative writing. There is an excellent vegetarian restaurant, as well as a museum and gardens; the whole area is accessible to those with disabilities. More details on 061-273 5673.

The **Workers Educational Association** have been organizing successful women's interest classes for years, but in 1990 they opened a special branch in Hattersley. They offer courses on everything from 'Women and Health' to 'Women's History'. Telephone 061-368 8513 for details.

For women aged between fifteen and twenty-five, **42nd Street** (see *Youth*) is a godsend, and offers advice and refuge for women with hassles at home as well as the general growing-up pressures. For details of the women's only sessions, call 061-832 0170. The **Old Trafford Community Centre** (Shrewsbury Street, 061-872 5445) offers evenings dedicated specifically to the interests of women aged between thirteen and eighteen. However, it also caters for those outside this immediate age-range with a wide variety of activities.

For specific **social events**, it is wise to check with *City Life*'s Women's section, or you can contact the Pankhurst Centre (see above). There are, in addition, a number of regular women's evenings on offer in venues throughout the city. On Saturday nights, **Follies** on Aytoun Street offer a women-only night. The first Saturday of each month is hosted by Lesbian Link and the third Saturday is generally the most popular. The décor is naff, but it's a welcome break from the 'd'ya come here often?' syndrome.

Above the Rembrandt, on Sackville Street, is a quiet women-only bar called **Sappho's**. It's cosy and friendly, and is licensed until midnight. In the **Old Steam Brewery**, near the Polytechnic on Oxford Road, is the curiously named **Fizz Booms** disco on Thursday nights. Likewise, on Sundays, **Archies** (next to Oxford Road Station) offers a women's social, the proceeds from which go towards women's support groups.

Black and Ethnic

Manchester has an extensive and varied multi-racial community, and race relations are of vital importance in the city's attempts to achieve and maintain social harmony. The effects of ghettoized and marginalized communities were graphically demonstrated in the Moss Side riots during the mid-1980s. All sections of the community are keen to ensure that these problems do not recur.

There are, however, some alarming signals that racism, far from being dead, is gaining momentum within the city. Indifference from society as a whole, thinly veiled in a patronizing 'oh they're all right, some of my best friends are Black/Jewish/Irish' attitude, has allowed a slimy undercurrent of racial hatred to develop. In 1989 and 1990, increasingly disturbing and violent attacks were mounted on Jewish graves. Elsewhere, racist graffiti is on the increase, and it would seem that it is only a matter of time before the ugliness rears its head more blatantly.

Nightclubs have long been sources of racial controversy. In 1990

Nayaba Aghedo, a reporter with *City Life*, noted anti-Black door policies at a city-centre nightclub one Saturday night. This is not an isolated occurrence within the club scene, more especially the mainstream club scene: such policies are one of the major sources of complaint reported to the groups monitoring and campaigning against racism in the city.

There are many groups, centres and facilities available to help Black and ethnic groups within the city to cope with a range of race-related problems, from racism to language and social difficulties. This brief guide is intended to serve as a pointer to those who can offer more detailed and comprehensive assistance.

Should you suffer from any form of racial harassment, be it in work, housing or in other areas, do not hesitate to contact the local **Racial Equality Council** (formerly the Community Relations Council). In Manchester this is at Maybrook House, 40 Blackfriars Street, Manchester, M3 (061-831 7782). The Manchester branch of the **Equal Opportunities Commission**, not to be confused with the council committees, is based on Quay Street and will be more than happy to take up cases of racism and offer advice. Details on 061-833 9244.

All the councils in and around Manchester have equal opportunities departments, with officers especially employed to deal with ethnic concerns. Manchester City Council has a **Race Unit** who are extremely competent and committed to the co-ordination and implementation of anti-racist policies throughout the council's jurisdiction. They will help to put you in contact with those groups out of their area, as well as smaller, more specialized groups for individual needs. The unit can be contacted on 061-234 3353.

If your problems are specifically related to immigration laws and their effects, specialized legal advice and support is offered by the **Immigration Aid Unit** on Cheetham Hill Road, M8 (061-740 7722). There is an active campaigning group on this subject that goes by the name of **MAGIC** (Manchester Against Immigration Control). The aid unit will be able to put you in contact with them if you want to get involved.

Zora Neale Hurston observed that facing the combined problems of sexual and racial discrimination, a Black woman was doubly downtrodden; 'de mule of de world'. In many ways, things really don't seem to be a great deal different for the majority of Black and ethnic women in Manchester in the 1990s than they were in the Harlem of the 1920s that she wrote about. There are, however, a great number of support services available to women of ethnic minorities with specific needs. One of the primary ones the **Bangladeshi Family Welfare and**

Advice Centre, 19a Birch Lane (061-225 4012), offering advice for all Asian women and their families. In addition, there is an **Asian Women's Aid** group, which will provide refuge, advice and support for Asian women and girls who have been sexually, mentally or physically abused. Contact Saheli at the Longsight Law Centre (details on 061-255 5111). **Abasindi** is a Black women's group offering help and advice on a variety of issues (061-226 6837). In Hulme, where racial ghettos are common, there is a self-help group, the **Hulme Young Black Women's Project**, which can be reached on 061-226 9814.

For Black lesbians and gays, who can be ostracized by many different communities, there is the excellent **Black Lesbian and Gay Group**.

For the large Irish communities, there are a number of social clubs and organizations. The **Irish in Britain Representative Group** has a branch in Manchester, which meets regularly at the St Brendan's Irish Centre, City Road, Old Trafford. There is also an active Irish club in Chorlton on High Lane. The **West Indian Sports and Social Club** on Westwood Street, Moss Side, is a club for the West Indian community in which regular meetings are held, as well as community events.

In November every year there is an **ethnic festival** organized by Community Understanding, which is intended to highlight and celebrate the cultures of Manchester's many ethnic communities. Wide ranges of food, dance, music and displays from groups all over the city are in evidence, and all proceeds are donated to charity. In 1990 the festival was held in the Ukrainian Cultural Centre in Cheetham. Watch the November editions of *City Life* for advance notice.

People with Disabilities

Not so long ago, the problems faced by people with disabilities were swept under the proverbial carpet by the rest of our caring society. Thanks to dedicated campaigning by disabled rights groups, problems of accessibility and acceptance are being challenged and changed. In all walks of life, from buses to jobs, understanding and facilities are being improved, but much ground is yet to be covered, and thus, while this section is intended to point the way to help and information, it cannot hope to cover the full extent of facilities available. Access to museums and theatres is dealt with in those particular sections; other useful sources of information can be gleaned from the groups listed below.

HELP AND ADVICE

If you have suffered from crime and are less able to cope because of your disability, contact the **Telephone Advice Bureau for Disabled People**, who will help with a whole host of queries, problems or enquiries that you may have. The Bureau is staffed Monday-Friday 1300-1700: 061-226 1694 (Connie), 061-436 4922 (Derek), 061-860 4482 (Marilyn) or 061-445 2603 (Sandra). The **City Council Disability Officer** may be reached on 061-273 3258.

The **Greater Manchester Disability Forum** is a campaigning group as well as a support group, fighting vehemently for disabled access rights. They can also provide you with details of specialist support groups, benefits and legal advice (061-273 5033 or 061-273 5083 for minicom). A group with many similar characteristics, but with a cutting, campaigning edge are the **Greater Manchester Coalition of Disabled People**, who would welcome new blood into the team. They can be reached on 061-273 5155.

TRANSPORT

One of the major, and largely untackled areas of difficulty for the disabled and the elderly is public transport. At present, a bye-law is passing through the city council to ensure that all black Hackney cabs are converted to cope adequately with disabled passengers with wheelchairs. The Disability Forum will be able to keep you abreast of developments on that front. For **Manchester Disabled Motorists**, telephone 061-436 4922.

As far as buses and trains go, it would be a grave overstatement to say that facilities were scarce. However, the **Metrolink** has been designed with the needs of disabled people in mind (see *Travel and Transport*), and there is a bus service in Manchester running specifically for people with disabilities, prams or cumbersome loads. **Localine**, launched in Wythenshawe in 1985, is the only bus service that can accommodate wheelchairs. Services now operate in and between Stockport, Altrincham, Manchester city centre, Wythenshawe and Bury. Telephone the Greater Manchester Passenger Transport Executive for details on 061-228 7811.

SPORT AND LEISURE

Several sports centres offer special facilities for disabled people.

Debdale Park in Gorton – just off Hyde Road (061-223 0816) – contains two reservoirs upon which wheelchair users can **sail** on specially designed boats. At the **Failsworth Sports Centre** in Oldham (061-688 5888/683 4438-Brierly Avenue, Failsworth) between 1900 and 2200 every first and third Saturday of the month, facilities are made available and adapted for people with disabilities in a variety of sports, including swimming, board games, basketball, badminton and archery. Those facilities plus athletics, rifle shooting, bowls and table tennis have also been won by a representative group at the **Whitworth Centre**, 761 Ashton Old Road (061-223 0532). This centre is the only fully comprehensive sports ground geared primarily towards people with disabilities. At Halliwell in Bolton (Darley Street, 0204-393321), the **Jubilee Pool** has been designed and is available for the exclusive use of disabled people and their companions. The **Stretford Sports Centre**, Greatstone Road, off Chester Road (061-872 0906), also offers swimming facilities – but only on Thursdays for an hour between 2000 and 2100.

To keep abreast of news and issues affecting the disabled people of the North-West, susbscribe to *Change*, the magazine of the **Disabled Resource Unit**, based in Liverpool (051-709 0990, extension 203). On the subject of reading, the city council have taken care to make the Town Hall and Central Library fully accessible. The latter provides extensive access for wheelchairs, as well as braille and aural facilities for the blind and audio visual facilities for the deaf.

The **Greater Manchester Interpreters' Unit** provide a sign language service for deaf people. The Unit can be contacted at 30 Broad Street, Salford (telephone for voice and minicom 061-745 9128 and for QWERTY 061-745 7872).

Lesbian and Gay

Home to the second largest lesbian and gay community in the country, Manchester offers a healthy selection of social life, political activities and support services for the tens of thousands of lesbians and gays in the city. Not for nothing did entire trainfuls of people converge on Manchester from all over the UK for the massive demonstration against the infamous Section 28 of the 1988 Local Government Act. There was no more obvious second venue after the capital.

Manchester is also the base for 'the voice of the gay North' *Scene Out* magazine, which comes out monthly and has a comprehensive selection of listings, events and features lurking deep within its pages. Well worth investing your pennies in – buy from your local newsagent, or contact them at 23 New Mount Street, Manchester M4 4DE (061-953 4045). There's also a new gay freebie, *All Points North*.

SOCIAL LIFE

For those who believe that London is *the* place, and that anywhere in the provinces can only muster one dingy and rather sad little pub, Manchester will come as a welcome and thoroughly pleasant surprise. However, much of the gay social scene seems to have stuck in the groove of 1970s glam rock, and serves only to confirm some of the worst prejudices and stereotypes. Despair not, however, for there are some excellent and varied haunts around that will prove a delight to explore.

The area around Chorlton Street, near Piccadilly Station, is known as the **gay village**, as it acts as a focus for many social and political activities for the lesbian and gay community (as well as a host of refugees from the nearby coach station). **Central Park** on Sackville Street (061-236 5196) is very popular and extremely lively. Friday nights are women only, as are Saturdays at **Follies** at 6 Whitworth Street (061-236 8149), a restaurant and estimably superior kind of bar/disco. The **Rembrandt Hotel**, at 33 Sackville Street (061-236 1311), is a little quieter, and is more generally recognized as a gay venue, especially as it hosts all kind of very different events throughout the week. Other recommended pubs and bars are **New York, New York** (Bloom Street, 061-236 6556), which is heralded by a camp Statue of Liberty at the entrance, the **New Union** (Princess Street, 061-228 1492), **Paddy's Goose** (Bloom Street) and **Archies** (Oxford Road, 061-228 2114) – a trendy bar next to Oxford Road Station.

The club with the most exciting music has to be **Number One** (1 Central Street, 061-834 1292), which is the only one to recognize the need for a mainly gay venue with strictly contemporary tastes. Kylie-weary lesbians and gay men flock here in their hundreds for an indie cure. Although Tuesdays are the best nights, the place is busy all week. **Rockies** (Whitworth Street, near Piccadilly Station, 061-228 3078) is just as popular and, with several levels, bars and dance floors, by far the biggest club. This is the place for the leather/denim/clone crowd, but there's plenty of room for all types. Unfortunately, the club scene trails off a bit from here. Take your pick from places such as **La Cage** (105-7 Princess Street, 061-236 4445), a sophisticated plastic-plant paradise, or **Napoleon's** (Bloom Street, 061-236 8800). If you're searching for the more alternative side of life, and that means where virtually anything goes, **Dickens** at 74a Oldham Street (061-236 1249) offers just about anything that you can take.

There are no specifically lesbian bars in Manchester, but there are some women-only nights: for instance, **Sappho's Bar** at the Rembrandt (upstairs) on Fridays and **Fizz Boom** at the Old Steam Brewery on Thursdays. See *Women* for other women's venues.

Well-established features of the village are the well-stocked gay shop, **Clone Zone** (Bloom Street, 061-236 1398), and the small, very cheap **Bloom Street Café** next door, which is a pleasant place for hanging out during the day. That's also true of the brand-new **Manto Café** (Canal Street, see *Restaurants and Cafés*), which is sure to prove popular with lesbians and gay men.

The social scene for lesbians and gays is ever-changing, and it is best to check for the latest information from the venues themselves, or from the informative pages of *Scene Out* or the national **Gay Times**. Check *Scene Out* for details of lesbian and gay pubs outside the city centre, such as the **Church** in Bolton and the **New Inn** in Stockport.

ADVICE, INFORMATION AND HELP

Relatively sympathetic and humane city councils in Manchester and Salford have kept the repercussions of Section 28 and other 'loony left' backlash pressures at bay. Nonetheless, as is sadly the case all over, homophobia and victimization are rife. Situated at the same address as *Scene Out* magazine (see above) is the **North-West Campaign for Homosexual Equality**. Don't hesitate to contact them for any advice or information that you may need: they are friendly and concerned, and have a great deal of experience at your disposal.

Manchester City Council has two sub-committees that work with lesbians and with gay men in order to represent their needs within the public sector, especially in relation to provision of services. Both Gay Men's and Lesbian Women's Officers can be reached on 061-234 3259.

The city also boasts an excellent **Gay Centre**, a broad-based lesbian and gay community centre that sees a load of different events taking place throughout the year. There's also a weekend coffee bar. Find the place at 49-51 Sidney Street, All Saints (061-274 3814).

Other useful contact numbers are:

Gay Switchboard:	061-274 3999, daily 1600-2200
Lesbian Link:	061-236 6205, Mon-Thurs 1800-2100
Transvestite/Transsexual line:	061-274 3705, Weds 1900-2200

Youthline: 061-274 3705, Sat 1200-1600
AIDSline: 061-839 2442, Mon-Fri 1900-2200

Youth

There is a high population of people aged between fourteen and twenty-five in Manchester. In recent years, the problems, pressures, worries and fears of this age group have become ever more obvious. To help counteract these, there are a number of sympathetic help lines and organizations who are able to offer moral support and concrete aid, without falling into the traps of preaching and patronizing. If you feel that you need help – either on leaving home and coping with parents, money and employment, or with something more personal – don't hesitate to contact one of the groups below.

42nd Street, based rather confusingly at 22 Lloyd Street, off Albert Square (its old address was at number 42), is the leading youth help group in Manchester, and its services are in great demand. It caters for the needs of people aged between fifteen and twenty-five; as well as offering information and advice, it runs sessions dealing with specific problems, holding women- and men-only group meetings. Advance notice of meetings can be gleaned from the pages of *City Life*, and further details from the place itself on 061-832 0170. Also for this age group is a telephone counselling service called **Signpost**, operating Monday to Friday 1000-1700 and Monday evenings 1900-2100 on 061-946 0695/0736.

The Café is a facility for those aged fifteen to twenty-five who feel isolated and stressed, or who just need a friendly retreat and a sympathetic and wise ear. The centre is a coffee bar, but inside are counsellors who are more than willing to offer advice and help on problems such as housing, benefits and careers – should such stuff be required. If not, there are games and events organized, or you can simply go along and have a very cheap drink and meal in a warm environment with other young people. The Café is at the Coffee Bar, Old Library, Cheetham Hill Road, and is open 1500-1800 daily. More details from 42nd Street on 061-832 0170.

Young people in the areas of M14, M15 and M16 (largely Hulme and Moss Side) are generally recognized to suffer from specific problems arising from conditions in the areas in which they live. With this in mind, the **Moss Side District Centre** offers counselling and training on 061-226 9257 on Mondays, Tuesdays and Thursdays 1400-1700.

If your specific problem lies in leaving home or moving from the one you already have, and you are aged between sixteen and twenty-five, help is at hand in the form of the **Shades City Centre Project Ltd**. They can offer practical and legal advice as well as moral support. Contact them on 061-834 7360 to make an appointment for one of their sessions at 48 Copperas Street, M4.

For students, there is a national network called **Nightline** providing a counselling service throughout the night for any kind of problem. It is more of a 'someone to talk to' organization, although they can put you in touch with groups who might be able to offer more concrete advice. The Manchester-based group can be reached on 061-275 2983/4.

Environmental Groups and Concerns

Perchance ironic how the most stereotypical industrial cities have taken the biggest steps to turn grey into green, eh? While the capital continues to jump on the bandwagon with lots of noise and very little action, other cities are branching out into all aspects of green life.

Good ol' Manchester was the world's first **Nuclear Free Zone**, and recently celebrated its tenth birthday as such. If you see any dubious radioactivity lurking around in your neighbourhood, don't hesitate to contact the Nuke Squad at the Town Hall on 061-234 3244. The Nuclear Free Zone Unit works closely with **Greater Manchester CND**, who are based at The One World Centre, see later, and if disarmament and life are issues that make you want to scream, shout or spit, cruise (ahem...) on down to one of their meetings.

Manchester was also the first ever Smokeless Zone, and questions over the ozone layer have injected huge amounts of enthusiasm into this zone-fond city. All topics of pollution control and energy efficiency are dealt with by the councils, with a varying degree of enthusiasm. Manchester City Council went so far as to produce an *Environmental Charter* to support local policies and groups. One of its commitments is to work towards improvements for that evergreen transport mode, the bike, which doesn't really explain why the Greater Manchester Cycling Project is suffering from a threatened lack of funds.

Ah well, perhaps the spare copies of this charter could be collected and used for **recycling**. All the councils provide extensive recycling facilities: telephone your local authority for details of locations of bottle banks and skips. A company called **Limited Resources** will collect paper, glass, plastic and aluminium for recycling, as well as delivering environmentally friendly products to the green, green grass of your own home. Their service is free, and more information can be obtained on

061-226 4777.

Friends of The Earth have two active groups up and running in Manchester. The Trafford Branch meets at Ashfield House, Ashfield Road, Sale and, as with all FoE branches, membership costs £4.00 (£2.00 unwaged). Details on 061-962 1546. The branch in the city centre is based at the One World Centre (see below) and can be contacted on 061-236 1558. **Greenpeace** (061-861 0146) and **Amnesty** (061-881 3102) both hold regular meetings in the city.

The One World Centre is based at 13 Paton Street near Piccadilly (061-236 1588), and plays host to FoE's office, and an extensive shop stocking all those non-biodegradable/E-free/ozone-friendly/non-drag-net goods for a truly environmentally and ideologically sound lifestyle. They are in touch with numerous environmental, human and animal rights groups too, and can put you in contact with most of those operating in Manchester, such as **Manchester Organic Gardeners** (0257 451440). The centre is open Monday-Friday 1000-1700 and Sat 1100-1700.

For up-to-date information on new groups and events geared to keeping our world around for a wee bit longer, check *City Life*, *Cahoots*, or *Globe*, a bimonthly green magazine about the North generally.

Working in the Voluntary Sector

It's all very well digging into the pocket in a desperate attempt to shut Terry Wogan up for *Children in Need*, but many of the hundreds of voluntary organizations desperately need help of a more practical kind. If you have a few spare hours, a few bags full of enthusiasm, and want to do your bit, pop along to your local library or council and extract a list of voluntary groups from their information desk.

Manchester Council for Voluntary Services, 57 Hilton Street (061-236 3206), acts as a supporting, co-ordinating and advisory body for the voluntary sector. From them you can obtain help and information from both sides of the fence. They can put you in touch with a suitable organization, or if you already are a suitable organization, they can help you survive. If the latter applies, and you need resources, there is a facility in the city that provides basic office equipment such as typewriters, photocopiers and suchlike to voluntary groups. The **Manchester Area Resource Centre** can be found at Brownsfield Mill, Binns Place, 104 Great Ancoats Street, Ancoats and is open Monday-Friday 1000-1630. Details on 061-236 0350.

Continuing and Further Education

If your brain is fed up with unemployment, under-employment or just plain boring employment, it could be a sound idea to head on back to the classroom. You get a little better treated now that you're a grown-up, and you have the added bonus of being able to study something useful or interesting. The local councils can provide you with infinite lists of courses and colleges available for adult education, and if you're a mum, there are several that offer crèche facilities.

The **Education Advice Service** is a weekly drop-in service for those adults who are keen to return to education but don't quite know where to start. They can put you in touch with colleges and schools, and advise you on what your options are. They are based at the Moseley Road Centre, Moseley Road, Fallowfield (061-224 8241).

The **Workers Education Association** is an independent voluntary body which organizes an astounding number of classes covering virtually every subject that you imagined existed, as well as a great many that you didn't. None of the classes is vocational in the conventional sense, although assertiveness training and other such courses can improve working conditions no end. The Association works very closely with the University and Manchester Education Authority. Fees vary depending on the course, but they are free for the unwaged. They also have a special women's branch (see *Women*). More information from their regional office on the fourth floor of Crawford House in the University Precinct on Oxford Road (061-273 7652).

Manchester University offers a wide selection of courses to the general public, ranging from *Educating Rita*-like summer schools of fun and frolics to weekly evening courses. Details on 061-275 3276/7.

9. GREATER MANCHESTER POTTED DIRECTORY

The list below is a short summary of contacts for services not mentioned elsewhere. Except that is for...

Tourist Information Centres

Manchester Tourist Information Centre:	061-234 3157/8
Castlefield Tourist Information Centre:	061-832 4244

Useful Contacts

COUNCILS

Manchester City Council:	061-234 5000
Salford City Council:	061-794 4711
Trafford Borough Council:	061-872 2101
Tameside Borough Council:	061-330 8355
Bury Borough Council:	061-705 5000
Oldham Borough Council:	061-678 4800
Stockport Borough Council:	061-480 4949

HELP AND ADVICE

AIDSline:	061-839 2442
National AIDSline:	0800-555777 (free)
Alcoholics Anonymous:	061-236 6569
Anorexic Line:	061-736 6541
British Pregnancy Advisory Service:	061-236 7777
Citizens Advice Bureau:	061-832 7028
Lifeline:	061-839 2054 (advice and needle-exchange service)
Mainline:	061-227 9299 (self-help drug support)
Samaritans:	061-834 9000
Men Overcoming Violence:	061-227 9931 (self-help for violent men)

HEALTH

Cut-backs on spending in the health sector have hit Manchester as hard as the next town (Bolton). Christie Hospital has been given little option but to take part in the new opting-out proposals, despite considerable public outcry. A recent glossy brochure produced contained photos of beaming staff – snapped without their consent. Just down the road, the old Withington Hospital faces closure as part of plans for a new multi-million pound development in Wythenshawe. The new hospital is good news for the University – it will become an affiliated medical school, and the gleaming environs will be pleasant for all those with cars who can reach the place. However, the poor and the old will be forced on to difficult transport routes out to the southernmost tip of the city. Safe in their hands?

Blood Donor Service:	0800-300333
Health Authorities:	
Central:	061-276 1234
South:	061-445 8111
North:	061-795 4567
Family Health Services Committee:	061-276 3136
Sexually Transmitted Diseases:	061-276 5200 (men)
	061-276 5212 (women)

INDEX

21 Piccadilly, 75
42nd Street, 124, 131
5th Avenue, 76

A

Abasindi, 126
Abraham Moss Centre, 80, 85
Academy, 76, 78, 79
ACCOMMODATION
  LONG-TERM, 23
  SHORT-TERM, 25
Adlington Hall, 104
Affleck's Palace, 105, 106, 107
AIDSline, 131
Airport information, 16
Albert and Victoria Halls, 86
Albert Memorial, 66
All Points North, 129
Altrincham, 28, 101, 111
American football, 118
Amnesty International, 133
And God Created Manchester, 78
Apollo, 77
Archies, 124, 129
Arndale Centre, 105, 107
Arsenic and Old Lace, 106
Artful Reporter, 36
Arts Festival, 73
Ashton-under-Lyne, 29
Asian Women's Aid, 126
Athletics, 116, 119
Avant, 36
Awareness, 75

B

Band on the Wall, 78, 79
Bangladeshi Family Welfare & Advice Centre, 125
Banshee, 76
Barley, 94
Barton Arcade, 67
Basketball, 119
BBC Philharmonnic Orchestra, 85
BED AND BREAKFASTS, 25
BEERS AND BREWERIES
  Boddingtons, 48
  Chesters, 48
  Holts, 48
  Hydes, 48
  Lees, 48
  Robinsons, 48
Beeston Castle, 104
Belle Vue, 29
Belle Vue race track, 119
Belle Vue Showcase, 81
BLACK AND ETHNIC, 124
Black Lesbian and Gay Group, 126
Blackpool, 88
Blezards guest house, 25
Bloom Street Café, 130
Boardwalk, 78
Bollington, 104
Bolton, 88, 90, 111
Bolton Octagon, 84, 90
Bramham Hall, 71
British Pregnancy Advisory Service, 121
Broadfield Park, 93
Brontë sisters, 96
Burnage, 30
Burnley, 88, 95
Burnley Pot Fair, 95
Bury, 28, 29, 88, 92, 111
BUSES, 19
Butterfly World, 91
Buxton, 99
Buxton Country Park, 100
Buxton Opera House, 86, 99
Buzz, 80

C

CABARET, 79
Cahoots, 36
Calderdale, 93
Camelot Theme Park, 91
Campaign for Homosexual Equality, 130
Canals, 69
Cannon Salford Quays, 81
Capesthorne Hall, 104
Car Share Project, 17
Castlefield, 19, 66, 69
Castlefield Carnival, 73
Castlefield Gallery, 64
Castlefield Hotel, 25
Castleton, 100
Cathedral, 19, 32, 67, 86
Central Library, 66
Central Park, 129
Chamber House urban farm, 93
Champion, Sarah, 78
Change, 128
Chatsworth, 100
Cheadle, 30
Cheetham Hill, 28
Cheshire, 100
Chester, 102
Chetham's Library, 65
Chetham's School of Music, 67, 85
CHILDREN, 72
Chinatown, 19, 68, 110
Chinese Arts Centre, 64
Chinese New Year, 73
Chorlton, 30
Chorlton Water Park, 113
Christchurch, 86
CINEMA, 80, 81, 82
City Art Gallery, 63
City Council Guide to Services, 113
City Life, 34, 35, 36
City Road Inn, 25
CLASSICAL MUSIC, 85
Clitheroe, 94
Clone Zone, 130
CND, 132
Coach information, 16
Cod Almighty, 105
Contact Theatre, 79, 84
Corn Exchange, 105
Corn Laws, 31
Cornerhouse, 19, 45, 64, 72, 79, 82
Coronation Street, 34, 69
Council for Voluntary Service, 133
Council housing, 23
Councils, 135
Counthill Centre, 113
Craft Centre, 105, 106, 109
Crèche facilities, 122
Cricket, 114
Crumpsall, 28
Crumpsall Community Festival, 73
Cycling, 17, 18, 114, 119

D

Debdale Park, 113, 128
Delamere Forest, 104
Delph, 92
Denton, 29
Derwent Dams, 99
Design Centre, 108
Dickens, 130
Didsbury, 30
Disability Forum, 127
DISABLED PEOPLE, 126-127
Disabled Resource Unit, 128
Discothèque Royale, 75
Disley, 104
Dobcross, 92

Dry 201, 74, 106
Dunham Massey Hall, 101
Dunham Park, 101

E

East Lancashire Railway, 92
Eccles, 28, 50
EDUCATION, 134
Education Advice Service, 134
Entwistle, 91
ENVIRONMENT AND GREEN, 132
Equal opportunities, 120
Equal Opportunities Commission, 125
Evening News, 24, 34, 35, 36, 108

F

Failsworth Sports Centre, 128
Fairholmes, 99
Fallowfield, 30
Family planning, 121
Fence, 94
Fizz Boom, 130
Fletcher Moss Gardens, 71
Flixton, 27
Follies, 124, 129
Football, 116
Forest of Trawden, 97
Free Trade Hall, 67, 79, 85
Fridays, 76
Friends of the Earth, 133
Frontline, 108
FURTHER EDUCATION, 134

G

G-Mex, 66, 77, 85, 118
Gallery of English Costume, 59
Gatley, 30
GAY AND LESBIAN, 128
Gay Centre, 130
Gay Switchboard, 130
Gay village, 129
Girl About Town, 36
Glossop, 99
GMR, 37
Golden Dawn, 109
Golf, 114
Gorton Tub, 114
Granada Arboretum, 103
Granada studios tour, 68
Granada TV, 34
Greater Manchester Cycling Project, 18
Greater Manchester Passenger Transport Executive, 19
Greater Manchester Play Resources Unit, 72
Greater Manchester Police, 34
Greater Manchester Police Museum, 59
GREEN CONCERNS, 132
Green Room, 45, 72, 79, 82, 83
Greenpeace, 133
Greyhound racing, 119
Grumpy, 72
Guardian, 34
Guardian/Evening News tours, 68

H

Haçienda, 74
Haigh and Hochland, 108
Haigh Country Park, 90
Halifax, 97
Hall i' th' Wood, 90
Hallé Orchestra, 85
Harriet and Dee, 110
Haunted Manchester tour, 65
Haworth, 96
Haydock races, 90
Hayfield, 99
HEALTH, 136
HEALTH WOMEN, 121
Heartlands, 76
Heaton Park, 92
Heaton Park and Hall, 70
Hebden Bridge, 96
Hebden Water, 96
Helmshore Textile Museum, 92
Help and advice, 135
Heptonstall, 96
Hidden Gem (St. Mary's Church), 66
Hillside Ornamental Fowl Park, 102
HISTORY, 31
Holcombe Hill, 92
Holden Gallery, 64
Hotel Martinez, 25
HOTELS, 25
Housing Aid, 25
Housing Associations, 24
Housing Co-operatives, 24
Housing Corporation, 24
Hulme, 30
Hulme Young Black Women's Project, 126

I

Ice hockey, 118
Ice-skating, 113
Immigration Aid Unit, 125
International, 77, 79
International 2, 76, 77, 79
Interpreters' Unit, 128
Irish in Britain Representative Group, 126

J

JAZZ, 79
Jazz Festival, 73
Jewish Museum, 58
Jodrell Bank, 103
John Rylands Library, 65, 67
Jubilee Pool, 128
Jumbles Country Park, 91

K

Kaufman, Gerald, 33
Keighley Moor, 97
Key 103, 37
KFM Radio, 37
KIDS, 72
Kinder Plateau and downfall, 99
King Street, 67
Konspiracy, 74

L

La Cage, 129
Ladybarn, 30
Lake District, 87, 88
Lancashire, 87
Lancashire County Cricket Club, 114, 119
Lancashire County Cricket Museum, 60
Lancaster House hotel, 26
Laser Quest Labyrinth, 72
Last Drop Village, 90
LESBIAN AND GAY, 128
Lesbian Link, 130
Levenshulme, 30
LIBRARIES OF INTEREST, 65
Library Theatre, 83
Lincoln Service flats and hotels, 25
Link Up, 36
Little Moreton Hall, 104
Longsight, 30
Loot, 24, 35
Lumb Falls, 96
Lyme Country Park, 104

M

Macclesfield, 103
MAGAZINES, 35
Man Alive, 74
Manchester All Saints, 118
Manchester and Salford Film Society, 82
Manchester Area Resource Centre, 133
Manchester City F.C., 116
Manchester Museum, 57
Manchester Polytechnic, 19, 26, 77
Manchester Spartans, 118
Manchester United F.C., 116
Manchester United Foootball Museum, 60
Manchester University, 19, 26, 78, 82, 134
Manchester University Music Department, 86
Markets, 110
MEDIA, 34
METROLINK, 22, 127
Midland Hotel, 25
Mobberley, 102
Moon Festival, 73
Moss Side, 30
Moss Side District Centre, 131
Mulberry's, 79, 80
Museum of Science and Industry, 57, 69
MUSEUMS AND GALLERIES, 57, 58, 59, 60, 61, 62, 63, 64
MUSIC VENUES, 77

N

Napoleon's, 129
National Museum of Labour History, 60
National Museum of Working Horses, 97
New Continental Club, 76
New Union, 129
New York, New York, 129
Newchurch-in-Pendle, 94
NEWSPAPERS, 35
NIGHT BUSES, 21
NIGHTCLUBS, 74-76
Nightline, 132
Norman's Guest House, 26
North-West Arts, 80
Number One, 75, 129

O

Oasis, 110
Odeon Manchester, 81
Old Steam Brewery, 124
Old Trafford Community Centre, 124
Oldham, 28, 29, 92, 111
Oldham Athletic F.C., 117
Oldham Coliseum, 84
Oldham R.F.C., 118
One-parent advice centre, 122
One World Centre, 132, 133
Opera House, 83
Ordsall Hall Museum, 71
Organic Gardeners, 133
Orwell, George, 32

P

Paddy's Goose, 129
Palace Theatre, 83
Pankhurst Centre, 61, 123
Paradise Mill, 103
Paramount Book Exchange, 108
PARKS AND HOUSES, 69
Parsonage Gardens, 71
Peak District, 98
Peel Hall, 86
Peel Tower, 92
Pendle, 88, 93
Pendle Hill, 94
Pennine Way, 97, 98
Peterloo Massacre, 31, 67
Piccadilly Gold, 37
Piccadilly Radio, 37
Platt Fields Park, 70
POLITICS, 31
Ponden Hall and reservoir, 97
Portico Library and Gallery, 65
Portland Basin Industrial Heritage Centre, 62
Precinct 13, 74
Prestwich, 28
Prince of Wales, 25
PSV, 76
PUBS AND BARS, 47
Pubs of Character tour, 65
Pulse, 122

Q

Queen Street Mill Museum, 95

R

Racial Equality Council, 125
RADIO, 37
Rail information, 16
Ramsbottom, 92
Rape Crisis Centre, 121
Real Ale tour, 65
Recycling, 132
Red or Dead, 108
Redesmere, 104
Rees, Roger, 33
Rembrandt hotel, 129
RESTAURANTS (City Centre)
Armenian Restaurant, 44
Basta Pasta, 42
Bouzouki by Night, 44
Cafe Yaqoub, 41
City Art Gallery, 45
Coco Ristorante Pizzeria, 42
Cornerhouse, 45
Courtneys, 46
Cuckoo Chef, 41
Deansgate Indian Restaurant, 40
Dick's Last Resort, 42
Dry 201, 45
El Macho, 44
Everest, 41
George's Taverna, 44
Green Room, 45
Greens, 45
Happy Seasons, 40
Henry J. Bean's, 43
Henry's, 46
Howling Scream, 41, 43
Kathmandu, 40
La Péniche, 44
Little Yang Sing, 39
Manto Café, 46, 130
Market, 43
Mina Japana, 44
Muswells, 46
Olive Branch, 43
Penang Village, 40
Plaza, 41
Ronnies, 46
Viceroy of India, 42
Walcots, 45
Win Wah, 39
Yang Sing, 39
RESTAURANTS (North)
Pepe's, 42
RESTAURANTS (South)
Armenian Restaurant, 45
Café de Paris (La Crêpe Rit), 44
Café Paradise Lost, 41
Casa España, 44
Greenhouse, 41
Greens, 41
Kosmos, 44
Lime Tree Café, 41
On the Eighth Day, 41

Pie in the Sky, 41
Sanam, 40
Tandoori Kitchen, 40
That Café, 45
Tootsie's, 43
Righton Gallery, 64
Ritz, 76, 78, 79
Rochdale, 92
Rochdale Pioneers Museum, 93
Rockies, 129
Roller skating, 115
Roughlee, 95
Royal Exchange, 67, 82, 86, 105, 106, 108, 110
Royal Northern College of Music, 79, 85
Rugby League, 118
Rugby Union, 118
Rusholme, 30

S

Sabden, 94
Sacha's, 75
Saddleworth Moor, 92, 98
Saddleworth Museum, 98
Sale, 27, 101
Sale R.F.C., 118
Sale Water Park, 113
Salford, 28
Salford Mining Museum, 62
Salford Museum and Art Gallery, 62
Salford University, 26, 86
Sappho's, 124, 130
Scene Out, 36, 128, 130
Science Museum, 57, 69
Scorpion's Nest, 105
Sett Valley Trail, 99
Severe, 76
Shades City Centre Project, 132
Shambles Square, 67
SHOPPING, 105
Books, 108
Clothes, 107
Crafts and gifts, 109
Markets, 110
Records, 109
Signpost, 131
Silk Museum, 103
Single parents, 122
Skateboarding, 115
Ski Rossendale, 113
Smith, Sir Cyril, 33
Soccer Six Championships, 73
Socialist Conference, 73
Soundgarden, 75
South Manchester Music Festival, 73
Southport, 90
SPECIAL EVENTS, 72
Speedway, 119
Spice, 116
SPORT
AS A PARTICIPANT, 112
AS A SPECTATOR, 116
Sports Council, 116
St Ann's Church, 67
St Ann's Square, 67, 108
St Mary's Centre, 121
St Peter's Children's Centre, 122
Stalybridge, 29
Stockport, 112
Stockport Indoor Pavilion, 114
Straw, Jack, 33
Stretford, 27
Stretford Athletics Club, 119
Stretford Sports Centre, 128
Stringer, Graham, 33
Styal, 102
Sunset Radio, 37
Swimming, 114
Swinton, 28

T

Taboo, 121
Tameside, 29
Tameside Leisure Park, 114
Tatton Park, 102
TAXIS, 22
TELEVISION, 37
Ten-pin bowling, 115
Tennis, 115
The Café, 131
THEATRE, 82, 83, 84, 85
Three Sisters, 90
Ticket Shop, 82
TOURING COMPANIES, 86
Tourist Information Centres, 135
TOURS AND WALKS, 65
Town Hall, 66
Towneley Park, 95
Trafford, 27
Trafford Ecology Park, 71
Trafford Metros, 119
TRAINS, 18
Transport Muuseum, 58
Transvestite/Transsexual line, 130
TRAVEL AND TRANSPORT, 16
Turnpike Gallery, 64

U

Under-Fives Unit, 122
Uppermill, 92, 98
Uptown, 36
Urmston, 27

V

Verdene hotel, 25
Viewpoint Gallery, 64
VOLUNTARY WORK, 133

W

Waddington, 94
Waddington, Lord, 33
Wardle, 93
Warner Multiplex, 81
Warrington R.F.C., 118
Weaver's Triangle, 95
Wessenden, 98
West Indian Sports and Social Club, 126
West Yorkshire, 87
Whalley, 94
Whalley Range, 30
Wheatsheaf, 79
White Lodge hotel, 25
Whitefield, 28
Whitworth Art Gallery, 63
Whitworth Centre, 128
Wigan, 89
Wigan Pier, 89
Wigan R.F.C., 118
Wilmslow, 102, 112
Wilson, Anthony H., 38
Witchwood, 79
Withington, 30
WOMEN, 120
Women's Aid Centre, 120
Womenkind, 123
Workers Educational Association, 123, 134
Working Class Movement Museum and Library, 61
Worsley, 28, 89
Wythenshawe, 30
Wythenshawe Forum, 83
Wythenshawe Hall, 71

Y

YMCA, 26
Yorkshire moors, 88
YOUTH, 131
Youth hostel, 26
Youthline, 131
YWCA, 26

Pub Index

32 Club, 53

Albert Inn, 52

Beehive, 50
Beerhouse, 49
Beerkeller, 55
Bird in the Hand, 51
Braziers Arms, 50
Briton's Protection, 50

Castle, 49
Charlton Irish Club, 52
Cheshire Cheese, 99
Church Inn (Bolton), 130
Church Inn (Stalybridge), 56
Circus Tavern, 49
City Arms, 49
Claremont, 52
Coach and Horses, 51
Corbière's, 55
Cornerhouse, 55
Crescent, 53
Crown and Kettle, 50

Dry 201, 54, 74, 106
Ducie Arms, 53
Duke of York, 50
Duke's Gate, 50

Flea and Firkin, 53, 55
Fleece (Glossop), 79, 99
Friendship, 54

Gardener's Arms, 53
Greens, 55

Higher Buck, 94

Jackson's Boat, 46
Jolly Angler, 49, 53, 56

King's Arms, 48, 52

Lass o' Gowrie, 48, 53
Lower Buck, 94

Marble Arch, 49
Mark Addy, 46, 53
Mock Turtle, 46
Moulders, 53
Mr. Thomas's Chop House, 49

Nags Head, 56
New Inn, 130

Old House at Home, 51
Old Steam Brewery, 54, 124
Old Wellington, 49
Osborne, 47

Prince of Wales, 46

Queen of Hearts, 46, 54
Queen's Arms, 51, 55

Railway (Newton Heath), 51
Railway (Pottery Lane), 51
Red Lion, 54
Royal Oak, 46, 52, 54

Salutation, 52
Severe, 55
Sinclair's Oyster Bar, 49
Sparrow Hawk, 95
Star, 50
Station, 52, 56
Strawberry Duck, 91
Sun, 46
Swan Inn, 56

Tommy Ducks, 50
Traveller's Call, 52

Vine, 46

Waggon and Horses, 104
White Lion, 46
White Swan, 95

Walter Har

The N vengers 3: To Catch A Rat

Based on an original script
by Terence Feeley

Futura Publications Limited
A Futura Book

A Futura Book

First published in Great Britain in 1977
by Futura Publications Limited

ISBN 0 8600 7474 9
Printed in Great Britain by
Hazell Watson & Viney Ltd
Aylesbury, Bucks

Futura Publications Limited
110 Warner Road
Camberwell, London SE5

Richardson

THE NEW AVENGERS 3: TO CATCH A RAT

Also in THE NEW AVENGERS series

THE NEW AVENGERS 1: HOUSE OF CARDS

THE NEW AVENGERS 2: THE EAGLES NEST

CHAPTER ONE

The noise of a car engine washed up the stark, narrow lane four kilometres outside East Berlin, a bow-wave of noise that violated the silence of the night. Higher up the lane, moonlight glittered on the rusty, corrugated roof of an old barn; nearby, what had been a farmhouse crouched in ruins.

Inside the barn a man waited. Gunner had a memorable face; high cheek-bones sheltered in the lee of a powerful nose freckled and crannied with pores. Beneath Gunner lay an envelope, and in his right hand was a Mauser, trained on the door.

The noise of the engine had stopped some way down the lane; the man on the beam could hear no footsteps creeping towards him, but he sensed them. He waited like a trap-door spider listening to insect feet thudding through sand towards it.

My God, I want him, Gunner thought. I'll give him one bullet in the belly and another in the heart. Maybe a third lower down. One for Jennings, one for Hart, and one for Julie Bennett. Hope he sees their faces in his mind's eye before he dies – the bullets'll be their gift from the hereafter.

Footsteps, almost inaudible, canvas on dried earth. He's come early, wants to have a look round first. Thought he might – that's why I'm early myself. Come on, White Rat, you treacherous bastard. I should worry if you die an hour sooner than scheduled.

He's standing just outside the door, I know he is.

Can't see him but I can sense him. Vibrations – that's what I'm getting. He's uncertain – wonder what tale Cledge told him to get him here, what does he think is in that envelope?

Gunner relaxed slightly as the man outside moved away. Maybe he thinks the place is booby-trapped – no, he's just one for punctuality, that's all.

A half-hour passed; there was the sound of a car starting, approaching, stopping. The footsteps returned. The door opened very slowly; the man who eventually came in wore a Tyrolean hat with a frivolous feather, and a muffler.

He looked at the envelope, moved towards it, head swivelling from side to side, eyes probing.

Gunner longed to leap down on him, throttle the life from him, but restrained himself. The Mauser was pointing straight down at the man's neck.

'Hello, Rat.'

With the reflexes of extreme tension, the man below leaped aside, wrenched a gun from his pocket and fired upward just as Gunner pulled the trigger of the Mauser; both men were motionless for a second, deafened by the double explosion, before the White Rat dashed for the door.

Hit in the arm, Gunner cursed, half jumped, half fell to the ground, steadied the Mauser and held it in front of him like a votive offering. As the Rat went through the doorway the Mauser coughed for the second time – the Rat screamed and fell, just out of sight round the edge of the door. What a marvellous shot you are, Gunner told himself savagely, the bloody bloke's right beneath you and you have to muff it.

He stumbled after his quarry, arrived in the doorway

just in time to see an Opel accelerate swiftly down the lane; he fired again, but missed.

'Winged him in the leg, anyway,' trying to console himself. 'Do him good to sweat. From now on, no sweet dreams, just a question: when will they try next?'

With difficulty, Gunner pulled off his black sweater, examined his arm and satisfied himself that he had only suffered a flesh wound. It was very painful at that – he hoped the White Rat's hurt a great deal more. Christ, what I wouldn't have given to see his face.

Gunner made his way to a Volkswagen parked at the back of the barn, forced himself to press down on the gear-shift, gritting his teeth, and drove back to Leipzig, where Cledge, his partner in both Section Five of Department DI 6, and a trapeze act known as the Fabulous Flyers, awaited him in their caravan.

Cledge was a tall, powerfully-built man with treacle-coloured hair and the eyes of a frustrated sadist. Although he had worked with him for some years, Gunner still occasionally felt uneasy when looking at those eyes, knowing that his life depended on Cledge's skill as they swung on trapezes high above the heads of the crowd chilled by the performance taking place just beneath the Big Top.

'So what happened?' Cledge asked, eyeing Gunner's bandaged arm. 'Did you get him?'

Gunner shook his head in disgust. 'I fouled it up. Had him there, right below me, and I did it in.'

'It happens. Did you get a good look at him?'

'No, he was muffled up to the eyes.' Gunner gave a slight grin. 'I'd know him again, though.'

'Oh?' Cledge opened a can of beer. 'How?'

'I winged him in the leg. Sent him over, but he managed to make his car. But he'll limp, he'll always limp – must have torn the calf off him.'

'I see. Have you told London yet?'

'No. I'm going to tonight, after the show. That's when I'm due to make contact.'

'Steed won't be too happy,' Cledge said.

'Nobody'll be happy. But I'll get him next time – the White Rat's properly branded now. But I shouldn't have missed!' savagely.

'You're lucky he missed you too, except for a flesh wound. Think you'll be able to make it tonight?'

'I'll make it,' Gunner said. 'It'll hurt, but that'll be a kind of penance.'

Cledge handed him beer, smiled thinly. 'You don't want to think of it like that,' and patted Gunner consolingly on the shoulder.

Later, the two men climbed the long, flexible ladders to their trapezes, stood on small platforms facing each other.

Gunner gritted his teeth against the pain in his arm, swung gracefully away from the platform towards Cledge, who was moving quickly towards him. The trapezes described two arcs over the heads of the crowd, came together a third time – Gunner jumped towards Cledge's outstretched hands, presenting his wrists to Cledge's grasp.

The grasp never came. Unbelievingly, Gunner knew that Cledge had withdrawn his hands, had condemned him to death. For a fraction of a second he stayed in mid-air, like a cartoon character running over the edge of a cliff without realising it, before he started to plummet at the appalled faces rushing up at him.

There was no time to fear death, no time even to scream. There was only the sensation of his stomach rising to the back of his neck, of open mouths and a mass gasp of horror filling the tent; in his last moment of consciousness Gunner heard a cracking sound heralding extinction.

In the early morning, a car drew up at a dockside in Warnemunde. Quickly and implacably, two men carrying a third hurried on to the quay, climbed aboard a cargo ship, looked down into the open hold.

'This should do,' one of them muttered. He and his companion lifted the third man, wrapped in a tarpaulin, on to the edge of the hatchway, pushed, listened to the soft thud far below.

An hour later, the ship sailed.

CHAPTER TWO

Steed was an elegant man with the head of a Janus both of whose faces had been rolled into one. One of the faces exuded easy charm, the club face which could shake off club bores without making them feel slighted; the other face belonged to a man as efficient as he was warm, as ruthless as he appeared to be superficially indolent. Steed was the swordsman who dealt in repartee as well as in steel.

'I have a nasty feeling,' he said, 'that Gunner's only the latest in a highly unhealthy campaign against us.'

The person to whom Steed had spoken was a girl, standing beside him in the small radio room of Section D6 of British Intelligence. She was young and lithe and formidable, and known to her colleagues only by her surname, Purdey. A specialist in unarmed combat, Purdey had all the femininity when on duty of a firing-pin poised behind a cartridge. There was about her a lethal quality, an untouchability which few men had seen discarded. One of the men was Steed.

'What are we going to do about it?'

'An excellent question, Purdey. Each death has been made to look like an accident; in Gunner's, for instance, Cledge says he missed a handhold and fell from his trapeze.'

'Dangling from a trapeze isn't my idea of fun,' Purdey observed.

'No, you prefer to kick a loaded gun out of some villain's hand.' Steed smiled.

'Quite,' Purdey agreed coolly. 'Shall I do some kicking behind the Iron Curtain?'

'I don't think so. Whoever is on to us seems to know as soon as we send someone new out. No obvious slaughter – just an accident. If a tough pro like Gunner can't take care of himself . . .'

'How can little me?' Purdey interrupted.

'I have every confidence in you, sweet Purdey. At the same time, there's no point in dangling you as bait until we have an idea where the tiger is.'

'*If* there's a tiger. They might have been genuine accidents. Not for a moment that I think they were.'

'I think our friend in the enemy camp is shrewd and subtle – could be one of their people with a gift for guessing our moves in advance – a first-class chess player, perhaps.' He grinned at Purdey. 'Chess makes me think of boards, and the thought of boards makes me feel festive. Will you join me for a snack at Prunier's?'

'I'd be delighted,' demurely. Steed opened the door, followed her out into the broad, dim corridor of the Ministry.

CHAPTER THREE

The White Rat sat in a small room with a sign on the door proclaiming him to be manager of a wine exporting firm. The room was in a dull building in a dull street in Potsdam; the Rat looked out of the window at a matching sky.

There was a knock at the door; Cledge came in. He was wearing a brown raincoat with a turned up collar – he looks like a Volkspollizei, the Rat thought.

'I've been thinking,' Cledge said, sitting down. 'Supposing I'm suspected in London? They couldn't link me with Hart or any of the others I looked after before I did in Gunner, but Gunner – that's different. They've got a direct link there.'

'That looked more like an accident than any of the others. You worry too much, Cledge.'

Cledge scowled. 'It's all very well for you. You've been playing a double game for a long time; you have friends.'

'But so have you,' softly. 'I'm your friend.' The White Rat smiled, absently picked a matchstick from a box and snapped it as though it were the head of something small. His ashtray was full of matchsticks that had been snapped.

'Now go and do as I say, Cledge,' he went on. 'Just carry on as though you were as innocent as the day is long, and don't kill any other British agents until I say it's all right. I'm sure our East German friends will keep you in murder fodder.'

Cledge rose, stared hard at the White Rat, nodded and went out. When the clump of his footsteps on the rickety wooden stairs had ceased, the White Rat's comforting smile disappeared. He looked tense and wary. There was a smell of danger in the air.

Still, there's nothing I can do about it now – I'm in too deep. Anyway, now that Lydia's dead, does it matter so much if they get me?

Of course it does, he admitted to himself, in the barn, for instance – I'm glad that Gunner missed me. First came the shock, then an immense joy that I was still alive.

Maybe one day – even today, perhaps – I might find another Lydia.

He broke another match. It still surprised him, the hard, chilly, secret centre of himself which nothing could touch. His own cache of self-sufficiency, for use on an emotional rainy day. He had not become a traitor for Lydia's sake, but because he gained excitement from doing something evil.

To be totally amoral, to be devoid of principle and heedless of the lives of those who trusted him, pleased him. He was proud of his ruthlessness; Lydia had come nearer to vanquishing the frozen emotional core of him than anyone else.

He would have given a lot to know what had happened to her.

Looking out of the window, the White Rat remembered the manner of his defection. It had been during his second assignment in Central Europe.

He had been approached by a Hungarian, charming but, like the Rat himself, coldly introvert beneath the bonhomie. They had discussed women, watched them pass the Cafe on whose terrace they were sitting, drinking slivovitz.

The Hungarian had expressed his ideal of a woman – big, full-bosomed, blonde. A woman who could take a great deal of sexual punishment.

In his turn the White Rat had discussed his own notion of perfection – small, raven-haired, green-eyed, tireless.

A few days later, a girl who might have stepped straight from his sensual design-board knocked at the door of his flat. Lydia. She was a gift that he could not turn down, and the string that was attached to her led straight to an office in a dim, Gothic building in East Berlin.

Behind a large desk under the flag of the Deutchesbund Republik and the hard gaze of a photograph of Ernest Ulbricht, surrogate dictator of East Germany, sat a small, thin-faced man. About him there was an arctic quality, a polar self-containedness which made even the White Rat feel uncomfortable.

Here, the deal had begun to evolve. Lydia in exchange for the White Rat's services. The betrayal of other British agents, which would be compensated for by money and privacy with Lydia in a government-owned apartment.

The White Rat had sat uncomfortably on an ornate chair with a small and wobbly seat – like the rest of the office, it possessed ostentation without comfort.

'You will have to be subtle,' the small man said, with a smile like a razor-cut. 'But of course I do not have to tell you that. We do not wish your Intelligence people to become suspicious of you, do we? They are bound to suspect, when you have started to lead their agents into the hereafter, that something is going wrong here. You are, we think, intelligent enough and shrewd enough to be able to keep ahead of them. We will help you by permitting you to achieve certain – successes. One or two of our own people, those of little importance to us, will be sacrificed to your ingenuity. So long as we catch whales, we can afford a few sardines.'

'I see.' The White Rat smiled appreciatively.

'Good. We believe that one of your compatriots will be willing to help you. He has certain qualities that we can use.'

'Oh?'

'Like yourself, he has certain weaknesses. Or should I say that he has needs that we can satisfy? Not perhaps quite as healthy as yours, but nevertheless interesting to us.'

The White Rat looked into the small bleak eyes across the desk. 'How do I make contact with this compatriot?'

'Tomorrow at four o'clock in the afternoon, you will go to the Lederstrasse. At the junction with Dekkershof, you will find a taxi parked by the butcher's. Your contact will be sitting in the back of the taxi. He is a trapeze artist code-named the Catcher – your people – your other people,' with the razor-slash grin, 'have shown unexpected ingenuity in using a circus as cover.'

'We aren't by any means useless,' said the White Rat.

'Precisely. You haven't been. We hope that your employment with us will rectify that situation.' The small man rose, held out a small hand.

The White Rat took it; it was like shaking hands with a sweaty canary.

CHAPTER FOUR

The Lederstrasse was a canyon blasted by bombs that had wiped out a block of houses between two streets. As a result, the Lederstrasse was spacious and dead, with hardly any traffic moving along its ten carriageways.

Sauntering along, the White Rat saw a Skoda taxi pull up at the place indicated by his new employer; a flight of ancient bicycles went by like metallic birds migrating from one cheerless winter to another.

The man on the back seat of the taxi was tall and slender, with a sullen face. Supposing he doesn't want to join us at all, thought the Rat, supposing I'm being set up for a kill?

'You the White Rat?'

'I am. Are you the Catcher?'

'That's right. Cledge to my friends,' with a tight, unfriendly grin.

'Changed sides, have you?' he went on.

'Not really. I've become – shall we say, ambidextrous?'

'Call it what you like. How does it feel – are you happy?'

'It feels all right. I'm content.'

'I'm thinking of switching too.'

'So I understand.'

'As a matter of fact, I don't think I've the option any more. Not after meeting you. If I don't switch they'll finish me off.'

'In that case, let's assume that you have switched.

That is to say, that you're working for both sides.'

'Exactly. Ambidextrous, as you said.'

'So let's talk.' The White Rat climbed into the taxi, looked closely at the new recruit. 'What are you in it for?'

Cledge grinned. 'Don't you think it's for politics? I'd have thought it stood out a mile that I'm sick of Capitalism and that Communism's the only answer for me.'

'It doesn't stick out an inch.'

'All right, then. I want freedom.'

'In a Communist state?'

'Don't sound so surprised. Freedom has its variations, like everything else.'

'All right then – what sort of freedom?'

'The carte blanche sort.' The White Rat felt something cold scutter up his spine. 'I doubt if you'll find that sort of freedom anywhere.'

'No? I've got special skills, that's why they're interested in me. If I have carte blanche, I'll be a one-man firing squad. I like guns, but what the hell's the use of a gun if you can't use it?'

'Don't you kill enough people in the course of your assignments, to keep you satisfied?'

'Not really.'

'But why do you like killing?'

'It's not a question of liking, really. I just feel it's good for me – good for my health.' He went on: 'Look at it this way. A lion's locked up, but he's free to eat meat when the keeper brings it. Regularly each day, a fellow comes with a trolley-load of meat, and he feeds the lions. That's what I call freedom.'

'And you want to be fed victims? A sort of emotional Walpurgisnacht?'

'I'm not with you.'

'The night of the witches. Evil descending on the mountain, perched on broomsticks.'

'It's not evil to me,' Cledge said. 'I just want to be free to do as I like – if you like, I want the freedom of the city. I always thought how nice it must be, to get the freedom of the city. To go anywhere, do anything, walk into a shop and help yourself – everything on the city.'

'A credit card honour, in other words, with the city picking up the tab.'

'Exactly. I help myself. Our East German friends say: we want someone bumped off, I do it. Just the way the Nazis did.'

'All crime and no punishment,' murmured the White Rat. 'And what would you be prepared to offer in exchange for your – freedom?'

'Well, for a start I'd sort out some of our agents here. I gather there's one or two our friends would be glad to get rid of.' He tapped the White Rat's shoulder. 'And it needn't be only here, either. I might, for an extra consideration, have a go at Steed, for example. I don't much like that smooth bastard.'

'Steed, eh? I must say that would please the Republik, but it would stir things up too much.'

'Why? How could an accident stir things up?'

'Do you know,' the White Rat said, 'you might have something there?'

'I'm sure I have, mate. I mean, Rat,' as the White Rat glared at him.

'We'll meet at Wittgenstein's cafe in the Leninplatz tomorrow morning at 10.30. In the meantime, I'll think about what you've said.'

'Good. Don't forget to mention it to the boys at the Ministry of Intelligence here, will you? Who knows, I might get a bonus before I start.'

The White Rat climbed out of the taxi, watched as it drove away. He was not given to self-doubt, but he could not help wondering about his ability to control Cledge.

He walked back to his apartment, breaking the loose matchsticks in his pocket and thinking of the kudos that would attach to Cledge himself for the death of Steed.

CHAPTER FIVE

A man called Hart was the first British agent to contribute to Cledge's notion of freedom. Hart was a drab, careful man who worked with the unassuming intensity of a woodworm.

Methodically, patiently, Hart assembled his facts and sent them to London, where they were processed and acted upon. A gun flared in an alley, a man lay dead, and Hart was able to start on a fresh lot of facts for another strike.

The Cafe Poland was a small, dim bar frequented by lower echelon bureaucrats and junior grades of the secret police. Always on the lookout for information, they sometimes unwittingly parted with it to the dry, downtrodden little man who so obviously regarded them as heroes. They were used to him, a quiet man hiding behind a stein of beer.

Hart listened without appearing to, spoke when spoken to, occasionally bought a round in the submissive way of one asking a favour which will benefit the person asked more than the person making the request.

Cledge came into the Poland, demanded beer, talked to the bartender in pidgin German. He was dressed in dungarees, gave the impression of being a sailor, probably from a Russian coaster.

Hart did not know Cledge, but he was sure the man was a fake. But a fake what? He smiled a timid smile and addressed Cledge in German. Cledge answered in his pidgin German, insisted on buying Hart a drink. He told Hart that he was a sailor – ah, thought Hart, he's a fake sailor, then. But what is he really? He asked a number of questions about the life of a sailor, commenting on the interesting aspects of a mariner's life, bought a drink in his turn. Finally, Cledge put his arm round Hart's shoulder and ushered him outside, telling him that there was a better bar a few streets away.

Hart had a sense of vivid danger, but was not sure how to act upon it. There was a knife in his pocket, but he could not bring himself to kill Cledge purely on suspicion.

Cledge suffered from no such inhibitions. He waited until he and Hart were a hundred yards from the Poland, in deep shadow; he still had his arm companionably round the smaller man's shoulder. Now he slid it up to his neck, slipped it under his chin, and squeezed relentlessly until there was a sharp crack.

Carefully placing Hart under the front wheel of his hired Opel, Cledge started up, lurched forward over Hart's neck, accelerated down the street. He was singing lustily, and laughing to himself as he thought of the small, dirty bundle in the gutter back down the road, and the commendation he would receive to-morrow.

There was no doubt about it, working for the White Rat was just the job.

CHAPTER SIX

After Hart, Cledge was given the enjoyable task of eliminating a new, highly promising young agent code-named Hummingbird. Hummingbird's real name was Julie Bennett, a small, alert girl whose speciality was dressing up as an old woman and getting work as a char in places where information might be gathered without much heed being paid to a heavily aproned hag with a mop and bucket.

Gunner had known Julie before she entered Intelligence, had in fact recommended her to Steed. Steed was doubtful about accepting an existing agent's girl friend, but in Julie's case had waived any fear he might have had that she might come to harm and be used as a weapon against Gunner.

Firstly, Gunner was not in love with the girl; instead, he had an almost paternal affection for her. Secondly, Julie was very tough, a girl who had been born and brought up in the Gorbals and won a scholarship to Edinburgh University. She lacked the appeal of a Purdey, but had the same steely ability to look after herself. It failed her when she met Cledge.

Julie finished her charring at the Ministry of Defence at midnight, picked up her heavy bucket, limped painfully down a corridor to the broom closet, put bucket and broom inside. Hand to the small of her back, she straightened up, wondering what it would be like to be really old and arthritic. Who knew, maybe forty years from now, she would become the woman she was playing at being. Ridiculous – she would remain working for British Intelligence for a few more years, then marry and settle down comfortably. There would be no chance of herself being as her mother and aunts had been, poor, undernourished and well-nigh illiterate. There would be a much better future for Julie, just as there was already a much better present than her mother had ever had.

Having put her accessories in the broom closet, Julie hobbled to the top of the stairs, leaned on the stone balustrade. Tier after tier of floors, the basement floor in distant perspective far below. When the lifts went wrong, which they often did, Julie and her fellow charwomen had to climb the stairs, clutching at the cold stone banisters to heave themselves upward; they stopped and gasped and went on, the stone rubbing painfully at their worn grey mittens.

To-night, a man was climbing the stairs, a tall, powerful man in a jersey and flat blue cap. Something nautical about him, Julie thought. Wonder what he wants, whom he's going to see. Not many officials left at this time of night.

''Abend,' touching his cap.

'Guten Abend,' echoed Julie in an old woman's high-pitched, respectful voice.

The man paused beside her. 'I'm a friend of Irwin Gunner,' he breathed.

Julie glanced at him sharply. 'Was haben Sie gesagt?'

'I said I'm a friend of Irwin Gunner.'

Julie did not reply, turned to hobble away. 'It's all right, Hummingbird,' with a grin.

'Did Gunner send you?'

'That's right. He gave me a little message for you.'

Something was wrong – not what the man was saying, although that did not somehow ring true, what the man was. There was a touch of Satan about him – he had wicked eyes.

The eyes came closer to Julie's; Cledge reached down and took off the steel-rimmed spectacles. 'You're not a bad looker, without these.' He snapped them in two, grinning as he reflected that that was what the White Rat did to matches.

Julie reached beneath her apron for the small pistol she kept there, but Cledge's hand clamped on hers and she knew at that moment that she was about to die.

'Naughty.' Cledge brought her arm up hard behind her back; the pistol clattered on the floor. Julie yelled as Cledge forced her on to the stone rail, saw the stairs in their frozen cascade falling distantly to the tesselated red star on the ground floor.

Desperately she brought up her right foot, kicking Cledge from behind in the genitals. He doubled up, but as he did so thrust his great hands forward. Flinging Julie outward, he sent her viciously over the banisters, watched her spin screaming past flight after flight of stairs. Finally he managed to stumble forward to peer through the balustrade as she hit the ground.

'The bitch,' he muttered, as he slowly descended the stairs. 'the bitch. My God, she got what was coming to her.' The sight of her pulped body scarcely assuaged Cledge's hate; later in the day, still not sated, he obtained the White Rat's congratulations and permission for a further operation against British Intelligence in East Germany.

So it happened that a third British agent died. Maurice Jennings was on a train sitting by himself, when the door of his compartment opened. A big man with a cruel smile came in, opened the door on the opposite side.

Oh my God, Jennings thought, he's going to commit suicide. Suicide was, however, not what was in the man's mind. He seized Jennings, tripped him, upended him.

Jennings saw the rail flowing by just below his nose, saw a haze of ballast, shrieked as Cledge carefully lowered him until his head was level with the two wheels of the bogey beneath the open door.

With his strong acrobat's arm, Cledge swung Jennings out, let his head come back to crash against the step, let him swing out again and then, on the return, let him go, to fall between the wheels.

Jennings was decapitated instantly; his head bounced at high speed from the rail and bumped and rolled down an embankment. Cledge laughed aloud, rubbed his hands in glee, closed the carriage door and sank on to a seat.

Freedom, that was what he had got for himself, freedom. And the great thing was, there need be no end to it.

CHAPTER SEVEN

'We've got to find out who the swine is!' Gunner was furious in grief, restless with frustration. He could not sit down for more than a moment, kept fetching beer for himself and Cledge, downing it, going to the tiny caravan kitchen for more. 'To kill Julie – my God, I'd give anything to have my hands round his neck. And to finish off Hart and Jennings—'

'But what proof do we have? They seem to have been accidental, all three of them.' Cledge tried to sound consoling – in fact, he was thoroughly enjoying himself.

'Three agents killed within the space of a few hours – by accident? Christ, that's stretching coincidence a bit far, don't you think? No, someone's on to us, someone who knows exactly what we're up to and what it's all about!'

'So what do you suggest?' Cledge asked softly.

'It stands to reason that whoever it is, is quite high up. No ordinary field personnel would have known about Julie and Hart and Jennings, what their movements were and so on. Not unless he was briefed. And you don't go round getting rid of people like that unless you have the authorities winking at you, do you?'

'I suppose not.' Cledge frowned, trying to look commiserating; Gunner made his way to the miniature bathroom and scrubbed his teeth in mineral water. He was uneasy – there was something about Cledge, something indefinable. Seven times a week Gunner trusted Cledge with his life, yet there was something there that he could not trust, deep as a maggot in an apple. He came back from the bathroom, laid down on the narrow bed in the grey-walled cubicle which was his bedroom. Exhausted by his emotion at hearing of Julie's death, he soon slept.

Cledge waited until he had started to snore, crept out of the caravan, made his way to a telephone and dialled a number. 'White Rat? I've an idea.'

'You're not supposed to call me here unless it's urgent.' The White Rat's voice was angry.

'Isn't getting rid of Steed urgent?'

Silence. 'All right, carry on,' resignedly.

'I want to receive some information,' Cledge said. 'Nothing official. My idea is this.' He spoke for some minutes.

You're more dangerous that I thought, the White Rat reflected. I'd put you down purely as an order-taker, but you're more than that. You're capable of good ideas.

'All right, Cledge. You'll receive that information.'

'We leave for Potsdam tomorrow.'

'Right. It'll arrive by post, the day after tomorrow.'

'Good. Sweet dreams,' Cledge said, and hung up; he returned to the caravan, wondering whether a pillow firmly thrust over Gunner's face would improve him, decided to let him live for the time being. Steed after all was the immediate, the valuable target.

Smiling to himself, Cledge prepared for bed.

Two days later, a letter arrived for Cledge, bearing an English postmark.

'It's my mother,' he told Gunner, 'she's been taken ill. I've been granted compassionate leave.'

'Sorry to hear it,' Gunner said. 'Hope she'll be better soon.'

'I hope so – as long as you can keep things going for a day or two.'

'I'll do my best.' Commiseratingly, Gunner patted Cledge's shoulder.

CHAPTER EIGHT

Down the Ministry steps came Steed to step into a Whitehall summer evening. Pigeons did their best to camouflage the dreadful postwar architecture perpetrated by philistine committees, buses pulled ponderously away from their stops or gleefully ignored them.

Parked by the kerb nearby was a grey Morris Traveller, with a grey man hunched behind the wheel. Grey hair, grey complexion, grey, shabby suit. Even the spectacles resting half way down his nose had a grey tint; he looked like a sick market gardener who had come to London to see a specialist.

Steed turned into the Ministry car park, retrieved his open blob-blob Bentley, and drove towards Trafalgar Square. He noticed in his mirror that the Morris had come to life, was following in his wake across the messy Haymarket–Pall Mall intersection and up Lower Regent Street.

So what – there must be hundreds of similar cars driven by similar people. So, his instinct told him, there's something odd about that car. Something wrong.

At the lights halting traffic at Oxford Circus, Steed leaped lightly from the Bentley, walked past a van, addressed the Traveller's driver.

'Hello, haven't we met before?'

Cledge was disconcerted. 'I don't think so,' in what he hoped was the tone of voice to go with his appearance.

'I'm so sorry.' Steed smiled, tilted his hat, ran back

to the Bentley in time to avoid too many impatient honks as the lights changed.

'I'll teach you to play games with me,' Cledge muttered under his breath. 'A belly-full of dum-dum bullets, that's what you're going to get in a minute.'

Reaching to the seat beside him, Cledge took a Schmeisser automatic and switched it to his right hand. He saw the Bentley turn off Portland Place into Weymouth Street, licked his lips in anticipation. A taxi interposed itself between the two cars, and with the consideration of its kind for other road users, double-parked alongside the Bentley, to emit a tall young blonde in sables.

'Darling, how well met,' said Steed, raising his hat. He went over to the cab-driver, paid him, approached Cledge. 'Are you sure you're not lost?' he asked blandly. Cledge fingered the Schmeisser and sweated. Steed looked benignly through the window. 'You look a trifle worried about something, old chap. Anything I can do?'

'I'm just waiting for your friend's taxi to move,' in high-pitched impatience.

'Ah yes, they can be a bit obstructive, our hackney friends. Never mind, he's going now,' as the taxi moved slowly away.

Steed stood back; Cledge let in the clutch. In his rear-view mirror he saw Steed escort the blonde up the front steps, and scowled, his lips assuming the bitter line of a man who has never been loved, but is aware that he has missed something.

'Damn, now I'll either have to wait all night and get him in the morning, or just go up to his front door later and plug him when he answers the bell. Unless he's got a butler or something – the Rat ought to have given me more griff about that. Should have asked for a thousand for doing this job, instead of a lousy five hundred,' he told himself.

Cledge steered the Morris into a mews, parked, walked round to the front of Steed's building, glanced at it as he passed. A massive, highly-polished front door, several brass plates advertising the presence within of numerous members of the medical fraternity, a plain brass tab with no name on it.

Frowning, Cledge went back to the Morris, leaned against it, thought of Steed and the blonde and was aware of a strange, unpalatable sensation. Lighted windows, a distant burst of laughter, taxis hurrying by on errands of entertainment, were destroying his self-sufficiency; all at once, Cledge felt unbearably lonely.

CHAPTER NINE

The record-player breathed muted music across the room. 'Baby, it's cold outside,' sang Louis Prima; Steed sympathised with his efforts to keep his girl in the warmth.

'Even though it isn't cold outside, you don't have to go, do you?' he asked, slowly running a hand across the shoulder of the girl who was bending over, pulling up a stocking.

'Darling, I have to. They worry if I'm not back by midnight.'

'But you're over twenty-one.'

'Only just.'

'And you're no Cinderella,' pulling her gently down and kissing the nape of her neck.

'No,' the girl said, 'I'm an ugly sister.'

Steed laughed. 'Are you now? I'd say you were a very beautiful sister.'

'But I really must go.'

'Nobody will be more disappointed than I,' as the record-player conveyed the last chorus of the lyric, hesitated, lifted from the plastic and returned to its rest. With a click of satisfaction, it switched itself off.

'I'm not exactly raring to go,' the girl said. 'Any time you make your bed, I'll lie in it. But I must go tonight. Don't forget – next week they'll be away.'

'I may be too.'

'Oh no!' with flattering dismay.

'Oh yes.'

'Where?'

'A little tour on the Continent.'

'Couldn't I come too?'

'I'd love to take you, darling, but it's business.'

'Can't it wait?' beseechingly.

In view of Matthew's lack of enthusiasm, of course it can. Steed, you old devil, you just wanted to see her reaction.

'I suppose it'll have to.' The lustre of appreciation in her eyes – she's still not old enough, or vain enough, to know that business ought to step aside in favour of a beloved woman, not the other way about. Still, how many men realize that?

'Well,' rolling off the bed, 'I'd better drive you home.'

'No. I can take a cab.'

'You'll do no such thing. It's not my gallantry that's withered.'

The girl laughed. 'It's no tribute to me that you can still stand on one leg,' as Steed pulled on his trousers.

He kissed her. 'I've paid all my tributes for one night.'

'Magnificently.'

Rotating the car keys in his fingers, Steed opened the front door, led the way down a wide staircase, stood aside to let the girl into the street.

Right opposite, Cledge watched with the eyes of a crocodile surveying a waterhole. The Schmeisser lay with its muzzle on the window-frame, its butt tucked into his shoulder. Impulsively, the girl stepped in front of Steed, kissed him – he embraced her in return.

Cledge again felt loneliness, a desire to be loved for his highly unlovable self; he could not comprehend that affection is a form of barter.

A seemingly endless American car with a proud chauffeur and humble-looking emissary crouched in the back, passed between Steed and the Schmeisser; when it had finally gone by Steed and the girl were in the Bentley.

Cledge started his Morris, following his quarry through the West End to Marble Arch and thence to Holland Park.

'Nice pad,' muttered Cledge, as the Bentley drew up outside a house in Addison Road. 'Maybe I'll look you up some time,' to the girl kissing Steed fifty yards away.

A final hug; the girl mounted the front steps with the sort of antelope grace that befitted one wearing sables.

Steed waited until the front door had shut irrevocably on his evening, swung away from the kerb, headed back into Holland Park Road, Cledge drawing up closer behind him.

The Morris's sidelights stared at Steed from his rear-view mirror, like the eyes of a determined but rather under-powered animal. He accelerated; the lights sank back, paused, began to move forward.

He's spotted me, thought Cledge, prepare for some tricks.

Steed made as though to follow Holland Park Road through to Bayswater Road, whipped the wheel over to send the Bentley on its hard, unyielding but stable suspension into Palace Gardens Terrace; hard right along Rabbit Row he sent the car, with an enraged bellow, then right again back into the main road.

Less agile, the Morris swayed in the Bentley's wake, nearly turned over as it keeled to the right; Cledge turned off the main road and began to travel fast through the back streets that might bring him out in front of Steed's building before Steed reached it.

Seeing that he was no longer followed, Steed allowed the car to lose way, coasted to a stop, sat behind the quietly turning engine and thought. He drove into a garage forecourt, left a note on the windshield, hailed a cab, gave an address a hundred yards away from his own.

Cledge, congratulating himself on arriving first, saw the taxi stop, hardly looked at it. It had come from the east; Steed would approach his home from the west.

'Where is the bastard? Don't tell me he's gone back to the bird.' Cledge slouched in his seat, lit a cigarette. Steed's taxi clattered into the distance, its passenger a deeper shadow in a shadowed doorway.

Steed saw the glow of the cigarette, took off his bowler, left it in the doorway, sauntered towards the Morris.

Cledge saw the aimlessly advancing figure, discounted it – Steed's flat was opposite, this bloke was coming along on the same side of the road as himself. About the same height as Steed, but not wearing anything on his head.

Might as well make sure – maybe he doesn't leave his car outside all night, maybe he's left it at a garage round the corner. Wait till he reaches that street lamp, that should show whether it's Steed or not. Can't be – he's climbed that flight of steps back there – and look, he's as tight as a tick. Hardly managed it, weaved all over the place. Cledge grinned. What a chance to roll him and pinch his wallet, though there probably isn't anything left in it – he's no doubt had a very expensive night.

Swaying, Steed stood in front of the door, holding up

keys and dangling them in front of his eyes. He staggered backwards, gave a dramatic impersonation of a windmill as his arms flailed helplessly.

Cledge laughed aloud as the drunk landed on the pavement, rolled over, tried to regain his feet. Headlights appeared ahead – he forgot the drunk, concentrated on them. Doesn't look like a Bentley – they're too small, set at the side like ears. Bentley's got goggles, frog's eyes near the top of the radiator.

The lights came nearer, showed a man levering himself lithely from the pavement, running towards a parked car.

Temporarily blinded, Cledge did not realise until too late that he had been careless; a pair of powerful hands locked on to his throat.

'Waiting for someone?' The melodious, ruthless voice gave him no time to answer, even had he been able to. 'I believe you were following me tonight – now tell me, what can I do for you?'

Cledge reached up, tried desperately to deliver a numbing punch at the biceps above his right ear. It landed too low; the hands did not loosen at all.

'Naughty,' Steed murmured, 'I can see I shall have to hurt you.' He drew back his hand, presented the edge of it hard at Cledge's Adam's apple. Cledge choked, blacked out, felt himself being hauled out of the car.

'What's going on here?'

'Good evening, officer. We've just come home – I'm afraid my friend is a little the worse for drink. It was quite a party.'

'He was driving,' accusingly.

'No indeed – I was driving. I'm just helping him out this side, that's all.'

The policeman eyed Steed suspiciously, smelled no alcohol on his breath, moved on with all the dignity of a night-watchman taking an antelucan stroll along a promenade.

Steed supported Cledge under the arms, manoeuvred him with difficulty up to his front door, began to lug him upstairs. Cledge vomited violently, so Steed dropped him.

'How unattractive of you,' he murmured; Cledge lashed out at Steed's groin and connected. As Steed doubled up, Cledge summoned all his strength to run down the stairs, wrenched the front door open, gritted his teeth and managed to reach his car.

'Thank God I had false plates on,' he told himself, surging down the street – 'the bastard, the bastard, I'll get him next time.'

Alerted, Steed made sure that there was no next time – baffled, unwilling to risk suspicion, Cledge had to return to East Germany, his mission unaccomplished. No one was pleased with him, and nobody less so than himself.

CHAPTER TEN

Like a virus, resentment ate into Cledge. Regarded with basilisk lack of cordiality by the White Rat, Cledge found dreams of his own brand of freedom fading; he had to redeem himself for his failure to kill Steed. He simmered and brooded and hated – someone was going to pay for his loss of face.

'What's up?' Gunner asked kindly. 'Still worried about your mother?'

'That's right.'

'Maybe they'll give you some more compassionate leave soon.'

'I hope so.' What happens when I next go to England – will Steed recognise me? That make-up was pretty good, but you never know. Don't they say that the ears can't be disguised?

Cledge imagined Steed poring over photographs, gazing at a back-of-head view of a man, recognising it.

That's all I need. Answer a summons to London, walk into the room, find Steed smiling as he tells me he knows I tried to kill him. Cledge tried to imagine what Steed would do – instant execution, perhaps? Lie down on that tarpaulin, old man – that's right. Don't want your blood to ruin my carpet. A gun in his hand, pointed at Cledge's heart. What would I do Cledge asked himself, say a few prayers? No, I'd go for him – that's the best way to die, when you're attacking.

Meanwhile, someone had to pay for his humiliation.

The White Rat – it was his fault. Yet the Rat was the key to the sort of life Cledge wanted, so that he could not be hurt directly. But indirectly? A devious plan insinuated itself into Cledge's mind. Kill several birds with one stone, or at least knock them unconscious.

'I think I know who the White Rat is,' he told Gunner one evening. 'I'm not sure, though – I'll have to keep him under observation for a few days – don't want to score a hit on the wrong guy.'

'I'm with you,' Gunner said eagerly.

'Later – I can handle it easier by myself, to start with. If I'm right, I'll call you in. You just stay on here as though nothing had happened.'

Reluctant agreement; Cledge packed a bag, checked into a dismal pension in Potsdam, telephoned the White Rat's number.

'Hello?' A woman's voice, husky as though she had just awakened.

'Hello,' Cledge said. 'Is – er – your husband in?'

'Not at the moment. Can I give him a message?'

'It's all right. I'll call back later.'

He hung up, grinned to himself. That bird sounded all right. Nice voice, probably sang contralto in the bath. Cledge thought about a woman in her bath, her serenity. It was so easy to disturb a woman's serenity, so easy to shatter her. A harsh word, a leer, and there was the terror, the satisfying and soothing terror. I wonder if I'd have been different if I'd been loved, thought Cledge; he had never asked himself why he had never been loved. The cruelty was luminous in him, an affliction of the spirit that glowed malevolently in the depths of his eyes, turned the ends of his mouth downward.

The Rat's woman – wonder if he'd miss her?

Later that evening, Cledge rang again. 'Is your husband in yet?'

'Not yet. Who is that, please?'

'A friend. Would you ask him if he can be at Wittgenstein's at three tomorrow?'

'I will tell him.'

'Thanks.' Disconnection. Cledge wished that he could project himself along the telephone cable, emerge from its conduit to see the astonished face of the White Rat's woman. What a game it would be, to be able to travel like a voice, to come upon the sources of intimate conversations. Cledge felt himself growing excited, saw a woman in a shabby raincoat standing in the shelter of a ruined arch, approached her.

God, she thought, he's a whipper. You can always tell the men who do not like women as women, who need something weaker than themselves on whom to vent unnatural longings.

'Are you busy, darling?' Cledge leered at her; she had a young but thin face, large, resigned eyes.

'Yes. I am waiting for someone.'

'Me?'

'Not you.'

Cledge wanted to strike her there and then – damned impertinence, who does she think she is, rotten little whore? – but restrained himself. Turned down by a tart; my God, someone was going to pay, pay for all the affronts, all the insult of not being attractive to women.

He walked on, leaving the girl staring straight ahead, trembling with reaction. The White Rat's woman, I wonder what she looks like? He looks the type to find himself something classy, something elegant and attractive. Like Steed's woman – Cledge clenched his fists.

My God, I'd like to take her. Know where she lives – no problem. If only I had the time – can't risk another visit to England without permission. Next leave, though – just wait until next leave, he told himself.

Meanwhile, there are other things to do.

He was looking forward to next day, at the Cafe Wittgenstein.

CHAPTER ELEVEN

'Well?' The White Rat's eyes were hostile; he broke several matches, stuffed them into an ashtray of mottled green stone.

Cledge suppressed a surge of anger at the Rat's tone of voice, looked at the crowded street beyond the terrace wall, sipped beer.

'I muffed killing Steed last time – I won't next.'

'I'm afraid apologies don't wash in our business. You either deliver or you don't.'

'Who said I was apologising?' Cledge gave a thin sneer. 'I was just making an observation – I made a mistake the other day, I shan't next time Steed and I come across each other.'

'If you do – we can't send you across to England every time your mother's indisposed, you know.'

Cledge chuckled without humour. 'If I'd known my mother, I might have been different. All I ever knew of maternal love was a photograph of a woman with a baby, and she wasn't even looking at it, just smiling into the camera.'

'What happened to her?'

'I don't know – I was a foundling. Dumped on the steps of an orphanage in a shawl with a note pinned on me – I've still got it. "Please take care of John." So they did – I don't suppose you've ever enjoyed the affection of an institution? It's not that they're over harsh, these days, but for every word of encouragement there's a rebuke, you never do anything completely right without being told that you've done well, except for—

'I'll tell you this, too,' Cledge went on, 'it's damn difficult to love an institution.'

'But surely there were individuals—'

'Oh yes, there were those. But they couldn't take too much of our love, or they'd have been swamped. So what happened? Naturally they chose the kids they wanted to love and could afford to be loved by – the rest of us were OK, but they couldn't emotionally afford to give us much.

'Anyhow, as I was saying, we can't send you across to England every time your mother – or your institution – is indisposed. By failing with Steed, you have tarnished my reputation, as well as your own. We—'

'Tarnished your reputation, have I? Which reputation?' Cledge was feeling savage, the crack about his institution had enraged him. 'Your reputation as a loyal member of British Intelligence, or your reputation among our friends here as a traitor?'

'Look here—'

'Nobody esteems a traitor,' Cledge went on, 'you know that. Nobody ever got any medals for betraying his own side. If you want to do that, you can't expect anything but money, privilege, and contempt. I can live with that sort of contempt, but you obviously can't. Not if you're going to talk about your tarnished reputation.'

The White Rat's face was pale, he was trembling with anger. Other habitues of Wittgenstein's sensed the sparks of antagonism flashing between the two men, watched with interest and embarrassment.

'Now look,' Cledge went on, 'I've got an idea. Steed has a woman – a good looker at that. I can get at him through her. I know where she lives.'

'You also know where he lives. Why go to all that trouble? Why not just shoot him as he comes out of his front door, or puff a dart tipped with curare at him?

'Alternatively,' the White Rat continued sarcastically, 'you could rent an Irishman to put a bomb under his car – just tell the IRA that Steed's their mortal enemy.'

'I prefer the oblique approach myself. Think how many people have bankrupted themselves to pay ransom for a kidnapped dear one,' sneering, 'or been willing to sacrifice themselves if only the nasty kidnapper would let the dear one go. It's effective and it's less dangerous.' He leaned forward. 'It's the end result that's important, isn't it?'

'We're discussing the end result. The easiest way to accomplish it is the direct one.' His eyes dropped before the intensity of Cledge's stare. 'Anyway, Steed isn't the only one. What about your colleague in the trapeze act? Gunner, you said his name was.'

'That's right, he's planning one or two surprises for the White Rat. Maybe you'd better prepare one for him.'

'Maybe you could. That would be a redeeming mark in your favour, I can assure you of that.'

Cledge allowed himself a smile. 'I'll bear that in mind. Mark you, redemption may be enough for most people, but don't forget the other things I'm interested in.'

'They won't be forgotten,' the White Rat said. 'Now, do you think you can get rid of him without anyone at home—'

'Where?' interrupted Cledge maliciously.

'In England,' flushing, 'suspecting that his death wasn't an accident?'

'I'll think about it.'

'Right.' The White Rat paid the bill, nodded at Cledge, walked briskly away. The chap made him feel positively unclean, positively – the word surged into his mind, unbidden – positively tarnished. How dare he make fun of him, try to reduce the Rat's estimation of his own value. Not to mention that of the East Germans – they respected him, no question of it, the Rat tried to convince himself.

He was so put out that he did not notice Cledge following him at a distance; he strode quickly along the pavement towards home.

Lydia respects me, Lydia loves me, Lydia will soothe me. The Rat smiled in anticipation of the restoring of his ego, turned into his apartment house, began to climb stairs.

Cledge sprinted to the building's front door, walked lightly up the stairs, marked the source of echo as the White Rat's door slammed shut.

Cledge made his way back down the stairs and out of the place. I'll show him, he won't be so superior in future. I'll show him and get some kudos from him and his mates into the bargain.

Who knows – I might even get some kudos from my own.

CHAPTER TWELVE

Lydia Quaritsch had the beauty of a black chrysanthemum. Her hair was jet, as were her eyes; both shone. Her body was supple and not too thin; when she walked, her buttocks rotated and her breasts formed a sublime outpost. Many men had wanted Lydia, and many men had enjoyed her, but since she had met him, the White Rat had been the only beneficiary of her affection.

She was waiting for him to return – when he was out, she became swiftly bored. She sat in a deep armchair, and wished that his lap was beneath her, fondled her breasts gently and wished that her hands were his.

A ring at the bell. Had her darling forgotten his key? She hurried to the door with anticipation, opened it to look into the face of a stranger.

'May I come in? I'm a friend of your husband.'

'Please do.' But who are you – I have never heard him mention a friend, an Englishman who was here, in East Germany. And this man's eyes – they are not the eyes of a friend.

'Would you like something to drink. A slivovitz, perhaps?'

'That would be nice,' Cledge said, 'thank you.'

Lydia went over to a cupboard, took out a bottle and one glass. Cledge watched the way she moved, with enjoyment, came up behind her as she was pouring, and slapped a chloroformed pad against her nose and mouth.

She struggled, tried to kick backwards, grazed

Cledge's shin. After a few moments, she sagged into Cledge's arms.

'That's my beauty. Nice and easy, nice and relaxed.' Cledge carried her into the bedroom, carefully undressed her, assiduously raped her. After that, he dressed her again, carried her to the back door, down the back stairs, and paused while he looked out into the street.

His hired Opel stood just in front of him, a venerable car mouldering under a patchwork quilt of various paints. Nobody about, everything nice and discreet – Cledge put Lydia on to the floor at the back and tucked a rug round her.

Squeezing behind the wheel, Cledge grinned to himself, wondered exactly what he was going to do with his captive. Everything else was clear, because it had to be, but the fate of the girl behind him was not as important. Not important at all.

The car ground away from the kerb, fended off some half-hearted bicycles at an intersection, moaned harshly along rough, traffic-free roads between buildings whose shattered masonry and brickwork were the tablets on which a history of violence from the air had been viciously recorded.

Clumps of moss and grass thrusting themselves from the ruins became withered and splintered trees, scraping at the sky with leafless vernal branches. Inserted in the branches, nests of optimistic birds waited for eggs to hatch in the renewal time of year.

Christ, thought Cledge, this country is a dump. I wonder if I could stand living here permanently. Not that I'll have to – I'm going to come out of this a bloody hero. To both sides. Now, let's see – the turn-off must be quite near now. Have to change down to get over these furrows – what I really need is a bloody tank. Ah, here we are, left up this lane, go on for a couple of miles.

The Opel lurched slowly along, forcefully pressing on rebellious springs. To one side of the rutted lane was a farmhouse, lying in pieces in its yard – a hundred yards away, set back from the road, a vast and shabby barn sagged hopelessly in a barren field.

'Here we are, my beauty.' Cledge lifted Lydia from the car, bore her into the gloom of the barn, laid her on a pile of fresh straw which he had gathered the previous day.

Undressing, Cledge lay on top of her, put his mouth on hers as though bestowing the kiss of life. Her breath tasted of ether – he spat into the straw. 'Wake up, my darling, and you can have a piece of chewing-gum to take the taste away,' feeling through the pocket of his discarded jacket. He held up a slender paper package in triumph. 'Wake up – John's got something for you. A nice piece of chewing-gum. Don't you fancy a chew?' He slapped her face.

'Must have given her a bit more than I meant to,' he told himself, pulling on his clothes; the warmth outside had not penetrated the barn. He looked down at the White Rat's woman, black hair fanned out round her, 'You look like those pictures I've seen of saints,' Cledge told her. 'Except that your halo's black. The black halo of Satan – are you a she-devil, duckie? If you are, wake up and show me.'

He knelt down, took her in his arms, began to shake her violently. Her head rocked, her lower jaw opened and closed with the tremors of Cledge's impatience. He bent down and kissed her again, bit her lips until they were lacerated – they did not bleed.

It was some time before he realised that she was dead.

'Bugger,' he muttered, 'I did give her too much. Never mind, make do with what you have – that's the way to be happy.' He undressed again, once more committed rape, rose feeling a more comfortable man. Picking Lydia up, he carried her to the back of the barn, piled straw on top of her, decided that she might be discovered too soon.

'Must find a spade,' he told himself, and came across one hanging on a rack nearby.

He went into the field, thrust with the blunt and rusty metal at the hard sun-dried ground, after much effort succeeded in digging a shallow grave.

He carried Lydia over to it, dropped her into the earth, cursed. 'You would have to have big tits and a large arse,' he grumbled. 'More digging for poor old Cledge.'

Two hours later, all that remained of warmth and beauty and the ability to give joy, was a ridge of stones and crusted earth that would soon turn to the same colour as the ground about it; Cledge looked at the grave and felt nothing.

There was nothing of Lydia that he had known.

CHAPTER THIRTEEN

'Lydia?' The White Rat paced from living-room to small kitchen, from small kitchen to bedroom, stood in the centre of the bedroom with wrinkled forehead. He hated to come home to an empty flat; it had not happened since he and Lydia had started living together. He hated this break in the emotional routine, which was not really a routine at all, this break in a habit which was too sweet to be a habit.

Down to the butcher's, perhaps? No, she always did her shopping in the morning. Perhaps she had just discovered that they'd run out of something – at any moment her footfall would sound on the stair, her dear face appear in the doorway, mocking him for his concern.

What was it about this empty place that relayed to him a mournful message, what impressed upon his mind the feeling that Lydia's going was not temporary, not the matter of an hour, but of a lifetime?

The Rat cursed himself – this was typical professional pessimism, the need to survive by reading every twinkle of the stars left-handed, to tense at the top of each jump for an instant change of direction on landing, to regard nothing as safe or secure or unchanging. The only thing you could be sure of was the continued undesirability of your existence in the eyes of enemies, and the fact that malign intent was focused permanently upon you.

The Rat hurried to the head of the stairs, ran down them to the street door, looked up and down and across, saw only a bustling peasant world, a world of grey moths, bereft of Lydia's candle. He began to be really afraid, to feel the chill of panic. Had she left a note? Of course she hadn't – he had looked in every room for her, and there had been nothing.

Something Cledge had said grabbed and twisted his entrails, he heard Cledge's metallic voice: 'I prefer the oblique approach myself – kidnapped dear one – I can get at Steed through his woman – I know where she lives.'

Christ, supposing someone's got at me through Lydia – God knows I've enough enemies. Yet surely I'm being a fool – just because she's not home when I get there I panic like a child in the dark.

Slowly, the Rat turned and went again upstairs, sat down and tried not to fidget. A drink – that would help. My God, two glasses.

He hurried over to the drink cupboard, examined both glasses, saw that one bore no fingerprints. Wiped clean – why? And what's that smell – just the hint of something in the air. Can't define it – a smell of childhood, of butterflies in cardboard boxes, permanently impaled on pins for the young entomologist's edification. Ether.

Whom to call? Could this be reported as an ordinary disappearance, for standard police handling? Or should it go higher, as it could bear on state security? Dangerous to involve the intelligence people – it was considered less than professional to allow yourself to be outwitted, to leave an essential part of your life unprotected against the enemy predator.

Who could it be? The Rat's normally agile mind had seized up, confusion swamped it, blotting out the ability to take any determined course of action. He was hypnotised by the certainty that Lydia had been taken, that the only way to retrieve her would be to make some lesser, but nevertheless severe, sacrifice.

Honour and principle had fallen victim to a frivolous form of moral atheism – what was there left that must be renounced? Nothing mattered but to have Lydia back. There would be a telephone call, no doubt, or a car would slide up beside him as he walked along a sunless street, to be motioned into the back seat.

'You can have her back if—' he longed to hear the words, to begin to implement the regaining of her; he looked at the telephone, as so many people in his position had done in so many cities across the world, and willed it to ring.

The Rat stared at the telephone for one hour, then for two, the tears glistening on his increasingly haggard cheeks, but the telephone remained silent.

The day faded into twilight, twilight into dusk, and still the Rat sat almost motionless, and sipped slivovitz without tasting its fire, and fought to keep the hope in him from dying.

Back in his caravan, a few kilometres from the Rat's flat, Cledge prepared for bed, grinned at Gunner, raised his arms and stretched. Gunner turned away from Cledge's toxic armpits, went into the minute kitchen for a beer.

Cledge showered, washing away the sweat of his grave-digger's exertions, told Gunner, as he dried himself: 'Remember I said I'd call you in when I was sure who the White Rat was?'

Gunner stared at him over the rim of his glass. 'I'm not likely to forget,' grimly.

'Right. I've found him, and now I want you to help nail him.' He talked, and Gunner listened, and by and by Gunner smiled.

'Clever,' he said. 'He gets a message saying he'll find a clue as to who's after him here, and I'm up there in the barn, waiting for him.'

'I'm glad you like the idea.'

'Oh, I like it. I like it very much,' raising his glass to Cledge. 'I can't wait to tell London that the traitor's out of it.'

'I'm sure they'll be delighted,' Cledge said.

CHAPTER FOURTEEN

The White Rat's telephone failed to ring. He subsided into a light, tormented sleep, crammed into his chair. When he awoke, it was mid-morning; his clothes were creased and soiled, his mouth filled with the coppery after-taste of plum brandy. The immediate sense of loss which struck him, was overwhelming. It pinned him where he sat, deprived him of initiative. He was afraid of leaving the flat, even for a moment, in case the phone rang with news of Lydia.

Several times he made up his mind to call the police, but each time desisted. In the first place bringing in the police might be dangerous; perhaps the kidnappers had the building under surveillance, would know instantly if the police had been brought in and act accordingly.

There was also the Rat's uncertainty as to the efficacy of the ordinary police, and his worry about the displeasure of those higher up if a stir were created. He had never felt so helpless in his life.

He undressed, took a bath, lay on his bed. The bed felt empty, echoed with the sound of Lydia's voice, her endearments, his own cries of pleasure as she caressed him.

I don't want to live without her. You're romanticising. There are so many other women in the world – Traitor. Do you have to betray everyone? Lydia, the cock crows thrice for – Nonsense. I'm not renouncing her I'm – I know what you're doing. You're preparing a comfortable philosophical mattress to fall on when you get the news.

What news?

What news do you think – the news that Lydia's—

No, don't say it.

Why not? Plenty of other women in the world, aren't there? The news that Lydia's dead.

The Rat let out a deep, braying groan of sorrow, lay in the silence following it, shocked at himself. To mew and bawl – was that the behaviour of a spy, a man esteemed dangerous as agent and counter-agent? For God's sake do something more constructive – go back to see Delbert at the Ministry. Ask help from that quietly vicious little man? I doubt if he's ever felt emotion, would regard anything to do with love as a kind of deformity of the spirit.

What's that? The clatter of his letter-box as something thrust back the metal lid. The Rat ran into the tiny hall, saw an envelope lying trapped in the cage behind the letter slit, flung the door open but saw no one. Anyway, they'd hardly have delivered it themselves.

Delivered what? Who says it has anything to do with Lydia? Of course it's to do with Lydia – no stamp, and in any case the last post was due hours ago, at lunchtime.

Trembling with apprehension and hope, the Rat tore open the envelope. Rough off-white paper, capital letters in green ink.

IF YOU WANT YOUR LADY BACK, COME TO THE OLD BARN AT THE END OF THE SELIGGASSE AT NINE TOMORROW EVENING, THE 20TH. BRING TWENTY THOUSAND MARKS WITH YOU. IF YOU INFORM THE POLICE THE LADY WILL DIE.

Who'd do this for money? Something doesn't ring

true about it. That kind of crime isn't East German, it's American. Here people are picked up and carted off without explanation or notification for political deviation, for alleged subversion, for anything likely to offend the masters, but not taken for money.

Still, what choice have I? Twenty thousand marks – I'll have to ask for an advance on my next assignment. That means telling Delbert after all. He won't mind, if he thinks it's going to bind me even more closely to the East Germans and the Soviet brotherhood. Thank God there's something to do, at last.

The following morning, the White Rat was shown into the ornate, crumbling room at the Ministry, was waved again into a chair by the little man behind the desk.

'Well?'

'I need money,' the White Rat said at once. 'I need it now, and I'm prepared to do anything to earn it.'

'I think I have a right to ask why you have encountered this sudden fiscal emergency?'

'My wife – my lady – has been kidnapped.'

'You mean you have been guilty of such a lapse of security that someone was able to take her?' He stared at the Rat with no trace of sympathy. 'From where was she taken?'

'My flat.' The Rat swallowed. 'At least, so far as I know. She may have gone out while I was out, and been picked up in the street, but I don't think so. She'd done her shopping for the day.'

'And you have a ransom note?'

'Here.' The Rat walked to the desk, handed it to Delbert.

'Do you ever use green ink?'

'What?'

'I have to consider the circumstances very carefully. You want money – I must make sure – first, that the lady has really been kidnapped, and that you have not hidden her away and written this note yourself in order to raise money. Secondly, I have to consider what you can do for us in order to earn this sum – I do not want to help you, and then find that you have discarded your obligation to us.'

He looked at the Rat's strained face, saw astonishment rather than outrage at his suggestion, decided that the ransom note was, at least so far as the man in front of him was concerned, genuine.

'I am inclined to believe you,' he said softly. 'If I advance you the money, and you do not get the lady back, you will still owe it to us. You will not be able to change your surroundings in an effort to forget, you understand? If we felt that there was the slightest chance of your going away, before we were ready to permit it, we would have no choice but to eliminate you.'

The Rat licked his lips. 'I accept that,' he said.

'They want you to come alone. Do you mind going alone? Or would you like our support?'

'I'd rather not take any chances, Sir.' Delbert grinned to himself at the Rat's token of respect – he had tended to be slightly arrogant hitherto, to behave as though he were doing the Communists a favour in permitting them to buy his services. Now he was a spider caught in his own web, paralysed with his own poison. That was good.

Delbert rang a bell; a uniformed guard appeared. Delbert scribbled on a piece of paper, handed it to the guard, sat back and steepled his hands.

'I am sorry about your difficulties,' he said. 'Have

you any idea who has abducted the lady?'

'None.'

'And you are sure that it is money they are after?'

Chill attacked the Rat's belly. Cledge's words again – try to dismiss them. He swallowed. 'What else?'

'You, perhaps.'

'I'm not difficult to get. I don't have a bodyguard, I try to live as normal a life as possible. But why should anyone want to get me anyway?'

'In view of your counter-espionage activities, that seems a naive question.'

'The British would kill me, not kidnap Lydia.'

'And that is, if I may say so, a naive observation. The British are capable of fighting as cleanly, or as dirtily, as anyone else.'

'I suppose so,' the Rat agreed wearily. 'But somehow I don't think this is a British Intelligence job. It's too – too personal.'

'Whatever it is, you are in our debt to the tune of twenty thousand marks,' Delbert told him softly, as the guard came back with an envelope. He handed it to Delbert, who passed it over to the White Rat.

'I'm most grateful, Sir.'

'Gratitude is not entirely out of place in our practical society,' with a thin smile. 'You can start earning some of the money back – shall we say five hundred marks? – by capturing the abductors, if they do happen to be British. I will be even more generous – five hundred marks for each abductor. Are you sure you would not like some support from our people?'

'No thank you, Sir.' That's all I need, a convoy of Volkspolizei cars, subtlety isn't the polizei's strong point.

'Very well then, you may go. Good luck,' regarding the Rat with unsmiling, fathomless eyes.

'Thank you.'

The corridor, the steps, fresh air. Twenty thousand marks in my pocket. Decent of them. Think they've bought me, body and soul. Maybe they have – when I get Lydia back, I might be almost ardent in their service. Christ, how am I going to kill time till this evening – I'm like a bee in a field of cacti, can't settle anywhere.

Wittgenstein's. I'll go to Wittgenstein's.

It was nearly one o'clock; the White Rat took a taxi to his favourite cafe, found a seat on the terrace, ordered a stein of beer and a plate of assorted sausage.

The passing parade. Always has fascinated me, the sight of people in hotels, cafes, meeting each other, hurrying to rendezvous. Who are they, why are they?

If only Lydia would come along now – the magic of it. The White Rat found himself looking for her, disappointment welling up in him as each face turned out not to be hers.

He drank his beer, ordered another stein, drank that, blinked as a face appeared out of the crowd that he did recognise.

Cledge grinned at him, came up the steps, sat at the adjoining table. 'What a nice surprise,' he said. 'You look a bit rough – had a good night?'

'I feel bloody, as it happens.'

'Sorry to hear it. Have one with me?'

The Rat shrugged. 'Thank you.'

Cledge ordered two steins. 'Better than an aspirin, the hair of the dog.'

'I suppose so.'

'You can have as many hairs of the dog as you like – that's the advantage. Doesn't apply to aspirin, does it?' He lifted his tankard; he and the White Rat drank together.'

'I suppose not.'

'As a matter of fact, you look as though you've been under a bit of a strain,' Cledge went on. 'Don't worry about Steed and Co. – I'll handle them. I know you must sometimes feel that they're breathing down your neck—'

'Shut up!' the Rat snapped. 'This is a public place – how can you be so indiscreet?'

'Sorry – there isn't anyonc close by who looks sinister.'

'Not many people do,' the Rat answered; he thought of Delbert, sitting behind his desk, malign as a mamba, and Cledge himself also had something about him which, although not at once apparent, made you uneasy. That first time in the taxi, when he sat back and looked at me – there's a dead, insect-like aspect of him which is sinister, though not obvious.

Thc White Rat felt a great need to confide in someone; in spite of Cledge's unsympathetic personality, he was at least English.

'It's strange,' he began. 'You know you suggested getting at Steed through his girl?'

'Yes. It would be playing real dirty, but I'm sure it would work.'

'It would be playing dirty, I know that. Lydia – my wife – she's been kidnapped.'

Cledge looked at him with concern. 'You're joking!'

'That's why I've had a somewhat sleepless night – not, I'm afraid, because I was out on thc town.'

'Christ!' Cledge said, 'I'm sorry to have suggested it. What happened?' Glee swirled intoxicatingly through him.

'I got home and Lydia wasn't there. I waited and waited – I had a feeling something was wrong.'

'Oh? Did you call the police?'

'No. In the first place I don't think they're all that much good at tracing missing people – too many go missing for reasons of official policy – and in the second – well, it's difficult to believe that someone hasn't just gone out for a walk, or to visit a friend or relative.'

'So what did you do?'

'Well, finally I fell asleep. When I woke up it was morning.'

'And then?'

'Then a ransom demand arrived.'

'Christ. What do you have to do?'

'Take twenty thousand marks to an old barn at the end of a lane just outside the city.'

'And you haven't told the police?'

'I told Intelligence why I wanted the money – I had to raise it from somewhere.' Imperceptibly, Cledge's hand tightened on his stein.

'And they're going to help you capture the people who are holding your wife, no doubt?'

'They offered, but I told them I'd rather tackle it alone.'

Cledge frowned thoughtfully. 'Any idea how many people you'll be up against?'

'No. I may be up against no one,' the Rat said bitterly, 'there may just be another message in the barn, telling me to go somewhere else. Kidnappers usually put you through the hoop, don't they? To test your goodwill, apart from anything else, make sure you haven't brought the police into the thing.'

'That's what usually happens, according to the cases you read about in the papers. Luckily that sort of crime seems to happen in America, not England. Or Europe.'

'Well it's happened to Lydia,' the Rat said savagely. 'My God, I hope I have a chance to get my hands on the bastards who've taken her.'

'You might have a better chance of doing that if you don't go alone,' Cledge said slowly.

'I've told you, I don't want the police involved.'

'I wasn't thinking of the police,' Cledge told him. 'I was thinking of me.'

'You?' the Rat stared at Cledge. 'You'd come with me?'

'Why not?' He gulped beer; the Rat ordered more. For the first time in thirty hours he felt a glow of hope.

'That's – good of you.' The Rat was aware of a surge of gratitude and relief – whatever you might feel about him, Cledge was undoubtedly a good man to have on your side.

The beer made its way to the Rat's eyes, was transmuted into water. 'You're a very present help in trouble,' he said. 'I'm grateful for your offer.'

'Then you accept it,' doing his best to keep the contempt from showing in his eyes.

'I accept it.'

'Good,' Cledge leaned forward, tapped the White Rat's arm. 'Now don't you worry, the Catcher's coming to the rescue.

'I don't suppose you'd guess,' grinning, 'but I've a lot in common with St George.'

CHAPTER FIFTEEN

The Opel, with the White Rat at the wheel, lurched and jounced across the ruts in the lane, crawled without lights along the cracked, dried-up verge. Far ahead, moonlight showed a black shape, tethered in a field. The barn.

Is Lydia in there? Will they bring her? The White Rat had come to the rendezvous an hour early in order to spy out the land and, if possible, trap the kidnappers.

He stopped the car, whispered to Cledge, lying uncomfortably half on the back seat, half on the floor: 'I'm going to reconnoitre on foot.'

'Shall I come with you?'

'No, you stay here.'

'Right.'

Cledge sat up, grinning as the White Rat crouched low and hurried through the shadowless landscape. The Rat was early, but Gunner would be early too – maybe they'd be shooting at each other in a few minutes.

Pity about the twenty thousand marks – it would come in useful, but I can hardly pinch it without German Intelligence realising it. Still, they may let me have some of it – say five thousand – for getting rid of Gunner after he'd killed their valued counter-agent, the Rat.

And British Intelligence – there could be a bonus there, for killing the Rat. Pity Gunner had to go too, but at least one half of the trapeze act would survive.

Good show, no bonus, any more than we'd pay overtime, ha, ha, but you may shake my hand.

Thank you, sir.

Think nothing of it.

I don't.

The White Rat approached the barn cautiously. Not a sign of life, but then one would not have expected it. He looked at his watch – eight o'clock.

Which would be best – to get into position first, or to come later, as planned? If only there were some sort of shelter – might be able to conceal the car behind that wreck of a farm-house. If the kidnappers come now, and find the car with Cledge in it – I'd better go back.

Inside the barn, Gunner tensed, as light footsteps approached. On the ground, prominently displayed, was an envelope. The White Rat would bend down to pick it up, and then Gunner would let him have it – he steadied his gun and looked down from the beam along which he lay, at the front door.

The footsteps outside paused. If he goes much further round, thought Gunner, he'll see the Volkswagen – I'd better get ready to chase him.

The footsteps returned, no urgency in them, faded into inaudibility. Gunner swung down, went to the door of the barn, loped after the figure hurrying along by the side of the road.

Shall I get him now, or at nine o'clock, always supposing he intends to come back? Haven't quite got time to bring him down now, not in this light. Gunner flung himself to the ground, rolled into the shade of a small tree, as his target reached the car parked down the road.

The whine of a starter, the firing of an engine – the

car came slowly towards him. Gunner rested his chin on his forearm, the cold metal of the gun touching his nose as it lay flat across the back of his hand.

Only one bloke in the car – good. Gunner leaped up, ran back up the lane, shielded from the Opel driver's view by its rear three-quarter blind spot.

As the car swung abruptly right, towards the ruined farmhouse, Gunner hurled himself to the ground, jumped up and ran for the barn as the car turned into the yard behind the house and stopped.

Up on to the beam, sight the gun, wait.

'I don't think there's anyone there,' the White Rat whispered to Cledge. He looked at his watch again. 'It's still only eight forty-five – we'll wait till nine, then I'll have another look.'

'Right. I'll wait here. If there's any action, I'll be there in a second.'

'Thanks.' The beer he had drunk was still strong enough in its after-effects to make the White Rat feel mellow towards Cledge, to feel grateful for his strong presence. A good man to have with him – the Germans would appreciate the recruiting of such an agent.

The night was soundless – the ground was so dry that there were no insects to make noise round vegetation. Only the whirr of a bat skimming overhead, the distant cry of a night-jar, disturbed the quiet.

Four more times the Rat looked at his watch – at last it was nine o'clock.

'Either it's a hoax, or whoever it is has been in there all the time,' Cledge whispered. 'Maybe you'll catch them having a pee.'

The Rat's lips twitched; lightly, he ran forward, headed for the front of the barn.

Gunner heard the rustle of earth under canvas soles for the second time in the past hour, knew that this time they would not go away.

The door opened noisily; a man stood in the entrance. He was wearing a muffler and a Tyrolean hat. He looked at the envelope on the ground, but took his time about coming into the barn.

'Hello, Rat.'

Two guns fired, almost simultaneously.

The grin on Cledge's face died as he heard stumbling footsteps, accompanied by gasps of pain, coming rapidly towards him.

'Quick – it was a trap. The bastards set a trap!'

The Rat flung himself on to the passenger seat, Cledge reversed the car savagely, swung it round, sent it crashing across ridged ground to the lane, accelerated brutally over the ruts.

'I should have stayed and killed him – but why risk a bullet, when I can finish him off any time?'

'It was a trap,' the Rat muttered through clenched teeth. 'She wasn't there – Lydia wasn't there.'

'Better luck next time,' Cledge told him. 'We'd better have your leg fixed up right away – know anywhere?'

'There won't be a next time,' the Rat said mechanically, his voice devoid of tone. 'She's dead.'

'Not necessarily,' Cledge spun the wheel, took the car on to the main road. 'Looks like they only used her as bait to get you.'

'She's dead – why bother to keep her alive?'

'If she's good-looking—'

'Shut up!' cried the Rat, unable to bear the thought of Lydia in the arms of another man, wishing her dead rather than that, with the selfishness of one adoring and bereaved.

Cledge sighed, as though wronged. 'Sorry,' quietly. 'I was only trying—'

'I know. I'm sorry.'

'Now tell me which hospital we're going to?'

'The Ullbricht Krankenhau in the Bahnallee.'

'Consider yourself there,' Cledge said comfortingly. 'We'll have you fit in no time. And meanwhile, I'll give you a treat.'

'A treat?' exhausted with loss of blood and his subtler loss, the look, the sound, the love of Lydia.

'I think you might call it that. I'll get rid of Gunner for you.'

The Rat uttered no word of appreciation – he had fainted.

CHAPTER SIXTEEN

East German Intelligence's idea of making small sacrifices of personnel and material in order to gain significant rewards from the other side, seemed to be working extremely well.

The fear of discovery still troubled Cledge, the apprehension that he might be sent for and find himself being grilled by Steed, but as the hue and cry over its lost agents died down in London, he began to feel safer. At the insistence of the White Rat and the East Germans, he refrained from killing anyone on the British side, concentrated instead on ridding the Republik of political undesirables, who met strange deaths in unexpected places.

Cledge's illogical animosity towards the Rat changed to sympathy for him; the Rat, in his own cold way, found himself developing with Cledge something approaching friendship, insofar as friendship is the sharing of one's loss with someone else. He did not, of course, suspect that Cledge had caused the loss.

When the White Rat was finally recalled to London and promoted, he took Cledge with him as espionage assistant, paid for out of public funds and not stationed in Whitehall, where there was still the chance that Steed might recognize him.

One year faded into the next; the White Rat acquired power and began to forget his hunted days.

Hart, Julie Bennett, Jennings and Gunner, became part of the debris of history.

CHAPTER SEVENTEEN

The hospital grounds were spacious and beautiful, almost park-like. There were swings for the children, an ornamental lake, a dozen long green benches, a large half-moon bed of rhododendrons. Rose-bushes were placed in sentinel positions at the corners of various walks; the hospital buildings were the colour of a Tudor mansion.

It was only when the visitor looked closely at the inmates of such a pleasant place that he noticed something strange about their eyes, a vacuous quality, an appearance of perceiving only their souls, of being unconscious of the beauty before them.

On closer inspection the visitor noticed, too, that there was a fence round the lake, and fine mesh grilles of wire reaching from floor to ceiling of the numerous balconies giving on to the grounds.

St Marcia's was perhaps the most pleasant mental hospital in England, but a mental hospital none the less.

Near one of the swings a man was playing with a child, pushing her gently skyward, then letting the swing drift upward and back of its own momentum. The momentum decreased, the child, a Mongol, uttered sounds that the man understood, and again he pushed the swing, and again it rose skyward.

The man had a kindly face, which was marred by a scar running across the brow, parallel with the hairline. The nose had been badly broken but competently reset;

the ridge was barely uneven, but had a Roman hook that had not been there before. The man's hair was white, but his arms were strong and heavily muscled, not at all those of an old man. He grinned at the back of the child's head and crooned.

'The old Rat-Catcher'll make a bird of you yet, my beauty. Up you go – try to kick a cloud, my darling.'

'He's marvellous with children, isn't he?' the child's mother remarked to a nurse.

'He loves them. I understand that he's been a sort of godfather round the place for as long as he's been here – nearly five years, I understand.'

'Five years? Then he wasn't born here?'

'Oh no. He wasn't' – the nurse paused; she had been about to say that the man had not been born insane. 'Something happened to him, an accident.'

'And why is he called the Rat-Catcher?'

'He's always mumbled something about having to catch a rat. A white rat. He calls himself the Rat-Catcher, so of course it caught on.'

'How strange,' murmured the mother. 'Have you any idea what sort of accident? A car crash, I suppose.'

'He was found, badly damaged, in the hold of a ship. It was generally thought that he'd fallen from the rigging, or tripped over the edge of a hatchway. Nobody knows for sure.'

The mother's mouth opened to ask another question, but instead of words it uttered a scream. 'Look out!'

The Rat-Catcher, recognising her, had turned to smile a welcome and wave; as he did so, the swing, moving fast on its rearward arc, struck him on the back of the head.

'Oh my God,' wailed the mother, 'oh my God.' She

and the nurse ran towards the unconscious man, from the back of whose head blood was welling fast.

Two orderlies with a stretcher dashed up, hurried off with their heavy burden.

The child cried for another push.

CHAPTER EIGHTEEN

Gunner came slowly to in a sea of dissolving and reforming images. Giant hands were outstretched in front of him, comforting hands, but when he tried to respond to them, to clasp them, they disappeared.

He sensed himself falling, kicked spontaneously at the bed-clothes, tearing a sheet. He was unaware of it, unaware of the nurse tending him, unaware of the saline drip presiding over him.

He only knew that he was plunging to the bottom of a well shining and spiralled as the barrel of a gun; he was tearing through the barrel of the gun towards the butt, burst into the chamber, crashed through the ejector into the hand of a man wearing a Tyrolean hat with a feather in the band.

'Rat!' Gunner cried. 'I've got you now, White Rat! And you, Cledge – I know all about you, now. Two rats – you wait. I'll have the two of you!'

The nurse tried to calm him, but Gunner was filled with the lost energy of five years. An impulse of overwhelming force propelled him out of bed, tethered to it only by the drip.

'Please,' the nurse begged, 'please. You'll injure yourself if you try to get up. You'll be up and about before long.' Where was Dr Maple, she couldn't cope with giving the patient an injection of sedative by herself.

'I must pay a debt,' Gunner said; his eyes were fierce but not mad. And where, wondered the nurse, was the gentleness that had so often filled her with wonder; had sanity swept aside the Rat-Catcher's essential goodness? Or had that goodness been only a by-product of insanity – she pressed down on Gunner's shoulders with imploring hands, and felt immense relief when he dropped back on to his pillows.

Must do as she says – no use going off half-cock after so long. How long – how much life have I been done out of? Gunner's throat contracted, there was foreboding in his stomach as he asked the question: 'How long have I been here?'

The nurse licked her lips – why on earth wasn't the doctor here, why should she have to give the terrible answer?

'You were brought here five years ago.'

Five years, the penalty for what sort of crime? Armed robbery, perhaps, a serious fraud, manslaughter? Five years knocked off your usual span, five years of loving women and breathing fresh air and maybe siring kids and watching them grow. Kids – Gunner smiled a rancid smile. I didn't even have a wife.

'I suppose it could have been worse,' Gunner said, managing to sound jocular. 'If that swing hadn't hit me on the head, I might have been here for twenty, or maybe the rest of my life.'

'It's always a good thing to be able to take it like that,' the nurse said, the meaningless words accompanying a meaningless smile. 'I expect you'll have quite a new world to discover.'

'Oh yes, I'll be a sort of Columbus, looking for places that are known to everyone but myself.' He grinned, trying to give the impression that he was not bitter. 'The only thing is, I'm not going to have too much time to go exploring.'

'Why not?'

'I have to go rat-catching, haven't I?'

The grin was still on his face, but it had nothing to do with the expression in Gunner's eyes. The nurse shivered.

CHAPTER NINETEEN

'My God, look at this.' Looking quite shaken, the duty operator in the radio room attached to Steed's department, came into his office. Steed took the piece of paper torn from the operator's scratch-pad, read it, frowned.

'Is it genuine, do you think?'

'I don't know, sir. But it's been coming through steadily for the last five minutes. It's always the same message: The Flyer has Landed.'

'But the Flyer was Irwin Gunner's codename, and as far as we know he died five years ago. Not that we ever had any proof of that.' Steed's extraordinarily penetrating eyes were fixed on those of the operator. 'Thank you, Stevens. Come straight back if he starts to transmit again.'

'Right, sir.' The operator went out; Steed pressed a buzzer. Shortly afterwards, Purdey came in. She wore a one-piece jump suit in lilac cotton, and looked, Steed decided, like every man's idea of a diversion.

'The Flyer has landed,' Steed said, waving the piece of paper at her. 'What do you make of that?'

Purdey frowned, decided not to make the facetious remark she had been about to utter. 'I don't know that I make anything of it. Who or what is The Flyer?'

'Ah, that's just it. The only person we knew called that is dead.'

'I'm sorry,' sitting on the edge of his desk, 'I can't keep up with all the codenames. The Flyer sounds a mite old-fashioned, though. Something of The Man On The Flying Trapeze about it.'

'Precisely.'

'Not – what was his name? – not Irwin Gunner?'

'The same.'

'Did it come through on the radio, or was it transmitted through an ouija board?'

Steed smiled. 'That's just it – for five years we've assumed that the only way to get in touch with Gunner was through a medium at a seance. Now he suddenly seems to have resurrected himself.'

'Unless some ham has accidentally tuned in to our wave-length. Or else we've accidentally listened in to a crime code. Supposing that Flyer is a codeword for jewels, and that the message means they've just been satisfactorily pinched?'

'No, I think the message is genuine.'

'Why? Hunch?'

'Yes, but if you go on walking round the room like that all my instincts will turn elsewhere.'

'Sorry,' sitting on the edge of Steed's desk.

'You really are indecently attractive today.'

'Well don't sound so disapproving about it.' She tapped her leg with an elegant finger. 'Why not ask Gambit?'

'He wasn't here at the time Gunner went missing.'

'He often has ideas. Isn't that why you employ him?'

'That and the fact that he's a good chopper pilot. All right, we'll see if he knows anything.' Again he pressed the buzzer; Gambit came in a minute later. He was a tall young man with a face weathered by experience. He wore a steel Rolex which had a dial that was more like a facia; in addition to the time of day, the month and the year, it could, one felt, tell the speed at which Gambit was walking and how far he travelled in a day.

'The Flyer has Landed.' Steed told him. 'Any ideas about it?'

'I was looking through the files with old Finder the other day – I was interested in what he was saying about some agents we lost a few years ago. Thought a fresh young mind might come up with something.' He grinned. 'I seem to remember that the Flyer was the codename of one Gunner – no doubt he was a marksman?'

'Among other things.'

'Ah. He was also a trapeze artist, one of those courageous characters who plays Tarzan across circus arenas. I don't like flying without benefit of aircraft.' He pursed his lips. 'He had a partner, didn't he – chap called Cledge.'

'How every euphonious,' from Purdey.

'Very,' Steed agreed. 'We'd better trace him.'

'Isn't he still one of us?'

'I seem to remember that he resigned some time ago.'

'Well with a name like that he can't sink too far into obscurity. Even if he's gone to live abroad – there can't be too many Cledges about.'

'Right. Let's go and see Finder – you never know, he may have an address for him in records.'

The three went out, walked along the corridor to Finder's office. Here, Finder, a dusty man, presided over his repository of filed history, and of molecular events. Everything was buried under the residue from torn-down buildings, shredded artefacts and plain fluff, all pulverised between the millstones of creation and finity.

'The Flyer? We looked him up the other day,' he said accusingly, looking at Gambit.

'Exactly,' Steed murmured. 'Therefore it shouldn't be too difficult to find his file again.

'It won't be difficult at all,' Finder rejoined sharply. 'Everything's in its place, and its place is directly under my hand.' He waddled over to a cabinet, began sifting through grubby cardboard covers, soon waved a folder in triumph. 'Here we are – the Flyer, name Irwin Gunner, recruited on April 5th 1968. Trapeze artist by profession, also did six months in the 'forties for a spot of theft. No doubt we were able to use that talent too,' drily. 'Disappeared in mysterious circumstances that were never resolved.'

'Does it say who his partner was?' asked Steed.

'Chap called the Catcher.' He drew himself up. 'That will mean looking at another file.'

'We can wait.'

'I can assure you it won't take me a moment to find it.' Back to the cabinet. 'Here we are – the Catcher, real name John Cledge. Also a professional trapeze artist, suspected psychopathic tendency. I suppose we used that quality too.'

'Regrettable, but no doubt true. If that's the sort of bloke he was, he might be in clink.'

'He resigned in May of the year before last, as a matter of fact. Present whereabouts unknown. Only address was a Poste Restante – 393651.'

'Worth checking on that. Will you do it, Gambit?'

Gambit nodded. 'Right.' He went to stand beside Finder, leafed through the files. 'I hope the PR is in some exotic city – with my luck it will probably turn out to be a tobacconist somewhere in Liverpool.' He looked at Steed, a grin on his elastic lips. 'By the way, didn't you have some fun with a wench in Istanbul some time back? I saw something about you in another file – what are Turkish girls like when they're unwound?'

'They've been wearing Western dress since Kemal Attaturk,' Steed told him, 'and they're like anyone else who isn't a Swiss roll. You're supposed to be spying on the enemy, not on me,' he added plaintively. He looked at Finder. 'Do you—' he was interrupted by the shrill, emasculated chatter of morse next door in the radio room.

Steed, Purdey and Gambit hurried out, instinctively aware that the morse was more than usually urgent; Finder followed. Steed peered over the operator's shoulder; watched the man's blunt pencil pressing a network of valleys and deltas across a piece of off-white paper.

The morse ended abruptly; the operator continued for a minute or so to scribble. 'That's it,' leaning back in his chair, 'same as before. "The Flyer has Landed" – repeated a half-dozen times. I haven't bothered to write it down more than three times.'

'Quite right,' Steed told him, 'we have to save energy.' He frowned. The morse began again. "Where are you?" Steed read, the words splaying out in a faded wake behind the pencil. "Dad – Did – Dud" – 'shit,' breathed the operator, 'how the hell do you spell Daedalus?'

'Never mind – take it as read,' from Steed.

'Daedalus?' queried Finder incredulously. 'Did you say Daedalus?'

'That's right. Witness to a rather sticky flying accident, I believe.'

The morse stopped again.

'God knows why the blokes who set up codes think all us operators have had a classical education,' the operator muttered resentfully.

'You ought to be grateful that a wicked world should lavish incomprehensibility on you,' Steed told him. 'Now, Finder old friend, you look like a man anticipating a souffle who's been stuck with a blancmange instead.'

'You must admit it's a bit of a shock when the supposedly dead come back like this. And Daedalus – it's almost as though the name was chosen because someone knew what was going to happen to our Flyer.'

'Probably coincidence rather than a rather macabre practical joke, but let's go back to your files and see what we can find,' leading the way back into the records room.

'Ah, here's something.' Finder held up a photograph. It showed a ruggedly handsome man with pale hair and a showman's smile.

Purdey studied it. 'Not bad looking, in a tough sort of way. Doesn't look like a crook.'

'Anyone who comes back after five years could be anything,' Steed said. 'Could have tried pinching something he wasn't supposed to, and wound up in gaol in East Germany, or for that matter he might have become a double agent.'

'Wouldn't that be too obvious?' Purdey asked. 'After all, that would be the first thing we'd suspect.'

'Exactly. Unless he had a story we couldn't break.'

'He looks a fairly simple sort of chap,' Gambit put in. 'He must have been, or he wouldn't have joined us.

Ahem,' clearing his throat at Steed's expression of rebuke.

'Daedalus,' Steed murmured thoughtfully. 'He watched his son's wings melt.'

'Gunner's controller, perhaps?' suggested Gambit.

'Perhaps. Let's see if we can locate him.'

Finder at once began to rummage amidst further clouds of dust; he resembled a genie diving into a soda siphon.

'Supposing Gunner didn't disappear involuntarily,' Purdey said. 'Maybe he left the service by just fading out.'

'That way he'd have missed his bronze handshake,' Gambit offered. He was leafing through Gunner's file, whistled. 'I say, he was about to make his monthly report – it's been due for five years.' He sneezed. 'Why don't you clean this place up a bit?' he asked Finder's back, reproachfully.

'In the first place it's a government department,' without turning round, 'and in the second, this stuff' – sneezing in his turn – 'saves me pounds a year on my snuff bill. Now leave me in peace, or I'll never find Daedalus.' He added under his breath: 'Probably won't anyway, as I don't have a proper name for him.'

The others left him to sneeze in peace.

CHAPTER TWENTY

The message which had caused such a flurry in Department DI 6 caused amazement and dismay elsewhere.

'It's him all right,' Cledge said, pressing his hands to his headphones and looking across a big, ornament-sprinkled desk at the White Rat. 'I'd stake my life that it's Gunner.'

'But how, for God's sake. You dropped him from a great height twice in one day – he must have been killed.'

Cledge shrugged. 'Maybe he was born immortal and none of us realised it.' He grinned. 'Don't worry – I'll get him and for keeps this time. Even Gunner won't be able to take a bullet in the heart and carry on living.'

'And how do you propose to put a bullet in his heart? You have to find him first, and you can be quite sure that our colleagues in the Ministry will be going flat out to find him too.' He broke a match in half, put the remains in an onyx ashtray.

'We've certain advantages,' Cledge assured him.

'Such as?'

'I knew Gunner. I know his habits, how he thinks. I'll find him before anyone else does.'

'I hope so,' as Cledge took off the headphones.

'He's packed up for today – tomorrow, I'll get a fix on him. After that' – he smiled a humourless smile.

'If you don't succeed, we're both sunk,' taking another match from a box and twisting it. 'But I still don't believe in ghosts!' vehemently.

'I didn't, till now. But don't worry, he'll be a ghost again before long. Then it won't matter whether we believe in ghosts or not.'

'I,' said the White Rat thoughtfully, 'have survived through not believing in anything.' He eyed Cledge intently, gave a cold smile. 'Even in your ability to kill Gunner.'

Cledge's eyes went red as a ferret's. 'I'll get him this time – I'll give you something to believe in!' savagely.

'Good,' the White Rat said, and snapped another match.

CHAPTER TWENTY-ONE

'The Flyer has landed. The Flyer has landed.'

'Can you get a fix on him?' Steed asked urgently. The radio operator shook his head, pencil poised above a map.

'Signal's pretty loud – don't think he's too far away.' He fiddled with a dial. Again Gunner's signal sounded sharply in his headphones, rose and fell as the dial turned. The operator made a mark on the map. 'It's somewhere round here – Bury St Edmunds area.'

'Right. Purdey, you and Gambit take the chopper up to Suffolk right away, and see if you can bring Gunner back. And keep a look out for anyone else trying to do the same thing – I doubt if we're the only people who have picked up Gunner's message.'

'We're off.' Gambit threw a merry salute – he enjoyed the thought of having Purdey to himself in a helicopter. If we don't find him, we might be ordered to spend the night in Suffolk and resume search tomorrow – he hoped that Gunner would not be found right away.

Meanwhile, Cledge also was making preparations to go to Suffolk. 'I place him at Framlingham,' he told the Rat. 'Country area – probably a farm. Gunner liked farms.'

'He damn nearly finished me in one,' the Rat said savagely. 'What will you use – a pistol?'

'I'll take one, of course, but on this sort of job I prefer a shotgun. A shotgun in Suffolk wouldn't attract attention, and besides, it's safer than a pistol against a chap like Gunner. If he's as good a shot as he used to be, that is.'

'He missed me,' with a spurt of malice. 'Almost.'

'That was because he let emotion get in the way. Had to warn you before he let you have it, like a cowboy refusing to shoot someone in the back in a Western. If he's got any sense, he won't be that sporting again.'

'Sporting? He was damned stupid!'

'Saved you, though, didn't it?' Cledge grinned, made for the door. 'Want me to bring back his head?' he asked.

'A paragraph in the papers about the unexplained death of a man shot in the neighbourhood of Framlingham, will do.'

'Right.' Cledge went out, hurried down an ornate staircase supporting a ton or so of Axminster, climbed into his MGC and drove quickly but unobtrusively back to his flat, where he threw a few things into a suitcase, picked up a double-barrelled shot-gun and ammunition. He drove east.

The usual trench warfare on the Southend Road, opposing traffic locked together as it battled for space alongside road-up signs; Cledge made his shifty way past lorries that would have crowded him aside if they had seen him, broke out into open country at last, headed north-east.

At Colchester, he decided to stop for a dozen oysters, found to his disgust that they were dearer than in London, guzzled a plate of mediocre chips with frozen scampi, resumed his way.

Near Framlingham, he parked the car in a field, ran up the aerials of a transmitter, listened. 'If he doesn't come through again, I could be sniffing around here till Christmas,' he muttered. 'Wonder what he looks like these days.' He tried to imagine a Gunner five years older than when he had last seen him – would five years have made a great difference? Probably the two falls he had inflicted on Gunner would have made more. Christ, what a survivor. He wouldn't survive this time, though. Both barrels through the face, blow his head off – that'll put paid to him.

Cledge licked his lips. And there's the White Rat, being saved as a retirement pension. Subtle, not to have put the bite on him all these years – he'd be so shocked when the bite does come that he'll be chewed out of his wits. Cough up like a baby – and my pension will be indexed to his.

At the entrance to a farm, Cledge pulled up, switched off the motor. Now if I was Gunner, what would I do? Would I choose a place that was really remote, or one that was near a main road with a chance of a getaway if I thought I was spotted? Cledge screwed up his eyes, thought there would be no harm in asking the owner of Holmwood Farm if he had come across a stranger looking for accommodation.

Would he ask outright, or help himself to a night in a barn, move on the next day? Fly chap, Gunner – and he'd not take it for granted that Steed's mob was the only lot that had received his message.

Cledge left the car, his shot-gun in its canvas bag lying across his shoulder, an innocent in the land of wild birds, come to see if he could bring down a duck or two, maybe have a go at an unmyxamotosed rabbit.

Sauntering up to the front door, Cledge knocked, was answered by a buxom woman in a brilliant apron.

'Good afternoon,' in a manner meant to be winning but which in fact was losing – there was something sinister about Cledge and the farmer's wife sensed it.

'Yes?'

'I'm looking for a friend of mine who's staying in these parts – I've lost his address. I wondered if you had anyone from London staying here.'

'No one.'

'Do you know if any farms about take in guests?'

'Kerry's, down the road a way sometimes do,' reluctantly.

'Right. Thank you very much.'

The woman nodded, closed the door. Friendly type, thought Cledge, armour-plated against charm. Ah, well. Let's try Kerry's. Maybe the people there aren't suffering from lock-jaw.

He went back to the car, was soon halted by a mutilated sign at the end of a long and muddy lane.

Cledge looked at his shoes, wondered if he minded their getting muddy. No reason not to drive up – they take in visitors, I'm a visitor. Besides, Gunner might not have time to sprint back indoors if he's outside. Won't know who's driving. Settling himself as deeply in his seat as he could without forfeiting a sight of the road ahead, Cledge swung up the lane, jolted and squelched for a half-mile before arriving in front of a freshly-painted farmhouse. Highly polished cows ruminated in a field nearby, pigs that looked as though they had just enjoyed a porcine bath-night rooted happily under oak-trees. Even the chickens looked as if their feathers had been shampooed and blow-dried.

Climbing out of the car, Cledge looked back, wondered how the farmer had managed a Canute which had stopped the mud so efficiently where the lane swelled into a yard.

'Good afternoon,' as the door opened; Cledge smiled into the face of a thin, neurotic-looking woman holding a broom. 'I believe you take visitors?'

'Used to. Made the place too dirty. Can't stand dirt. So we don't any longer.' This is a different one, thought Cledge, polishes the cattle and speaks in morse.

'I'm looking for a friend of mine. He's staying in this neighbourhood, but I've lost his address.'

'No strangers hereabouts. None I know of. Could be at Rack's. 'Bout two miles down the road, Framlingham way.'

'Thank you very much.' Cledge turned to go, frowned at sight of a well-weathered barn a hundred yards away. Looks as though she's forgotten to varnish it. Nice hiding place. I wonder. 'Mind if I look at your barn? I'm a student of barns. That looks like Tudor.'

'Grandfather put it up. One before fell down.'

'I see. It looks very old.'

'Grandfather was fifty when he built it. Not old at all.'

'May I have a look anyway?'

'Don't see that it'll advantage you.' She looked at Cledge suspiciously.

'Just that I'm interested,' he said lamely.

'Good afternoon then.' She closed the door, leaving Cledge to scowl uncertainly. Has she said I can look, or refused? Damned if I know. Don't want to be accused of trespassing. Suppose I'll have to come back at night. No, why the hell should I? If anyone calls out, I'll be all injured innocence. Cledge advanced towards the barn.

'Hey, you!'

'Yes?'

'What do you want?' A gnarled little man approached, holding a pitchfork.

'Oh, good afternoon. I was just talking to your wife—'

'Don't have a wife.'

'Oh.'

'Got a daughter,' with no great joy in conveying the information.

'I asked her if I could see your barn.' Cledge's tone was hurt – he was not used to being on the defensive.

'Well you're seeing it. That's the barn there,' pointing at it.

Defeated, Cledge gave a smile of acknowledgement that would have done credit to a pouncing leopard whose prey has unaccountably evaporated, and returned to the MG.

'Have to come back tonight,' he growled to himself. 'If they're so cagey about letting me see inside – maybe they're just naturally unfriendly.'

Two more farms yielded similarly reticent inhabitants; just after dusk, Cledge came back to Kerry's. Shrugging, he left the car at the foot of the lane, did his best to walk along the verge – his shoes did not matter, but the car's interior did. The MG was the only thing Cledge loved.

How many watch-dogs do they have? Didn't see any this afternoon – maybe the chickens are trained to bark. Cledge crept along in the shadows of the oaks, shot-gun out of its bag and ready to fire. 'If anyone gets in my way now, I'll let him have it. It'll be a pleasure.' No sound – the animals have probably all been given aspirin and hot milk and tucked into beddy-byes, thought Cledge sourly.

The barn was close now, looming against the stars. There's nobody in there, I've got the sort of feeling I have when I ring at the bell of a house which is empty. Waste of bloody time – the White Rat'll have to up my pension for this. No use telling me I'm doing it for Satan and the Republic.

Gently, Cledge eased the latch on the barn door, stealthily opened it. A creak – why couldn't they oil the ruddy hinges? Everything else has been tended to.

Cledge crept forward, suddenly receiving the full impact of a pair of size tens in the face. He flew backwards, the shotgun thudded into the straw a few feet away.

Gunner grabbed Cledge by the hair, gave him a karate chop at the base of the ear, scooped up the gun and hurried out.

Keeping to the trees as Cledge had done, he reached the road, grinned to himself as he spotted the car. He lifted the bonnet, crossed wires, crammed himself into the driving-seat and accelerated hard into the darkness.

CHAPTER TWENTY-TWO

'You what?' The White Rat's voice was distorted with anger and apprehension.

'I told you – I lost him.'

'He outsmarted you? You've always said he wasn't very bright.'

'If he'd been bright,' said Cledge softly, 'he'd have killed me when he had the chance. Just as he would have killed you.'

'Shut up! I don't have a scrambler on this phone. Why didn't he kill you – didn't he have a gun?'

'I don't know. I reckon he's soft.'

'He strikes me as being too bloody durable. Well, you'd better get back here and wait till the next time he calls. He may be miles away by now.'

'He pinched my car.'

'I hope there weren't any incriminating papers in it.'

'I'm not a filing cabinet, *Sir*. He pinched my car!' Cledge repeated, almost in tears.

'In that case you'd better make your way to the nearest station and take a train.'

Cledge banged down the receiver. The sod – didn't he understand, didn't he *feel*? My car's gone.

Rage took over from sorrow. 'God help him next time!' Cledge said aloud. At that moment he was overwhelmed by a universal hatred which made it difficult for him even to breathe.

Cledge did not hear the helicopter which passed over

Framlingham whilst he was on the telephone, its navigation lights blinking in the dark.

'Doubt if he'll come through again to-night,' Gambit shouted. 'How about a romantic dinner in a luxurious pub I know near Ipswich?'

'I'm certainly hungry for food!' Purdey shouted back.

'You can have romance as dessert.'

Purdey smiled at him. 'I know, but I think I'd prefer an ice-cream by itself. A strawberry one.'

'Wait till I have you opposite me, by candlelight.'

'I'm sure you'll prove irresistible. Except that I'm rather tired. I'll settle for your company but not your embraces. Not tonight.'

'That leaves me with hope for tomorrow,' with a grin.

'Tomorrow we shall be looking for Gunner again.'

'While there's lust there's hope,' Gambit said.

'Now, now – concentrate on the job. This thing feels as though it's flying upside down.'

'It's just on the tilt, that's all.' Purdey clutched the handrail in front of her as the helicopter skittered in a broad sweep over the darkened landscape, passed over a line of pylons marking time across a valley.

On the top of one of the pylons, a man sat, skilfully tying himself into the circuit.

'Hope to Christ they can hear me this time,' he muttered, watching the helicopter's lights receding. 'It's about time I got some reaction from my own side. Unless I don't have a side – they could all have gone as rotten as the Rat. I must be barmy, to have let Cledge off with a kick in the chops and a slice under the ear. Though that would have killed most people, I doubt if it even dented that swine. I'm not thinking straight –

Cledge could have led me to the Rat – I could have made him talk. Or could I?'

Gunner shrugged to himself, cleared his throat, began to speak. The result was an instantaneous interruption of a disc-jockey's inanities, a woman discussing her experiences as a nursing sister in Malawi was temporarily blotted out, and a concert orchestra was flung into a dissonance that did nothing for its reputation.

'This is the Flyer. The Flyer has landed. This is the Flyer, calling Daedalus. I repeat: The Flyer has landed.' He paused. 'I can nail the White Rat.'

Steed, who was driving up St James Street after an excellent dinner at his club, pressed his foot hard on the throttle, sent the Bentley careering along Piccadilly and back to Whitehall. He took the steps of the Ministry two at a time, and as soon as he arrived in his office, called his chief.

'Minister? Sorry to disturb you, but we've just had another message from Gunner. Hooked himself into the broadcasting system.'

'Good God. I'll come down at once.'

A half hour later, the Minister, whose name was Quaintance, walked under the portico of the Ministry, poised on stilts that resembled decayed Edinburgh rock, and was soon standing in front of Steed.

'Anything more?' Quaintance had grey hair and a face that did not really go with it; it was the face of a cherub who had stepped from his niche in a discreet part of a cathedral to a discreet niche in the Civil Service, exchanging wings for shoulder-pads.

'No, sir. If he's still in Suffolk, where we last placed him, Purdey and Gambit may be able to contact him – I sent them up by helicopter.'

'Good. We'd better have Cromwell in.'

'I've just telephoned him too – he should be here in a minute.'

Quaintance beckoned Steed to sit down, sank into a leather easy chair. Not long afterwards, Cromwell arrived. The chief of DI 6 was a man in early middle age, who combined Harris tweeds with the complexion of a townsman. His face and hands were white, his eyes black.

'Good evening, Minister. Steed.'

They returned his greeting.

'So we've heard from our friend again, have we?' Cromwell frowned. 'I suppose there's no chance of this being a hoax. After all, the man died five years ago, so far as we know.'

'Perhaps we don't know enough,' Steed said.

'It could be a hoax,' Quaintance murmured thoughtfully. 'But if it is, the hoaxer knows that we used to have someone codenamed the Flyer, which means he must be, or have been, in our organisation.'

'Whoever it is, he's certainly set the cat among the pigeons now. All the media will want to know the meaning of the interruption tonight.'

'I think we ought to put out a blanket call,' Steed suggested. 'I've an idea he used the BBC because he wasn't getting a response from us.'

'How could he, when we don't know his wavelength?' from Cromwell.

'That's a point,' Quaintance answered, looking enquiringly at Steed. 'What exactly did he say?' he asked.

'This is the Flyer, the Flyer calling Daedalus. The Flyer has landed – the same message as before. Then he added something peculiar.' Steed rested his head against the chair-back, looked down his nose at the two men.

'It all seems peculiar,' Quaintance observed.

'And idiotic,' from Cromwell. 'What did he add?'

'He said: I can nail the White Rat.'

Silence in the room.

'Absolute nonsense, by the sound of it,' Quaintance said.

'I don't really think you should have troubled the Minister with this.' Cromwell frowned at Steed and gnawed a hang-nail.

'I disagree. I think we have to take this very seriously, gentlemen.'

'Indeed?' Cromwell refrained from any sign of encouragement.

'Why do we have to assume that it is really significant?' asked Quaintance, eyeing Steed closely.

'Because there was a White Rat. You must remember,' turning to Cromwell. 'In the '60s – he was a suspected double agent working right here in Whitehall. Successor to Philby and MacLean. We lost several good agents on account of the Rat, then he disappeared. That is to say, we heard no more about him.'

'It was a rumour, a theory,' Cromwell said. 'There was never any proof that he existed.'

'Corpses are proof. How else did our people die, if they weren't betrayed?'

'You don't have a life guaranteed danger-free if you're a spy,' Cromwell answered. 'You're bound to lose out occasionally, and if you do, the chances are that your loss will be permanent.'

'I concede that. But not that the people I'm talking about died as a result of the law of averages. Firstly, there wasn't just one, or two, but a batch, all killed within a short time of each other.

'Secondly, Irwin Gunner wasn't a myth – he existed. Judging from his morse fist – and some people still remember his style – he still does. Minister, we have to locate him.'

'I don't disagree with that. I'm only concerned that you don't waste vast amounts of time and money chasing a chap who isn't there.'

'We won't.' He looked enquiringly at Cromwell, who nodded agreement.

'Have you any idea where you're going to start?'

'I was just saying to the Minister – Purdey and Gambit are in Suffolk, which is where we last located him.' The telephone on his desk shrilled; Steed snatched up the receiver.

'Good. Fine. Thank you.' He replaced the receiver, smiled. 'He's still up there,' he said. 'We start at a radio pylon near Lowestoft.'

CHAPTER TWENTY-THREE

'Talk about needles in haystacks. And blacked-out ones at that.' Gambit was a disappointed man; dinner for two had abruptly been cancelled by Steed's radio message. Now, instead of Purdey's face opposite his, with a large steak apiece between them, he was having to fly slowly through the dark above the moon-silvered pylons just below.

'I doubt if he'd remain perched on top of the pylon all night,' Purdey said. 'It must be a trifle chilly, not to mention the drop if he happened to fall asleep.'

'Probably carries a safety harness amongst his other tibs and tabs.' He pointed ahead. 'He might be in that car – seems to be the only one about.'

'Try an interception, then.'

Gambit looked at her admiringly. My God, you're a cool one, yet I'm damn sure you're not as impenetrable as you make out. He sent the chopper swooping after the car, hovering above the dim ridges of hedgerows, prayed that telegraph wires would not suddenly leap from the darkness and bring them down in flames.

The car was travelling fast; Gambit brought the chopper's speed down to sixty, kept a straight course as the car burrowed its way between the hedgerows and along the winding road.

'I can't intercept him without hovering over the road just ahead of him.'

'All right, do that,' said Purdey calmly.

Gambit had a sudden urge to show off, but managed

to restrain it. He longed to send the chopper skidding round the sky, shadow-box the trees, skate across fields at ground level. Instead, he accelerated forward, flew over a pair of S-bends, came to rest a few feet above the roadway a half-mile in front of the car.

'I'll get out and thumb a lift,' Purdey shouted, opening the hatch.

'For God's sake, it might not be Gunner. And even if it is, he's likely to shoot first and ask questions later.'

'I doubt it,' coolly. 'Lift her up a bit, we don't want to frighten him.' She jumped lightly to the ground; Gambit sent the helicopter up a hundred feet, and waited.

The car swept round a bend, braked hard as Purdey stepped into the glitter of its headlights. Lithely, she hurried up to the driving door, peered inside.

'I'm going to Ipswich,' she said, 'can you give me a lift?'

The driver stared at her; he was wearing a clergyman's dog-collar. 'Ipswich?' He looked at Purdey in astonishment. 'This is the road to Stowmarket.'

'Oh well, all roads lead to Ipswich eventually, no doubt.'

The clergyman looked at the helicopter's lights, then at Purdey again, a self-possessed and wingless angel who had just climbed down Jacob's ladder.

'Please get in, then,' he murmured.

'Not the Flyer?' queried Purdey.

'The Flyer?' He shook his head, wondered if after all he ought to give a lift to someone who might not be entirely sane.

'It's all right, I've made a mistake. So sorry.' Purdey stepped in front of the headlights, signalled to Gambit, who immediately dropped to road level.

'Good night,' Purdey shouted to the clergyman, 'thanks for the offer.' She climbed into her seat alongside Gambit, a moment later was dangling high above the dazed reverend.

'No?' asked Gambit.

'No. The only sort of flying he might do is strictly celestial. He was a member of the cloth,' she explained.

Gambit laughed. 'Well, well, you certainly gave him a miracle to believe in,' and concentrated again on the countryside below.

There were no other headlights in view; only the pylons continued their static journey across the landscape.

On none of them was there the figure of a man.

CHAPTER TWENTY-FOUR

It was two days before Gunner made contact again. Immediately after his usual message about the Flyer, Purdey and Gambit were airborne, bound again for Suffolk.

In a rented Ford, Cledge too was headed again for Suffolk, and lamented the loss of his sports car every yard of the way. This time he would not come back till he had found Gunner and finished him off; the shotgun lay on the floor behind him.

Arrived in the neighbourhood of Framlingham, he stopped, stepped out of the car with a large-scale ordnance map, unrolled it on the bonnet.

'Now,' muttered Cledge, 'what would you do? You like farms, and you also like churches, I remember. This time I've a feeling it'll be a church – I wonder which one.' He stared at the map for some time, finally marked three circles on the map with red crayon.

He folded the map, put it on the seat beside him, and drove off.

The first church was early Norman, a squat tower which looked out over the countryside like a battlement. Cledge drew up some way down the road, stared up at the church in case there was any sign of movement. Nothing.

He strode along the grass at the side of the road, covered from view of anyone in the church by the hedgerows. Quickly, he opened the lych gate and went through it, entered the church quietly through a side door.

The church was still, with the atmosphere of a museum, religion a distant abstract, mummified and remote. Cledge tiptoed down the aisle like a bridegroom who hopes at the last moment that the bride won't see him, so that the whole thing will be off and he can regain his freedom.

Nice, open church this, thought Cledge, even Gunner wouldn't be able to hide up there. Not many pillars, open ledges. Where's the organ loft? Ah, there we are. I can't sense anybody hiding behind it – doesn't feel as though there's anyone else here.

Silently, Cledge emerged from the shadow of a pillar, went quickly past the altar into the vestry.

All was quiet and empty. Cledge glanced at the altar-piece, wondered how much it would fetch, made his way to the door and out again into the open air. Cross that one off the list – now for the next.

Cledge drove for a quarter of an hour, came in sight of the second church, stopped, entered with the same caution as before. Rows of pews too narrow for most bottoms to sit in comfort, flowers on the altar, stained glass windows shedding a red and purple glow. Cledge craned his head back, could not see any vantage point where Gunner might be lurking.

He went into the vestry without knocking at the door, found himself almost colliding with a priest who was about to leave.

'May I help you?' looking sharply at this burly intruder carrying a shotgun in the House of God.

'Sorry, I was looking for someone. A friend.'

'Indeed? With a deadly weapon?'

'I like shooting,' Cledge said. 'Grouse, mostly. Or pheasant. Legitimate, of course.'

'You must remember in future not to carry a gun into a church. I am surprised that you did not think to put it down outside.'

'I'm sorry,' beginning to feel anger well up in him.

'What does your friend look like?'

'Why?' asked Cledge suspiciously. 'Have you seen him?'

'I thought it might have been a she,' the vicar answered. 'I was unexpectedly accosted the other night by a girl who descended from a helicopter – I could well imagine her being friendly with a man who behaved as peculiarly as yourself.'

'Look,' said Cledge, 'do me a favour – don't lecture me on behaviour. It was a lapse, that's all, just a momentary lapse. Doesn't your memory ever let you down?'

'As a matter of fact, it doesn't,' the vicar said with acerbity. 'Now if I can be of service to you—' he gasped once as Cledge struck him, crumpled on the ground. Cledge struck him again, with the butt of the shotgun, felt the wild joy rise in him as he transformed the vicar's sleek grey head into pulp.

Dragging him to the door, Cledge looked carefully about, saw nobody, lugged the dead man to a newly dug grave, dropped him inside and began to cover him.

When he had finished, he drove on to the third church, his hand fondling the shotgun, butt clean after Cledge had wiped it repeatedly in the long grass beyond the churchyard.

'This must be it, unless he's gone off churches,' Cledge muttered. He cursed as a helicopter came in sight, clattered overhead, disappeared above and behind him.

'I wonder if that could be our friend,' Gambit said, 'let's play it cool. No stepping into space today, Purdey.'

Purdey smiled sweetly. 'I hear and obey, O Master. What do you suggest we do?'

'Frankly,' Gambit answered, 'I'm not sure. But we can't stop every car we see and ask: Is your name Gunner?'

'That car we've just flown over – it's stopped.'

Gambit banked steeply, making Purdey clutch her stomach, hovered a mile or so away from the stationary car, landed gently in a field.

'So?' Gambit raised an eyebrow. 'A car stops in front of a church, and—'

'But it didn't stop in front of it, it stopped several hundred yards from it, and there are no other buildings anywhere near. Doesn't that do anything to your adrenalin?'

'You do far more.'

'Come on,' Purdey said. 'I have a funny feeling about that car.'

'All right, I'll drop down a bit nearer.'

'And scare him away? What's the matter with your athletic prowess – it oughtn't to take more than four minutes to reach that church. Let's go.'

Gambit cut the motors; the chopper blades ceased to swirl and drooped like the ears of a disconsolate rabbit.

Cledge frowned at a gargoyle that was frowning at him. This church was baroque, its face florid and lumpy with strange beasts grinning in far from celestial fashion. A cluster of yews in the churchyard had been treated as objets d'art, if not of vertu, by the local topiarist – a cock crowed at the church steeple, something between an ostrich and a guinea-fowl looked ready to defecate on any passing worshipper.

Inside the church, the pattern continued; everything was carved and curlicued, and even the stained glass windows were fussy. Virgin and child, satyr and goblin, rested in every niche and alcove or leaned precariously over scalloped ledges.

In front of the altar, two matrons were arranging dahlias; they regarded Cledge curiously as he tried to look like a penitent. He sank to his knees, assembled the shotgun, which he hoped had looked like a disassembled fishing-rod.

Head bowed, Cledge studied the beams in front of him, raised his face as though vouchsafed a vision and had a good look at the rest of the church's architecture. His hair was rising; Gunner was here, he was sure of it. Maybe he was looking down at this very second, grinning to himself as he saw Cledge screwing the shotgun together, a revolver in his fist aimed at the back of Cledge's neck.

He never shoots without warning, that's what I must gamble on. The fool won't plug me in the back, I'll have time to throw myself sideways and bring the gun up. That'll do him. Where is he, where the hell is he?

The two ladies finished their business, went out, whispering. Sheltering between pews, Cledge found himself becoming jumpy. 'Gunner,' he murmured, 'are you here, Gunner?'

No answer, though it seemed an answer had echoed from the vaulted roof: 'Gunner, Gunner.'

The church door opened, and Purdey came in.

Cledge jumped as the door moved, relaxed as he saw that it was a girl. Pretty good-looker, too. She made her way up the aisle towards him, knelt in a pew nearby.

Damn, that makes it awkward. I hope to God my instinct's wrong and that Gunner isn't here after all. Come on, Miss Mantis, hurry up and get on with it and get out. He stared at the nape of Purdey's neck with hatred, again glanced up and along the vaulted beams above. He saw a silhouette, a shadow, a figment of imagination. Gunner.

'Gunner,' he whispered, unaware that he had spoken.

'Cledge,' the answer echoed in the taut quiet.

Purdey rose, stepped out of her pew, bowed in the direction of the altar, leaped backwards in a powerful, inverted kangaroo movement which brought her alongside Cledge.

At the same moment, Gambit rushed in, paused as he saw Purdey take a big, treacle-haired man who was shouting up at the ceiling: 'I've come to help you – can't you see we've been betrayed?'

Purdey leaned back, sent her right foot flying at Cledge's chin. He crashed backwards, dropping the shotgun – as Gambit began to run, he was flung down by the weight of a man jumping on to his back.

Gunner ran for the door, slamming it behind him; Cledge cursed and propelled himself forward into another kick. He caught Purdey's foot, twisted it; moving with it, she lashed out with her other foot and caught Cledge under the ear. He grunted, sagged, but managed a vicious sideways movement upward to Purdey's groin; she grunted, chopped down with her right hand at Cledge's neck, then pulled his face hard forward into her knee.

The two women who had been tending the altar flowers came running, let out a harrowing descant of screams as they saw Gambit lying in the middle of the aisle, and a tall, slender girl beating up a hefty and blood-stained man.

'It's all right,' Purdey called, 'just a local disturbance.' She grabbed Cledge by the hair, as he took a pistol from his pocket, let him have one last tremendous kick which sent him upwards and back; there was a loud report as a pistol went off.

Far down the road, Gunner drove intently, shaking with the reaction of recent events – who was friend, and who foe? Anyway, thank God for another of Cledge's cars.

CHAPTER TWENTY-FIVE

'So Cledge is dead.' Quaintance looked at Steed sombrely.

'He evidently went to catch a flyer. But it was the catcher who was caught.' He let a yellowed photograph of a tall, powerful man drop on to Quaintance's desk. 'John Cledge, Gunner's partner in the trapeze act. Died of a broken skull augmented by a gunshot wound – could have been a dead heat.'

'A somewhat distasteful observation.'

'But not tasteless, I'm sure you'll agree.' He tapped the photograph. 'This is the man who actually got to Gunner, although we pulled out every stop to do so. How? What was his intention? That's easier to answer than my first question – he went there to kill him.'

'Don't you think you're being over-suspicious, Steed?' Quaintance frowned. 'There's such a thing as being too theoretical.'

'I disagree. You can't say that it's all theory, because it's backed up by fact. How did Cledge know where to find Gunner? Presumably because he listened in to Gunner's transmissions. No problem there. How did he know where to find him? Because he was able to pinpoint his position, or because, remembering Gunner's habits, he had a theory' – grinning at the minister – 'which was correct. "Chap likes to hole up in churches," he told himself, 'so I'll have an ecclesiastical tour of the vicinity in which he located him.' His eyes narrowed. 'We'd have found life much simpler if Gunner had trusted us sufficiently to make more direct contact, or if, for that matter, he'd just toddled up to the office. He didn't. Why? Because, Minister, he's been suspicious of us from the start.'

'What you are implying is that there is today someone in our organisation who is, to say the least, untrustworthy. That is an appalling implication.'

'It's happened many times before, and I'm afraid it'll happen again. The last time it happened, that we know of, was when our friend the White Rat was active. What's happened to him? Was he killed in action, has he retired to grow roses in Dorking? Or, far more likely, has he been promoted for his pains? He'd now be far more powerful, carry far more weight, than a mere traitor in the field,' Steed continued bitterly. 'Lunch at the club, dinner as some hostess's honoured guest, and now and again a brief flipping over of the pages of his memory, a savouring of some spot of doublecross that left one of his colleagues to the mercies of East European secret police.'

'You're over-reacting, in my view.'

'That's better than not acting at all.' He and Quaintance stared at each other; Quaintance's eyes dropped first.

'Look, sir,' Steed said persuasively, 'Gunner comes back, a living ghost and won't stay comfortably glued in a scrapbook. He's all ready to pull the rug from under the White Rat, whose identity he knows, or at least strongly suspects. What more natural reaction on the part of our treacherous friend than to have Gunner safely pasted back in the scrapbook?'

'Why Cledge?'

'Presumably because Cledge was part of the original

White Rat cell.'

'Let's see what Cromwell thinks.' Quaintance reached towards the buzzer, stood up instead. 'I could do with a walk,' he said. 'Let's go to the ops room.' He followed Steed out.

In the ops room, Cromwell was listening to a voice that came huskily from a loudspeaker brooding from its perch on the wall.

'White Rat? I'm calling you, White Rat,' the voice croaked. The girl operator looked pale and unsure. Cromwell was glaring at the speaker, swung round to greet Quaintance. 'Good afternoon, Minister. Sorry about this – I have a feeling that we're up against someone who isn't quite right in the head.'

'I'm inclined to agree. It's Steed who keeps preventing me from reaching total conviction that the chap's mad.' Cromwell eyed Steed unlovingly, the three men gave their attention to the voice which now increased in volume with burgeoning anger.

'White Rat – this message is for you; I know what I'm up against now. I'd forgotten how quickly rats breed. I suppose there's a whole department of you now?'

'Outrageous,' muttered Quaintance.

'Disgraceful,' from Cromwell. Steed remained silent.

'Rats can hide, or scuttle away, but not from me. Oh no, White Rat. We both know, don't we, that you can't hide from me. I've put my mark on you, and I'm going to destroy you. Goodbye, White Rat – why don't you drink to our next meeting? I suggest you fill your glass with strychnine – that's the only way you'll avoid me.'

Cromwell was white. 'Well?' to the operator.

'I'm sorry, sir. I couldn't get a fix – it was very close by.'

'Very close?' Quaintance asked.

'Yes, sir.'

'Then he could be in London,' Steed said. 'If you'll forgive me for stating the obvious.'

'He must be found at once!' from Quaintance, compounding the obvious.

'Well, sir, we've done it once and I'm sure we can do it again.'

'You'd better!' Cromwell snapped.

Steel smiled forgivingly at him, carefully placed his bowler on his head, and went out.

'I think that fellow's becoming a trifle tedious,' Cromwell observed.

Discreetly, as befitted a minister attached to the Foreign and Commonwealth Office, Quaintance merely nodded.

CHAPTER TWENTY-SIX

Septimus Grant was a man who had not progressed very far in life, having been born with nearly everything. He lay back in his bath, a Montecristo in his mouth; an onyx ashtray, a bottle of Talisker and a Waterford tumbler on a salver rested within easy reach.

The displacement of the bath-water was considerable, Grant being rotund, as befitted a bon vivant, but was compensated for by an Everest of bubbles which welled up round his chin like a Puritan's frilled collar.

On an ingeniously adapted music stand, a copy of the latest salacious novel was positioned a few feet from Grant's eyes; he turned the pages with a loofah.

So intent was he on the doings of a nymphomaniac heroine and her covey of worn-out lovers, that Grant did not notice the window above him slowly open; beyond it was a rooftop view of that part of London still enjoying residential status between the Strand and the Thames. The scenic view was now augmented by the addition of a face, rugged and broken-nosed; above the nose a deep scar ran across the forehead.

''Evening,' Gunner said.

'What the devil—' Grant surged partly out of the water, sounded, fell back with his mouth open.

'Not really,' Gunner replied. 'Though I have plenty of the devil in me, these days. Don't say you don't recognise me.'

'I'm not accustomed to strange men accosting me when I'm in my bath.'

'I'm not accosting you, Grant. And I'm not strange, either. Look at my face closely.'

Grant would have far rather looked closely at the face of the nymphomaniac heroine, but he obeyed. 'Well?' shrugging under his bubbles, 'am I supposed to know you?' He added petulantly: 'I do have a front door, you know.'

'I don't doubt it. Doors can be traps, and in any case I wasn't sure you'd let me in.'

'Well, now that you have gained some sort of ingress, what do you want?'

'I'm Gunner.'

'Gunner?' incredulously.

'That's right. Glad you haven't forgotten the name.'

'Of course I haven't. But why are you behaving like a cat burglar? Someone chasing you?'

'Simpler than that, Grant. I want to be anonymous, so far as anyone else in the house is concerned, because I may have to kill you.'

'Oh?' Grant went pale, insofar as a man of vinous complexion in a hot bath can go pale, then grinned. 'Is this a joke?'

'I hope it turns out to be that. For the time being, let's just say it's a reunion.' He thoughtfully regarded the gun which rested on the window-ledge, and which Grant had not hitherto noticed. The sight was not reassuring, but a fat man in a bubble-bath is not really equipped for evasive action. Grant did his best to relax.

'We were a tight, happy little group, weren't we?' Gunner went on. 'Comrades. Yet one of us was a traitor, did you know that? In fact, more than one. But the other's dead now, I understand.'

'Oh?'

'At least he died in church,' Gunner observed. 'But he wasn't the White Rat.' He fondled the gun. 'I'm kind of curious as to who he was. Not you, by any chance?'

'For God's sake, man, do I look like a white rat?'

Gunner grinned, pointed the gun. 'No, but then you don't look like Venus, either.'

'I'll overlook that.' Grant tried to smile amiably. 'Look, old chap, I'm out of that now – moved on to higher places.'

'So has the White Rat.'

'Can I offer you a drink – a cigar – a bit of soap?' Grant asked, hoping to reduce the tension that was filling the steamy room.

Gunner ignored the offer. 'You were in the Navy, weren't you?'

'Yes. Quite a long time ago, now.'

'What do they say when they're getting the men up in the morning?' climbing through the window to stand poised above the bath. Grant stared up at him, cigar ash floating under his chin.

'Look, do you mind standing back, Gunner?'

'They say: "show a leg", don't they?' Abruptly, he leaned forward, raised one of Grant's fleshy legs; where his head had been there was only the ash and a dead cigar floating soggily on the foam.

Gunner released his grip; Grant reappeared, gurgling and trying to dash soap from his eyes. When he could see again, he glared at space – Gunner had gone.

'Confound the impertinent ass!' He tossed the remains of his disintegrating Montecristo into the ashtray, turned on the shower, stepped out of the bath into the embrace of a vast turkish towel.

He shook his head mournfully; although he believed in encountering as many novel experiences as possible in this life, the interruption of his bath grieved him.

'The White Rat,' he mumbled to himself, wondering if the code name would conjure up a portrait, trigger off a significant flash of instinct whose end product might be at least an MBE.

The name conjured up nothing but the vision of a white rat. Shaking his head, Grant left the bathroom, made his way downstairs to find another cigar. It was a long time before he felt able to go to bed – for all he knew, Gunner might appear in the bedroom and stuff a pillow over his head.

'Anyhow,' he muttered to himself, as he snuggled down between the sheets, 'there's one consolation. At least I'm not the White Rat. And I don't specially envy the chap who is.'

CHAPTER TWENTY-SEVEN

Regency Gate was a block of flats that relied on the illusion of historical association to make one forget the 30s façade, the narrow flanking streets, which forbade any real attempt at grandeur.

Free from vandals, but not from neglect, Regency Gate at night had the careworn aspect of a working mother returning home to a large family and indolent husband; its windows loomed sadly over the rest of the district, squat and unambitious, and its semicircular drive-in had all the invitation of a man-hating whore in her sixtieth year.

Purdey parked a few yards from the building, walked swiftly up to the peeling doors giving on to the shabby lobby, and entered. She pressed the button, without much hope, of a lift whose doors were blemished beyond repair, changed her mind about entering when they hesitantly slid open, and took the stairs two at a time.

Arrived at the third floor, she walked lightly down the corridor, stopped in front of a dead man's door. 'John Cledge' stated a brass plate.

Purdey produced a pick-lock and skilfully employed it, opened the door just sufficiently to squeeze through into the flat beyond. She was taut, ready for combat, even if her opponent was nothing more substantial than the dark. She groped along the wall for a light-switch, found her arms grabbed from behind and rammed excruciatingly towards her shoulders.

Allowing herself to go limp, she aimed a murderous rear kick, missed, was grappled to the floor. A shape bent over her – she raised her leg and caught it sharply under the chin.

Her adversary grunted, fell backward; Purdey leaped on to him and sent him sprawling on to a settee. In the dim light from outside she recognised him.

'Good Lord, Mr Cromwell.'

'Right,' panting. 'It seems we both had the same idea.'

'A very obvious one,' Purdey said coolly. 'If Cledge got to the Flyer before us – how? And also – why? Although Steed has a theory about that.'

'Steed has too many theories. And I'll tell you this, Purdey – the answer isn't here. I've searched the place thoroughly.'

'I see.'

'I did find one thing, though.'

Purdey eyed him enquiringly. 'Oh?'

'A surprisingly good malt scotch. Join me?'

'All right.' He rose, moved to a light switch, went over to a small cabinet.

'You play rough, Mr Cromwell.'

'You play rougher, Purdey.'

'I wasn't playing.'

'Neither was I. We're both lucky.' He poured two drinks, carried them over to her. Devilish attractive girl, but something distant about her, sex lost beneath the boiler-suit of her efficiency. Love to crack that veneer – or is it a veneer? maybe she's all veneer – peel it away and you have the Invisible Woman.

'You'd better take your trousers off,' said Purdey.

For one moment Cromwell was filled with disbelieving joy. 'I say—' stopped when he saw that she was pointing lower than he would have liked.

'You've torn your trouser-leg – or I've torn it for you. You really are lucky – I was aiming a fraction higher.'

Cromwell shuddered. 'It's forbidden to emasculate the boss,' he said.

Purdey gave him a slight smile, professional and devoid of warmth. 'Was Cledge a bachelor, do you know?'

'Eh? I think so – I don't know.' He stood just in front of her, wondering if arousal were possible. 'Why?'

'Because it'll have to be black thread if he was. That's all bachelors ever have.'

'I'm a bachelor,' Cromwell told her. 'At least, I'm a widower.' Play the pity bit – she might succumb. 'Cancer, you know. Of the liver.'

'I'm sorry to hear that,' dispassionate as usual. Was there no way to light up this girl, was she really a female eunuch? Surely not, not with that figure and those legs. Good for kicking, but also—

Impending daydreams of lecherous intent were interrupted by Purdey rising, walking round him to a small Italian worktable, whose lid she lifted.

'I knew it – black thread only. Never mind, it'll suffice to bestow respectability till you reach home.' Cromwell stared at her. 'Come on, come on,' Purdey insisted, 'I'm about to do my Mother Earth bit.'

'Off?'

'Well I can hardly sew them in situ, can I? Far too dangerous.'

'Very well.' Slowly he removed his trousers, wondered whether to risk giving Purdey the preliminary embrace that might lead to temporary paradise. She began to sew, aware of need burgeoning in front of her. Must hurry, otherwise the department head will either be grappling with you again, from in front, or grovelling for every crumb you can spare from your table. Yet I have to admit he's rather attractive – it might be fun to prise the butterfly from the chrysalis. No, too complicated – it would be bound to end messily. Either I'd be out of a job, or he would. Anyhow, I'm not built for momentary sexual aberrations. All the same – he's a big man.

'Purdey—' Cromwell's voice was thick.

'Mr Cromwell?'

'Couldn't we forget – just for a few minutes—'

'I don't go in for short leases,' Purdey told him.

'Please – I want you.'

'I'm complimented. But removing your trousers isn't really a passport to my favours – anyway, they're done now,' handing them to him.

'Do you really want me to put them on?'

'There wouldn't have been much point in my making them respectable, if you proposed to dispense with them altogether.'

'I'm not joking,' his face a few inches from hers. 'You're a marvellous girl, Purdey.'

'Oh, I have all the virtues. I can sew, iron, create a splendid cheese soufflé – and break a man's back in three places.'

'I know. But you could also break a man's heart,' Cromwell said. 'You know, I don't want to boast, but I'm pretty good.'

'I'm not all that sold on goodness. Now be good and put your pants back on.'

Cromwell did not answer; he took Purdey's shoulders and moved his face forward to kiss her. 'I've never been more vulnerable than I am now,' he whispered, 'to either a kiss of a kick.'

'I won't make a choice,' answered Purdey softly; his lips pressed hard against hers but she did not respond. Christ, does she want to be raped? How do you play a woman who won't reveal anything of herself – with a dry fly or a spinner? He was a man unaccustomed to feeling helpless – it was irritating, to say the least, to be made to feel unworldly when you sought to feel out of this world.

'For the moment,' Purdey murmured, 'I think esprit de corps, camaraderie, what you will – ought to come first. Later – who knows?'

Cromwell swallowed, could still not quite believe, in the heat of male need and male pride, that he was resistible. As Purdey walked towards the door, evading his outstretched hands, he forced a smile and slipped his trousers on as bidden.

'You're a tough girl, Purdey.'

'That's why you employ me, isn't it?' and gave him a glance so serene that his passion was virtually poulticed.

CHAPTER TWENTY-EIGHT

'It's not that I'm a complaining man, sans sensibility, sans proportion, but I'm not all that keen on gun-toting ex-pugilists invading my bathroom.'

'He's not an ex-pugilist, actually,' Steed answered, raising his glass to Grant and closing his mind's eye to the vision of the man in a bubble bath. 'He used to be a trapeze artist.'

'Whilst I am of course indebted to you for any biographical note you may proffer, the fact remains that the fellow was in my bathroom a half-hour ago and I'd be grateful if you could assure me that he won't appear again. God damn it,' Grant said plaintively, 'I've disbelieved in genies all my life in spite of several childhood visits to Aladdin, and I'd infinitely prefer to remain a disbeliever. Your chap Gunner looked as though he'd come into being without benefit of a rubbed lamp anyway – a rusty frying-pan scraped across a cast-iron stove would be more his cup of tea.'

'He's not really our chap at the moment – we're trying to find him, but he keeps darting away just as we think we have him.'

Grant scowled. 'What's it about, Steed? I haven't been involved in any cloak-and-dagger stuff for years – you know that. Too old to go chasing across the cosmos with a gun in my hand and a death-wish in my brain. Death-wishes are for the young – when you reach my age the life-wish takes over.'

'However, you did work with Gunner in the days of

your cloak-and-daggerism, didn't you?'

'In a vague sort of way – he was a contact, not much more.'

'Who else was on that team?' intently.

'Hard to say, really. You know what it's like. Agents anonymous, mustn't know more than is good for you. Can't give away secrets then, no matter what they do to you – better be tortured to death than relay useless information if the cyanide pill misfires.'

Steed grinned. 'Ever heard of a chap called Cledge?'

'Cledge?' Grant took Steed's glass, topped it up with more whiskey. 'Wasn't he with Gunner? The name does ring some sort of bell. Ah, he was a trapeze artist too – when you mentioned that that was Gunner's profession, I had a faint idea he didn't practise it alone.'

'That's right – he needed someone to catch him.'

'Of course – not a pastime for a solitaire player, is it? So what happened?'

'There came a time when Cledge didn't catch him. At least, so I suspect. Cledge bumped into Gunner a couple of days ago, and now Cledge is dead. So I have a feeling that either Cledge did the dirty on Gunner in the Big Top, or somewhere else, but the Big Top seems the more likely theory.'

'What about a safety net?'

'They're not compulsory, and a lot of performers still think they're a bit cissified.'

'You wouldn't get me up on a trapeze,' Grant said, admiring his ample paunch.

Steed mentally agreed. He drank the last of his scotch, eased himself out of his chair. 'Thanks for your help – and for your hospitality.'

'Sorry I couldn't have been of more use – thanks for

being so prompt anyway. Makes a fellow feel uncertain – the thought that some bloke with a grudge can appear at the window and duck you in your bath.'

'At least he let you up again,' Steed told him consolingly.

'There is that. Anyhow, good luck with your search.' He eyed Steed commiseratingly. 'I should have some sleep, if I were you.'

'Oh, I shall, I shall. As soon as we've found Gunner, I'll metamorphose into a giant sloth, and hang upside down from the FO flag-pole.'

He tilted his hat, trotted down the steps to his car.

Back at the office, Steed found red-eyed Finder studying some files. Only one light was on – Finder would rather go blind, Steed thought, than add a penny to the office's fuel bill.

'Find anything?'

'Not much – I've gone through everything from 1960 to '70.' Steed looked at the pile on the table, bent forward and gave the files an intense scrutiny.

'Have you had these down before, Finder?'

'Not till this evening. Why?'

'Well, well, well. With all due respect, old fruit, dust is almost mandatory in this place, but behold' – tapping the pile with his walking-stick – 'no dust on these.'

'I can get you some,' Finder offered sarcastically. 'The 1930s files – now the only dust to touch the quality on those is moon dust. In fact, I wouldn't be surprised if some of this floated up there over the years for Neil Armstrong to bring back again.'

Steed grinned. 'I'm more interested at present in no dust. Why? Has anyone asked to see these lately?'

'Yes, most of the people in the department working

on the Gunner case. Messrs Gambit, Purdey, the minister—'

'Quaintance was in here?'

'Not exactly. He sent for the files. Then there was Mr Cromwell, and—'

'All right,' Steed interrupted. 'I suppose it was fairly obvious that one person's tracks would be obscured by the herd's.'

He sighed. 'So. Let's see if we can find something no one else has tumbled to. You never know. Has anyone made any unusual requests lately?'

Finder grinned. 'No more so than usual.'

'Oh well, that's what I expected. You'd better get some sleep. It'll soon be time to come back.'

'Thanks. I could do with a few hours.'

'The next incarnation will no doubt see us both as nocturnal animals. I wouldn't mind being a badger – sporting animals. Game, set, and match. How about you?'

Finder stared at his visitor reproachfully, made for the door. 'I don't really care what I come back as, as long as it doesn't make puns,' he said. 'Good night, Mr Steed.'

'Good night,' Steed turned over another page, whistled softly. 'I wonder,' he murmured; 'Gilpin, old man, you might just be worth a visit.' And went out.

CHAPTER TWENTY-NINE

Fingers probed into drawers, displaced ornaments on a desk. Fingers that searched with an almost desperate diligence, the toccata of the thief, flipped over papers, scattered on the carpet delicate particles of personal history unheedingly.

The fingers briefly paused; in the dark by the light-switch, unheard, unobserved, Steed stood ready to jump the other intruder.

The fingers started to flicker again, pushing aside documents, rustling through old cheque-books, flicking away bits of dust and lint. Two empty drawers, no results, four more drawers to go.

'Good evening,' Steed said, depressing the switch; in the abrupt glare of an overhead light and the reproving glow of a standard lamp, Quaintance went rigid. Steed, curved like a bow, straightened up. 'Good evening, Minister.'

'Steed, what on earth are you doing here?'

'Wondering what you're doing. I know the ethics of government are changing,' blandly, 'but rifling a citizen's desk – shouldn't you leave that to the Inland Revenue? Or at least the Customs and Excise?' He smiled, watching Quaintance's hands – if he reaches for anything, I'll spring. 'Also,' he added, 'you broke the lock – it would have been so much kinder merely to have picked it.'

'I'm not particularly well versed in breaking into people's homes.' Quaintance was red with embarrassment. 'However, I can explain my actions.'

'I hope so.' Steed's voice was hard. 'As I am responsible for security, I must insist on an explanation.'

Deprived of the writ of his authority, Quaintance seemed to shrink slightly; the tough politician and seasoned cocktail campaigner did not even seem resentful of being spoken to in tones of distrust and rebuke.

'Mark Gilpin was in the same spy cell as Irwin Gunner in 1960.'

'Yes, I knew that.'

'It's therefore not unreasonable to suspect that Gilpin might be the White Rat, then.'

'Have you found anything to confirm your suspicions?'

'No.'

'Tell me,' smooth as a rapier going into a rubber duck, 'what did you expect to find?'

'I don't know – clues don't exactly proclaim themselves in advance, do they?' Quaintance sounded aggrieved. 'A diary, a photograph – something like that could incriminate him.'

'Perhaps it might be a better idea to have a word with him when he comes back. After all, if he's not the White Rat, he might be able to guess who the White Rat is.' Steed sat on the edge of the desk, allowed himself a slight smile. 'You see, Minister, I have to be professionally suspicious of everyone, even myself!'

Quaintance decided to be magnanimous. 'You're a good man, Steed.'

'I do my best.'

Quaintance was about to say that it was an excellent

best, but decided that he would be overstepping the boundary between the cordial and the effusive.

'Gunner visited a chap named Grant who used to be with us,' Steed said.

'I had an idea that Gunner might be doing the rounds. As a matter of fact, Grant was next on my list.'

Steed nodded. 'I've seen him. I don't think he's our man.'

'Oh? When was that?'

'About three hours ago.'

Quaintance yawned. 'Don't you ever sleep?'

'A catnap here, a catnap there. That's when I'm on an assignment like this one. I'm not a man who can sleep with something on his mind, so the best thing to do is to stay awake until circumstances have put my mind at ease.'

Quaintance yawned again. 'I'll push off, I think. Gilpin may not be coming back at all.'

'Didn't you ask at the lodge gate?'

'I naturally asked if Gilpin was in – I didn't enquire what time he was going to return.'

'I did, and they said they thought about midnight. There was a strong suggestion of a leer – do you suppose dons do that sort of thing?'

'I don't see why the anatomy of a don should atrophy more quickly than anyone else's. After all, Gilpin can't be much over fifty. You can't expect celibacy at that age – not as a guiding principle.'

'I suppose not. Unless you get paid for it,' Steed said absently, his gaze focused on the dark quadrangle below the window. 'There are times when the monastic life appeals.'

'I didn't know you got paid for being a monk.'

'I don't think you do – in cash. But think of the kind.'

Quaintance was about to reply, but Steed shushed him. 'Look,' he whispered, 'isn't that Gilpin?' as a splash of moonlight fell on a tall, angular man coming along the path towards them.

'Yes,' breathed Quaintance. 'Hadn't we better meet outside – don't want him to—'

'Look!' Steed pointed, turned, sprinted from the room. Quaintance remained at the window, temporarily transfixed by the sight of what looked like a large gorilla, which swung from the lower branches of a tree a few yards away and took a neck lock on Gilpin. Gurgling, the unfortunate don was suspended without dignity for a moment, before being propelled into the shrubbery, followed thither by his assailant.

Steed ran towards the bushes, forced his way into them. Almost at once, he came upon Gilpin's recumbent body.

'The man's mad,' Gilpin gasped. 'Pounces on me like an ape, flings me to the ground, and does this!' He held up his left leg, a sorry, skinny, pallid affair revealed to the moon because its shielding trouser had been ripped to the crotch.

'A pretty near thing, I'd say.'

'How do you mean? What do you suppose he was after?'

'I'd hate to guess,' Steed told him, extending a hand. He heaved Gilpin to his feet. Gunner, hidden in the branches of another tree, grinned to himself, longed to add to the repartee. He stiffened, as Quaintance came hurrying up.

'The bastard!' he muttered, chill with anger. 'That's him – it must be.'

Quaintance limped to a stop. 'What on earth was that about?'

Gilpin repeated his story. 'It was like encountering the Missing Link,' he explained. 'There I was, on my way back to my room, when I was—'

'We saw,' Steed interrupted gently.

'Of course. That explains how you came to be here so quickly.'

'Quite.' Steed tucked an arm round Gilpin's body, just below the arms, escorted him to the building just ahead. Up the stairs, into the don's sitting-room.

'Good heavens – someone's been here!' Gilpin looked at his desk, which Quaintance had neglected to tidy.

'I'm afraid I was responsible for that,' he said, leaning against the door.

'I don't understand.' Gilpin screwed up his eyes, stared at Quaintance. 'Aren't you the Foreign Minister?'

'I am.'

Gilpin shook his head. 'If you hadn't been, the resemblance would have been most startling.'

Steed smiled, considerately helped Gilpin into a chair. 'Supposing you tell us who pounced on you,' he suggested.

'I haven't the slightest idea. A large creature, but not wearing anything over its head.'

'It didn't need to,' said Steed.

Gilpin gave a thin smile. 'Quite so,' he said, 'a face like that hardly ranks as an aesthetic experience.'

'You didn't recognise it?'

'I would scarcely have forgotten it. No, I did not recognise it.' He looked at Quaintance. 'I seem to be answering your questions,' turning back to Steed, 'yet surley I am the one who is entitled to some information.

You come here, break in, pry into my affairs, make a mess – is there any reason why I should not report this matter?'

'We thought we might be saving your life,' Steed said smoothly.

Gilpin stared at him in astonishment. 'Why should you think that? Who would wish to take my life, for heaven's sake?'

'You were in an Intelligence cell in the late 60s.' Steed's eyes were suddenly cold. 'There was a traitor in that cell, codenamed the White Rat.'

'Ah,' Gilpin nodded. 'We all had peculiar names, it was really rather childish. Perhaps it was because we played games, though hardly of the nursery kind.'

'Hardly. You could be the White Rat. That is why your life is perhaps in danger.'

'How dare you, sir! Are you implying that I was a traitor?'

'I am not implying anything. However, the chap who had a go at you just now was betrayed by the White Rat, and wants to see that he doesn't betray anyone else. Also, he wants to punish him for what he did in the past.'

'In that case, why didn't he finish me off, instead of my trousers?'

'A sound question. What do you think, Minister?'

'Perhaps the White Rat had a birth-mark of some kind on his leg. I can't think of any other reason. It wasn't because Gunner—'

'Gunner?' interrupted Gilpin.

'That's right. Remember him?'

'He once gave me a couple of seats for a circus. I was most impressed by his agility, which was matched only by his courage. No safety net, you see.'

'Did you know him at all – outside the circus?'

'Only casually. We had met once or twice at briefings at the Ministry of Defence. Apart from that, I had no opportunity to enjoy the presence of his company.' He frowned in puzzlement. 'But the person who leaped on me from the tree wasn't Gunner. It didn't resemble him at all.'

'He had an accident; one of the reason's he wants to have a settlement out of court with the White Rat is his face. The Rat gave it to him.'

'Good heavens.' Gilpin sniffed. 'In that case, he can hardly be blamed for wanting revenge.'

'Quite. Anyhow, he let you go, which seems to indicate that you're in the clear so far as being the Rat is concerned. On the other hand, someone else may want to eliminate you, in case you can guess who it is.'

'What? Do you mean to say that—'

'We don't want to alarm you – we're busy tracking down the other members of the cell. The chances are that we'll find the Rat soon.'

'But in the meantime—?'

'In the meantime, don't walk under any more trees,' Steed said cheerfully. 'And don't let in strangers.'

'I find your frivolity unsettling,' Gilpin said with asperity.

'Don't be unsettled,' Steed advised him. 'We'll turn the heat on the White Rat so much that he'll be too intent on saving his own skin to worry about spoiling other people's.' He tipped his hat, bowed to Quaintance, who limped out in front of him. 'Goodbye,' he said.

From his vantage point in the nearby tree, Gunner clenched his fists and scowled, which made him look more like a gorilla than ever.

CHAPTER THIRTY

Quaintance was not normally a nervous man. As a politician who had clawed rather than clambered up the ladder to authority, he was prone to sacrifice anyone or anything on the altar of his ambition. He was an affectionate father, and like so many of his kind, a fond but absentee husband. He went forth into the fields, his wife could till or sew as she liked, or even indulge in minor flirtation with shepherd or herdsman, so long as it wasn't too obvious.

Instead of love-filled beds, Quaintance went in for smoke-filled nights, flung the mantle of his personality over anybody he could find in the Commons bar, alcohol the wood, charm the nails, determination the hammer, with which he continued to construct the rungs of the ladder which would take him to the top.

Women were a necessary frivolity, physical solace, mental sop; Quaintance preferred intelligent women to stupid, educated to illiterate, but if forced to a choice, opted for beauty irrespective of the person on whom it was bestowed.

This evening, as twilight hovered and settled, Quaintance found himself uneasy, unable to concentrate. Last night had been a bizarre experience – thank God Steed had showed up. Yet Steed now had something on himself – not of course that he would ever use it, but nevertheless—

And Gilpin, that fellow could go about saying that he had discovered one of Her Majesty's senior ministers raiding his desk. Quaintance frowned – he must be losing his grip. Nobody in his position could afford an Achilles heel – last night he had incurred all sorts of vulnerability.

Now, in addition to being almost under an obligation to Steed – a fairly pleasant fellow, but inclined to be arrogant to the point of being supercilious – he had to face the fact that an improbable ex-agent called Gunner was living up to his name. Fellow must be crackers, swinging about in trees and ripping people's trousers. Nevertheless, not to be taken lightly.

Quaintance's frown changed to a scowl. I resent being a target; I'm the one who's used to having a finger on the trigger, who's accustomed to manipulate other men – I'm damned if I'm going to be manipulated by apprehension. There's something so undignified about bodyguards, the intrusive aspects of the convoy of privilege. I'm ceasing to be an individual and becoming an entourage, and I don't like it. That fellow Gunner must be caught as quickly as possible – Steed seems actually to sympathise with the man. I suppose in a way I can sympathise with him myself, but the fact remains that he's a menace.

Grant – Grant carries sufficient weight in every sense of the word, to throw it about if he wants to – supposing he starts to talk about his disturbed bath night? Sort of chap who'd turn it into a joke, and our security with it. Quaintance stared moodily from his study window across his lawn and flowerbeds.

This house is no fortress. When I bought it I didn't anticipate physical attack – it's only lately that I've had to have it protected. I don't like it – if you put up too many barriers between yourself and the world outside, you become the prisoner, not the world. Power in a carapace of helpless impregnability.

Impatiently, Quaintance slammed a steel grille across the window of his study, stared at a group of oaks which as he watched merged with the dusk and became amorphous, ill-defined as his next move.

A guard walked by the window, an alsatian on a leash loping beside him. Quaintance, who had an unresponsive soul where dogs were concerned, wondered if the alsatian was well-trained when it came to faecal deposits; he could do without that sort of fouling of his lawns.

He reached for the telephone, desisted. It would be a sign of weakness to ring Cromwell for another progress report – everything possible was being done, of that he was sure. Cromwell tended to regard Gunner's resurrection as an impertinence – in his eyes, unsolved mysteries had an undesirable impudence.

Steed too – in addition to the pride of a man who had elevated sartorial elegance to the point of commanding the same sort of reverence as most of the major deities, he was proud of his team. The virtues of vanity – none of the team would accept anything but victory.

One man against the department – it's only a matter of time before they get him. For God's sake stop worrying.

He limped over to a cocktail cabinet, poured out a large scotch, sipped it at first, then gulped it.

High in a tree across the lawn, Gunner grinned, curled and uncurled his fingers, flexed his muscles. Getting nervous, are we? Good, that's what Gunner likes to see. The White Rat getting into a state – how many of your victims behaved like that, before they got the chop?

Wonder how Hart felt – they said it was an accident, being run over like that, but I never believed them. And Jennings, winding up under a train without his head. Another accident, just like Julie Bennett's.

Gunner's hands were white as they clasped a bough. Poor Julie – how lovely she was. A real sweetheart. The only girl I ever had a real feeling for, who I loved, for Christ's sake, though she thought of me more as an uncle.

He could hardly bear to think of Julie – misery reached a certain point and after that it was impossible to feel any more miserable. The thought of Julie lying smashed on the stone floor had tormented Gunner since he had found out what had happened to her. The White Rat had been responsible, the White Rat specialised in causing accidents.

And there he is now, limping round the room with my bullet in his leg. I'll get him in a few minutes, I'll rip his trousers up the leg and say: where did you get that scar, then? and watch his mouth working as he tries to think of an answer.

When he's had a little time he'll start to beg, and that'll be when he gets it in the belly. Five minutes after that, I'll give him another in the heart.

Gunner thrust himself back against the trunk as a guard passed below; his alsatian paused for a moment and Gunner reached for his pistol, but the dog merely lifted its leg against the tree.

'Come on,' the guard muttered, and towed the animal away.

'Value our precious life, don't we?' Gunner sneered. 'Good – we'll hate all the more to lose it,' watching Quaintance limp over to the light switch. The light went out; Quaintance reappeared in the drawing-room a few seconds later.

A tall, elegant woman looked up from her book to greet him; Quaintance kissed her.

'Julie, my darling Julie,' whispered Gunner, and found his vision blurred by tears.

CHAPTER THIRTY-ONE

During the time that Quaintance and Gunner, in their respective ways, were tried, Cromwell put into action an invasion that he had been contemplating for forty-eight hours.

Cromwell was a man whose lusts partook of a volcanic quality. Long periods of comparative quiescence were abruptly terminated in a series of eruptions, after which sated Cromwell was able to continue on a fairly calm course until the next Vesuvian onset.

A period of tranquillity had ended in Cledge's flat, and Purdey's even and dispassionate voice became orchestrated in Cromwell's mind with a subtle, pianissimo accompaniment of sensual overtones. Not only did it tell him to take off his trousers, but it had a different intonation – Cromwell was addicted to sensual command.

'Darling, do take off your trousers. Let me see your offering.' From pianissimo the sensuality became overt, anglo-saxon, unendurably stimulating.

In the ops room, Cromwell had scarcely dared look at Purdey, in case his inflammable need were too evident. Desire for her eclipsed even plans for the apprehension of Gunner; he longed to feel her body close against his in amorous, rather than lethal, combat.

Accordingly, armed with a large cellophane tube of various exotic flowers, including one orchid, Cromwell stood in front of Purdey's front door.

Hope to God she's not in bed with someone, that would be tragic. The way I feel, though, I'd turf him out, take his place, show her what marvellous damage I could do to her. He rang the bell.

The door opened almost at once; Purdey was wearing a leotard. She wore no make-up, but there were traces of indigo paint on her forehead.

'Oh, hello, Mr Cromwell. I'm in the middle of decorating the bathroom.'

'Sorry to barge in,' with a complete absence of sorrow. 'I was just passing by—'

Purdey shook her head. 'Try again. You don't just pass by a basement flat a hundred steps down.' However, she was smiling.

'All right then – away with feeble excuses. I had an overwhelming longing to see you.'

'But you see me every day – at least, you do when you look at me.'

'I'm sorry if I've seemed neglectful the past couple of days. I didn't want to spread an aura of passion round the ops room.'

'I see. Then you've come here with evil intent.'

'I've come here because I was driven to come here. Purdey, I want you madly.'

'Indeed? You've survived my presence pretty well for a long time – why the sudden urgency?'

'I've never believed in – in wooing anyone on the staff. But after the other night—'

'When I nearly rendered any forays like the current one permanently futile—'

'I had to see you again – socially.'

'Well,' waving him to a settee, 'make yourself at home. Would you like a drink?'

'I would like you.'

'I told you – I'm in the middle of decorating. A rather greasy girl wearing peace-paint.'

Cromwell grinned at her, handed her the flowers.

'How sweet – I'm not often given flowers.'

'I'm afraid you're too good at hiding your essential femininity – people – that is to say myself, find it – have found it – difficult to think of you in unBoadicean terms. The other night was the first time I saw you out of armour, so to speak.'

'You're very kind. But don't you think that, for the sake of the section's esprit de corps, you ought to forget your amour de corps?'

'I can't,' thickly. 'Please tell me to take off my trousers again?'

'It's a tempting thought, but I think not. Unless they're torn.'

'I'll tear them with pleasure,' Cromwell said, taking cloth in his hands and pulling.

'Please don't – you might strain yourself.'

Cromwell desisted. He was a man who could not light a bonfire, but had once accidentally set fire to a wheat-field with a cigarette-end – why did his trousers have to show their quality at this moment?

'Purdey—' he decided to wheedle. 'Be a darling – it's not fair to deny yourself to someone who needs you so badly.'

Purdey poured drinks, handed him one, sat down in a chair. 'Needs, or wants?'

'This is no time for semantics,' Cromwell said as soulfully as he could. 'This is a time for desire to erase all other feelings and thoughts, and I desire you, my God I desire you.'

'Do you now? Shall I tell you what I desire?'

Cromwell saw the laughter in her eyes. 'I don't think you'd better.'

'All right.'

'Unless you're referring to me.'

'Only indirectly.'

'Oh?'

'When I've put these flowers in water, and washed the paint off my face, would you like to take me to dinner?'

'What will the dessert be?'

'Dear Mr Cromwell, I do admire subtlety.'

Cromwell grinned. 'Very well. I'll take you to dinner. I'll take you to dinner until you consent. And after you've consented I shall be happy to go on taking you to dinner for as long as you like – you have that rare phoenix quality of resurrecting desire as soon as you've quenched it.'

'You make me sound quite messianic,' Purdey told him. 'A hint of the second coming.'

'For God's sake!' Cromwell was on his knees in front of her, hands on her thighs. 'Don't you know that that sort of thing in the mouth of a lovely girl drives a man mad?'

Purdey gently removed his hands. 'I'll go and wash,' she said, walking to the door.

Cromwell remained on his knees, quivering.

CHAPTER THIRTY-TWO

Gunner scanned the darkness. No sign of movement, only one light on in the house now. Probably the bedroom. He envisioned Quaintance undressing, saw the scar on his leg. No doubt he'd explained that away easily enough to his wife – not to me, he won't, thought Gunner, not to me.

Quickly and quietly, he climbed down the tree, stood in the deep shadow at its foot. Gun in hand, he ducked and ran across the lawn to the house, braced himself against the wall by the french windows giving on to the drawing-room.

Taking a pick-lock from a capacious pocket, he inserted it, heard the click of the lock, pushed gently.

'Damn, they've bolted them.' He crept along the side of the house, dived into an ambitiously flowering hydrangea. Its blooms were augmented by a face peering out at the police car which had come fast up the driveway.

Faint voices. 'Nothing to report – enjoy yourselves—' three policemen and a dog spread out and went their separate ways. Shortly afterwards, a car started up, and a police car that had been parked in front of a set of garages accelerated away.

'All right, boy?' the voice was only a few yards from the hydrangeas. Gunner raised his pistol.

I don't want to shoot a copper, or a dog, for that matter. Better, if I'm found, to leave the gun here. But then the Rat'll get away – they'll never believe me when he starts gabbing.

The policeman stopped just in front of him. The dog sniffed at the flowers, sneezed; the policeman laughed. 'Try the roses,' he said, and sauntered on.

Gunner wiped the sweat from his forehead, found that he was trembling. His mind began to wander, to ask a question which Gunner fought fiercely to suppress: supposing Quaintance isn't the one? And if he is, will you help Julie and the others by killing him? Why not expose him instead?

You damned fool – we've been all through that before. Who'd believe you instead of this big shot, with his fine house and police guard and a wife who looks like a magazine advertisement? Besides, you know what the Lord said about vengeance being sweet – my God it is, I can almost taste it, like honey.

Gunner slithered from the hydrangeas, stole round to the front door. Moonlight broke through cloud, to show a policeman standing a few yards away, his back to the house. He stood there for a long time, Gunner in full view had he turned round.

Go on, you bleeder, for Christ's sake go away. Gunner willed the constable to disappear, at the same time afraid that such ardent longing would make a telepathic impact on the constable, spin him on his axis to reveal the man behind him.

At last the policeman moved away; Gunner sprang at the lock of the front door, clicked it back, found again that he was baulked by bolts.

A wave of ivy alongside the porch looked tempting, but Gunner decided that it would be safer to try the back door. Another guard came towards him, and again Gunner sought botanical refuge, this time in some rhododendrons.

The back door turned out to be bolted too; Gunner swore, decided to find other means to liquidate Quaintance. Retreat came hard, but tonight there was nothing else to do.

He moved quickly away from the house, marvelled at the capacity of alsatian bladders as one relieved itself three times in ten seconds on three different treasures of the gardener's art, and retrieved his bicycle from a hedgerow.

Vengeance would not lose its sweetness for being slightly delayed.

CHAPTER THIRTY-THREE

Quaintance was not accustomed to being grilled in his own office. In fact, he was unaccustomed to being grilled at all. He looked up at Steed and Gambit with resentment, fiddled with a paper-weight from Malta in the shape of a sea-horse.

'Well, Minister?' Steed's face was set, his expression uncompromising. There was no civil service deference here.

'I didn't think it was relevant,' Quaintance said lamely.

'You were working with Gunner in 1960 and you didn't think it was relevant?'

'Perhaps a better word would be politic. How can I, a Minister of the Crown, be expected to broadcast the fact that I was once an associate – for a very brief period – of a man who's rushing round the countryside in a state of near insanity, settling old scores.'

'If he had settled an old score with you, you'd have wound up between a pair of brass handles with arum lilies scattered over you.'

'Oh, all right. I should have told you. But I'm sure you see my position?'

'Only too clearly,' Steed told him.

'Well then – Gunner is after the White Rat, not anybody else.' He looked at Steed's face, at Gambit's which wore a similar look. 'Good God, you surely don't think that I'm the White Rat? It's ridiculous—' his voice in his own ears sounded like bluster.

'It probably is,' Steed said. 'All you have to do is convince us.' He paused. 'You see, if you can convince us, we might be able to convince Gunner.'

Quaintance fought down his anger at Steed's attitude, thought that convincing Gunner of his innocence might not be a bad thing. 'Very well,' he said. 'I was only actively in the field for a few weeks. As for working *with* Gunner, I never actually met him.'

'Be that as it may, someone working with him, whether he actually saw him or not, was the White Rat.' Gambit leaned over Quaintance, added softly. 'In fact, still *is* the White Rat.'

'I'd come to that conclusion myself,' Quaintance answered icily. 'That was why I went down to pay a visit to another of his colleagues, after I had studied the files. And you found me there,' to Steed.

'Convinced?' Steed looked across Quaintance to Gambit.

'No.'

'Neither am I.'

'Oh for God's sake!' Quaintance banged a fist on his blotter. 'What else can I say? I worked in the Eastern Zone for a few weeks, then I had to get out in a hurry. Fell over the Wall, literally, and broke my leg. Mind you, my replacement didn't have much better luck.'

'Replacement? What replacement?' asked Steed.

Quaintance looked at him, a spark of pleasure in his eyes. 'You seem to know everything else – don't you know that?'

'No,' Steed replied severely.

Quaintance decided to tease him a little. 'He stopped a bullet in the leg. We never quite got to the bottom of that. He'd been out about a year when it happened.

Shipped home after that – he's done very well, too.'

'Let's stop playing games, please. *Who* was your replacement?'

Quaintance sat back in his chair, permitted himself a slight smile of satisfaction.

'Well, gentlemen, it seems that I must enlighten you. It was Cromwell.'

'Cromwell!' exclaimed Steed and Gambit simultaneously, and hurried from the room.

Cromwell looked across the dining-table at Purdey and set his will toward conquest. Candles burned in silver splendour, appropriate music samba'd softly through stereo speakers, giving the room the feeling of a night-club for two.

Purdey leaned back, decided that Cromwell was a charming man with a peroxide streak running through his personality. Something about him did not ring true, the hollow behind the panelling, the calculation beneath the warmth. In a way, the flaw she suspected added to the man's allure; Cromwell would take a lot of knowing.

'That was delicious,' Purdey told him, savouring the after-taste of the creme brulée and lighting a small cheroot. 'With your cooking and my sewing we'd be a first-rate example of domesticity.'

'Do you want to be domestic with me?'

Purdey regarded him demurely. 'Who knows? If you can cook like that—'

'To be honest, I had it sent in from outside. However, I don't rely on restaurants for the other things I can do well.' He stared at her intently, as though mesmerising her to leave her chair, come over to him, stand before him to be fondled.

'I see.' Purdey remained seated. 'You don't look very domestic at the moment.'

'How do I look, then?'

'Distinctly predatory.'

'You'd hardly expect me to resemble a herbivore.'

Purdey chuckled. 'That's true.'

'So come and be devoured – gently.'

'I'll think about it.'

'I hope you're not teasing me,' tautly.

'I don't go in for teasing,' Purdey said gently, with a hint of reproach. 'It's just that I have always sacrificed quantity to quality, so I don't go in for affairs lightly.'

'What about Steed?'

'What about him?' still demure, but with an imperceptible hardening of her voice.

'I thought you might be – very fond of him. It's difficult for a man to judge these things, but I'd say he was very attractive to women.'

'He is a very attractive man,' Purdey agreed.

'And efficient. Don't know what the department would do without him.'

Purdey said nothing, waited for Cromwell to continue. This was hardly the standard seduction scene, with the intended seducer intent upon praising a rival. Why?

'For instance, this business of Irwin Gunner – he seems to be getting to grips with that all right, doesn't he?'

'I don't know. He doesn't tell me everything.' Damn, thought Cromwell, her voice is different, if I'm not careful her ardour will go off the boil.

He's pumping me – I don't like being pumped. Monstrous thing to do, especially in the middle of trying to persuade a girl to relinquish the vertical.

'I thought he did. Because I thought you and he – hell, I'm sorry. I just didn't want to be disappointed. Have a glass of brandy.'

'Thank you – that seems an excellent idea.' Was he pumping me about Steed the professional, or Steed the lover? Give him the benefit of the doubt, at least for the time being. Don't think I'm going to succumb to him, though.

Cromwell came over to her, poured wine into her glass, bent down to kiss her mouth. As he did so, the telephone near Purdey's chair began to ring – she reached out and picked up the receiver, used it jokingly as an excuse to move her mouth from Cromwell's.

As he ignored it, preferring to kiss rather than speak, Purdey pressed it to her ear.

A hoarse voice. 'Cromwell?'

Purdey pushed Cromwell gently away. 'Who wants him?'

'Tell him the Flyer wants to speak to him.'

'The Flyer?' as Cromwell made to kiss her again. He stopped, almost snatched the receiver.

'Cromwell here.' His eyes were on Purdey's; with a slight shrug he tried to convey that this was all a bore, that it was typical of a crazy ex-agent to ring him just as the atmosphere was right for romance.

'Don't talk, Cromwell – just listen.' Purdey listened to the harsh metallic tones echoing in the ear-piece. 'I know you're head of DI6.' Cromwell began to say something, but Gunner cut him short. 'Don't ask me how I know. The fact is that I do. And I've got some information for you.'

'What information?' Purdey could feel the tension in Cromwell's body.

'I know who the White Rat is.'

'You do? Then who is he?' Cromwell's voice was quiet, controlled, only the colour of his face had changed, had grown a little paler.

'I'm not going to say over the phone. The White Rat's powerful these days – he's got authority, whereas what am I? Everyone thinks I'm a clown, a bit touched in the head, wandering round the countryside with a transmitter and a grudge.'

'Where are you, Gunner?'

'I need your protection, Cromwell. Do I get it?'

'Of course you do. Where are you?'

'I'll be at an empty warehouse on the North Circular Road, near Hanger Lane. There's a board in front, saying it's for rent.'

'I'll be there in twenty minutes.'

'And you'll be alone?'

'Of course I shall. 'Bye.'

Replace the receiver, turn to Purdey. 'You heard that?'

'I certainly did.'

'Good. I'm going there right away. Ring Steed and tell him—'

'Gladly. Afterwards.'

'What do you mean – afterwards?'

Purdey rose elegantly to her feet. 'You don't think you're going to leave me out – not at this stage. I can't wait to see what Gunner is like.'

'My dear girl—'

'Yes?' a lazy smile on her lips.

'If I let you come—'

'No conditions.'

'Perhaps conditional surrender – later?'

'Perhaps.'

'He would have to ring at this time.'

'If you ask me nicely there could be others.'

Cromwell turned abruptly, headed for a bureau, took from it a Walther automatic. 'Just in case,' he said softly.

'Quite. I agree with precautions.'

Cromwell grinned at her, held the front door open. They hurried across the road to his car, surged away into the darkness.

A minute later, Steed and Gambit arrived.

CHAPTER THIRTY-FOUR

Cromwell's block of flats, so far as kitchen odours were concerned, was smellproof. No hint of the gastronomic delights enjoyed by his neighbours wafted under their doors, to conflict with the heavy trails of Guerlain and Rochas which had been left, like vapour trails behind a jet, by the local exotica.

'Shall we follow our noses?' murmured Gambit hopefully. 'If we did, we both might wind up lucky.'

'No, unless Cromwell wears that sort of thing, and so far as I know he doesn't.'

Gambit grinned, fell into step with Steed as they percolated Cromwell's corridor, saved from the need to tiptoe by the thickness of the carpet.

'Ring, or shove?' whispered Gambit.

'Ring. Then shove.' Gambit pressed the bell. 'He isn't there,' as the electric chimes echoed emptily.

'In that case, no need to shove.' Steed produced his pick-lock, within a minute they were inside.

'He had something beefish for dinner,' from Gambit.

Steed hardly heard him. 'Do you recognise that handbag?'

'My God – it's Purdey's.'

'Precisely.'

'Dining with Cromwell? I didn't know she cared.'

Steed did not answer, began riffling through drawers and cupboards.

'Do you think Purdey has any idea?' Gambit asked, joining in the search.

'I doubt it. She always carries her gun in her bag, and her bag's here.' Steed opened it. 'Reprehensible, looking through a lady's handbag, but – ah,' holding up a small pearl-handled derringer. 'Belonged to her grandmother, I gather – American. Quite a gal out West in her youth.'

'Well, I hope they haven't gone anywhere more lethal than the pictures. If Cromwell got an inkling that she was on to him—'

'You don't have to spell it out,' Steed interrupted grimly. 'Let's have a word with the porter.'

'Mr Cromwell, sir? Went out with a girl about a half-hour ago.'

'Tall, slender, good-looking girl?'

'That's right, sir.'

'Any idea where they went?'

'I'm afraid not, sir.'

'Is there anybody about who would know?'

'Doubt it, sir.'

'Right. Thank you.' A pound note changed hands.

Frowning, and beginning to feel an alien emptiness in his belly, Steed again led Gambit upstairs. As they reached Cromwell's door, his telephone rang.

Steed flung back the door, rushed inside, reached the instrument just as it ceased summoning someone to pick it up. He stamped on the floor, frustrated and fearful. The telephone rang again.

'Yes?'

'Cromwell? I've been waiting for you – you're late.'

'I'm not Cromwell, I'm Steed. Is that Gunner?' Silence. 'Don't put the phone down,' Steed said, 'please wait till I get to you.'

'It's a trap.'

'It isn't. I swear it isn't. Where are you?'

Gunner hesitated. 'I'm in a warehouse on the North Circular Road. To Let sign in front of it. Not far from Hanger Lane, on the left hand side going east.'

'We'll be there right away?'

'We?' suspiciously. 'I told Cromwell not to bring anybody. You aren't Quaintance by any chance?'

'No. As I told you, I'm Steed. I'll be with you in a few minutes. And if anyone else comes first, keep mum. Hide behind a box or something. 'Bye.'

'North Circular Road?' asked Gambit, as they sprinted to the door.

'Right. Salubrious spot – lots of traffic and the odd killer. Come on.'

They dashed down the stairs, ran for Steed's Bentley, took off down the quiet street with a howl like a rabid wolf.

Steed drove with intense concentration, cornering hard and flat, the Bentley's big blunt nose pointing at impossible corners and taking them without a tremor, which was scarcely true of Gambit.

'What sort of G Force do you think we're taking?' he asked as the car tore across a junction and veered right.

Steed did not reply, did not in fact hear the question. All he heard was the slow, steady piston-beat of the great engine, and Purdey's calm, sardonic tones. Except that they were no longer as calm, no longer as sardonic, as the White Rat regretfully aimed at her and fired.

Cromwell was the sort of man who would apologise before doing irreparable damage.

CHAPTER THIRTY-FIVE

Gunner squatted on an old tool-box in the shadows. Steed, Cromwell, Quaintance, Cledge – what a merry-go-round. Telling Cromwell about Quaintance will be the only way I'll get to see his leg – every copper in Britain seems to be standing on guard over him.

Christ, Gunner thought, but I'm looking forward to the moment I look at his leg and see my bullet in it. I don't half owe him something, what with being dropped from a trapeze and then being left in the hold of a ship like some foundling on a door-step. The hospital told me when I was discharged that when I was brought there, they thought signing my death certificate would be just a formality.

There was the sound of a car slowing down, turning into the car-park. Gunner looked up at the beam above him, swung himself up. The opening of car doors, the closing. Footsteps. Just like that time in the barn – Gunner remembered the tension, the sound of the car engine coming up the lane, the abrupt silence, the foot-steps sensed rather than seen.

He watched again the barn door opening, the figure creeping through the doorway to look at the envelope lying on the floor. He quivered.

'Gunner?' Cromwell's voice boomed round the empty warehouse.

Gunner did not answer. Who's that with him? – I told him to come alone. Christ, it's a bird. I don't want to tell him what I know in front of his girlfriend.

'Gunner?' again. 'I'm Cromwell.'

How do I know who it is? I haven't seen Cromwell before. You can't suspect everyone. Of course you can – if you don't, in this game, you die. Gunner remained silent, held his gun ready. His hand was slippery on the butt – don't get in such a lather that you drop the thing, he told himself.

Why worry, though – if he's Cromwell.

'I've brought an assistant. There's no need to worry about her – she's on our side,' reassuringly.

Still no answer. Cromwell edged forward, eyes probing. 'That's far enough!' Gunner called sharply. Cromwell stood still, poised on the balls of his feet. 'How do I know you're Cromwell?'

Without answering, Cromwell slowly put his hand in his breast pocket, carefully pulled out his wallet, extracted his ID card and threw it in the direction of Gunner's voice.

Agile as an ape, Gunner swung down from the beam, picked up the card, looked at it in the light of a match.

'Satisfied, Gunner?'

'I'm satisfied,' as the flame went out. 'I've some news for you.'

'Yes?'

'I'll tell you later.'

'You can talk in front of the lady. As I told you, she's my assistant.'

'About five years ago, I got on the trail of a traitor in East Germany. I never knew his real name, but his codename suited him. The White Rat. Now I know who he is!' with fierce triumph.

'Who?' Cromwell's voice was calm. 'I'm delighted to hear it.' His hand was firm on the gun in his pocket – if

Gunner shot first, so much the better. I had to kill him in self-defence.

'Quaintance.' The name echoed through the big, cold room; Purdey stood poised behind Cromwell.

'Quaintance? The Foreign Minister?' Cromwell's voice was incredulous, had in it also a trace of something else, Purdey thought? Relief.

'Is that what he is? Can't say I'm surprised – a double-dealer like that would be bound to do well for himself, especially in politics. Fancy, a Foreign Minister who's a traitor.'

'Prove it.' Purdey's voice was crisp and clear. Cromwell turned his head towards her.

'I'll prove it all right. It was in a barn in East Germany, just outside East Berlin. I set a trap for him – I and a colleague of mine called Cledge. A right one he turned out to be, too – dropped me fifty feet to the ground from a trapeze.'

'The proof that the White Rat is Quaintance,' Purdey insisted.

'He carries my bullet in his leg. He got away from the barn but he took my bullet with him.'

'Which leg?' asked Purdey.

'The left.'

'Whereabouts?'

'Can't tell exactly,' Gunner said thoughtfully, 'but I reckon it was the calf. I was lying on the ground, you see, winged myself, and—'

'He's right,' Cromwell put in. 'You've seen Quaintance – he limps heavily on his left leg.'

'How long ago did this happen?' asked Purdey.

'About five years. I told you.'

'I doubt if he'd carry your bullet that long. It was

probably removed shortly after you'd wounded him.'

Gunner fingered his automatic. 'Who's side are you really on?' he growled.

'I'm not interested in seeing an innocent man punished,' Purdey said. 'I'm on your side, in wanting to nail the right one.'

'He limps!' shouted Gunner. 'He limps on his left leg. Isn't that enough?'

'No,' Purdey said slowly, 'it isn't.'

'You must be crazy,' Gunner whispered. 'You're covering for him.'

'Of course I'm not. I'm only saying that the man you shot wouldn't be carrying your bullet now, and for that matter might not even limp. All he'd have would be a small, puckered scar.'

If only I hadn't left my bag in Cromwell's flat – I'd feel happier with my gun.

'What are you saying?' Gunner's voice was scarcely audible; his automatic was pointed towards Purdey.

'You have a scar like that,' Purdey remarked casually, looking at Cromwell.

'Purdey. *Purdey*. I know I have. A war wound – thousands of us were hit in the legs. Not to mention the arms and so on.'

'I'd like a look at that scar,' Gunner said tersely.

'All right, if you insist.' Cromwell stood taught; watching his face in the dim light, Purdey saw a flicker of expression, promptly kicked upward, throwing him off balance. As Cromwell tried to regain his balance, Gunner leaped forward, seized Cromwell's arm, jerked his hand from his pocket with a ripping of expensive cloth. It held a Smith & Wesson.

'You didn't really suppose that the head of DI6 would

come on an assignment like this unarmed?' as casually as he could, with his arm gripped by Gunner.

Gunner knocked the pistol from Cromwell's hand, stepped backward, his own Walther rock steady on Cromwell's belly button. 'Let's see your scar,' he demanded.

'Certainly. Anything to allay your suspicions.' Cromwell bent over, pulled up his trouser leg. He turned slightly, so that Gunner could not see the small pistol taped to his calf. He snatched it from its sticky cradle, fired it whilst still crouching.

The shot took Gunner in the chest, lifted him and carried him backwards for several yards – his gun flew into distant shadows.

Purdey braced herself, waiting for the bullet that would momentarily exchange the cool metal chamber of Cromwell's automatic for the warmth of her flesh.

'I'm sorry, Purdey. I really am.'

'So am I. Lust doomed in the name of self-preservation.'

'It's a damn shame. If you hadn't seen that scar when you stitched up my trousers—'

'You would still have been found soon, by the process of elimination.'

'And now you're the one who has to be eliminated. Want to say anything before I finish it?'

'Just do it. Do it quickly.'

'All right. But I don't want to see your eyes – turn round.'

Slowly, Purdey turned; right in front of her was a brick pillar. Placing her hands against it, she hurled herself backward, smashing into Cromwell and sending his gun skittering across the floor.

'Now we're even. Don't forget – your back in three places.'

Cromwell shook his head sadly. 'No, Purdey. I never come on a mission like this without plenty of artillery. I'm sorry.'

Oh God, another gun. The creep really is a walking armoury. I've had it now.

'I shan't make the same mistake twice,' Cromwell said in the tones of someone at a funeral commiserating with the nearest kin of the dear departed.

Purdey shrank back as he raised the gun, was vaguely aware of a shriek of brakes outside, the beat of running feet. Too late. She leaped sideways, dived for the floor, prayed that Cromwell's bullet might hit her somewhere that was not vital. The ugly cough of a gun, the whirr of a bullet, the soft, sickening thud as flesh absorbed it.

I can't feel anything – where did it get me?

'Purdey!' Steed's voice held a note of flattering concern; Purdey looked up as he rushed towards her, held out her hands to be helped to her feet.

She shook her head, unable at first to understand why Cromwell was lying in front of her, blood welling from a hole in the middle of his forehead. 'I didn't have a gun,' she said, dazed, 'I was unarmed.'

'Of course you were – you left your bag in Cromwell's flat.' Steed made a clicking noise with his teeth. Purdey gently punched his arm.

'So how—?'

Steed nodded in the direction of Gambit, who was kneeling beside Gunner, supporting his head. 'Must have been him.'

They walked over to the two men; Purdey smiled down at Gunner, who was just conscious, placed one of his worn hands between hers. 'Welcome back,' she said, and to Gambit: 'Thanks for saving my life.'

'I didn't fire a shot,' Gambit answered. 'It was our friend here.'

'Did I get him?' asked Gunner anxiously, 'have I finally bagged myself a Rat?'

'You certainly have,' Purdey told him. 'A big White one. And thank you for saving me.' She bent over and kissed Gunner, who in a state of pleasure drifted into unconsciousness.

'Poor chap, Cromwell didn't do him much good,' Steed observed, as they waited for an ambulance.

'Well at least he didn't spoil his record of unsuccessful attempts to kill him.' Gambit grinned. 'Nasty wound, but ought to be all right.'

'Even after your first aid?' Steed took Purdey's arm. She smiled at him.

'I suppose you've already dined once tonight,' strolling slowly through the warehouse.

'Yes, as a matter of fact. Delightful meal, marred by a small interruption.'

'The death of the host?'

'Precisely.'

'Enough to make you want reassurance. Such as another dinner with another host. Just to demonstrate that hosts can often survive meals.'

'You know, that sounds like quite an attractive idea.'

'How could an idea that concerned two attractive people be anything else?'

Purdey laughed. 'I hadn't thought of that.' Emerging into the moonlight, they embraced, stopping only when the ambulance arrived.

Much later: 'You're dying to know how I knew about that scar on Cromwell's leg, aren't you?'

'Good gracious no. A gentleman would never pry into a thing like that. How did you know?'

'I made him take his trousers off, you see.'

'Ah, that's why you forgot your bag. You were lost in ecstasy.'

Purdey gave him a mock rabbit punch, looked down at him with a mocking smile.

'I'd better search you for scars now,' she said, and began lingeringly to do so.

THE END